AF531244

# SOCIAL WORK
# AND
# SOCIAL DEVELOPMENT

# SOCIAL WORK AND SOCIAL DEVELOPMENT

**P.R. Gautam**
**R.S. Singh**

**CENTRUM PRESS**
NEW DELHI-110002 (INDIA)

**CENTRUM PRESS**
**H.O.:** 4360/4, Ansari Road, Daryaganj,
New Delhi-110002 (India)
Tel: 23278000, 23261597, 23255577, 23286875
**B.O.:** No. 1015, Ist Main Road, BSK IIIrd Stage,
IIIrd Phase, IIIrd Block, Bangalore-560085 (INDIA)
Tel: 080-41723429
*Email:* centrumpress@gmail.com
*Visit us at:* www.centrumpress.com

*Social Work and Social Development*



First Edition, 2011

ISBN 978-93-80836-05-8

PRINTED IN INDIA

Printed at Balaji Offset, Delhi.

# Contents

# Preface

Social development is a process which results in the transformation of social structures in a manner which improves the capacity of the society to fulfil its aspirations. Society develops by consciousness and social consciousness develops by organization. The process that is subconscious in the society emerges as conscious knowledge in pioneering individuals. Development is a process, not a programme. Its power issues more from its subtle aspects than from material objects.

Not all social change constitutes development. It consists of four well-marked stages — survival, growth, development and evolution, each of which contains the other three within it. The quantitative expansion of existing activities generates growth or horizontal expansion. Development implies a qualitative change in the way the society carries out its activities, such as through more progressive attitudes and behaviour by the population, the adoption of more effective social organizations or more advanced technology which may have been developed elsewhere. The term evolution refers to the original formulation and adoption of qualitative and structural advances in the form of new social attitudes, values, behaviours, or organizations. While the term is usually applied to changes that are beneficial to society, it may result in negative side-effects or consequences that undermine or eliminate existing ways of life that are considered positive.

Social development can be summarily described as the process of organizing human energies and activities at higher levels to achieve greater results. Development increases the utilization of human potential. In the absence of valid theory, social development remains largely a process of trial and error experimentation, with a high failure rate and very uneven progress. The dismal consequences of transition strategies in most Eastern Europe countries, the very halting progress of many African and Asian countries, the increasing income gap between the most and least developed societies, and the distressing linkage between rising incomes, environmental depletion, crime and violence reflect the fact that humanity is vigorously pursuing a process without the full knowledge needed to guide and govern it effectively.

The book endeavours to provide all requirements of students, teachers, social workers, social work institutions to enable them to achieve success in social work and related activities.

*—Authors*

# 1

# History of Social Work in India

One Discipline, borrowed from America, taught in India at the university level is the discipline of Social Work. We have graduate, post graduate, MPhil and PhD degrees awarded in this discipline, as is in the case of most other disciplines. But Social Work is a professional course. It can earn a living directly.

Starting with one institute offering a programme in Social Work in 1946, we have today a hoard of such institutes functioning from all across the country. The earliest graduates in Social Work migrated to the United States of America or Europe because Social Work is a recognised profession there. A degree in Social Work offered good employment opportunities as well as scope for private practice.

In India Social Work never got established as an independent profession. The government social welfare departments, hospitals largely employed trained social workers against lower middle rung posts. When Indian labour laws made it compulsory to appoint welfare officers in the factories, Social Work degree became a passport to appointment against these posts. With time, welfare officers saw themselves becoming personnel officers and later human resource development (HRD) managers. People with Social Work background thus got higher status in society.

When management education came to India (also from the USA), HRD became a preferred area of specialisation and management graduates soon replaced Social Work graduates from HRD jobs. A new attractive field opened for the Social Work graduates when some non-government organisations (NGOs) adopted corporate culture under the influence of its foreign donors. But these employment opportunities were limited in numbers because how many NGOs in India would find foreign funds? High profile jobs for Social Work graduates were therefore ruled out.

The scope for practicing Social Work as private profession in India is next to nil. Petty political party workers who also call themselves social workers appear to be doing better. The image of a social worker amongst the general public is such that if a trained social worker were to introduce himself/herself the response coming from the opposite person most likely is to be: I am a social worker too.

It is difficult for the Indian people to conceive that there could be professionals around called social workers to be approached when facing personal or family problems. The reason is not far to see. Helping each other in the Indian traditions is a noble cause. Every body therefore shows eagerness to help every body else. Why in that case someone pay a social worker? Since the very concept of professional social work is missing from the Indian minds, trained social workers are going to find it very difficult to establish roots in this country. It is also to remember that profession wise it is the clients who approach the professionals and not the other way round.

If we look at the methods of professional social work, they talk of helping people individually (Social Case Work Method) helping people in groups (Social Group Work Method) and helping people's communities (Community Development Method).

It may be seen that of these, the last two methods can not be practiced by trained social workers in private practice since these require a larger setting. Only organised bodies such government, corporate houses, NGOs can afford it. Trained social workers therefore have to be necessarily employed to be able to practice these two methods. This leaves Social Case Work method as the only method that can be employed by trained social workers to earn an independent living.

In Social Case Work method, the trained social worker interviews his/her client, in private and takes down the personal history. Through this he/she makes an assessment of the likely cause for the problem faced by the client. The process of interviewing is simple chitchatting. The client may not even know if he/she is being helped or having a street corner talk. One interview with the client is not sufficient; more have to be arranged.

Some clients may not be prepared for repeat visits. Even if the cause is discovered successfully, the solution that is offered to the client may not be out of the ordinary. It consists of plain suggestions and motivational talks. Unlike doctors and psychiatrists who prescribe medicines, professional social workers prescribe no such thing. This leaves the clients a bit disappointed. In fact, many people (the household social workers) have been giving advises to them.

Experience shows that people in India are happier discussing their personal problems with astrologers, tantrics, priests and saddhus for they offer mantras, tabeej (locket), bhasma (ashes), flowers, etc said to be containing charismatic powers or ask to perform certain rituals such as feeding the fish, donating mustard oil, performing puja etc that heal all the problems. People have no hesitation in paying them; sometimes even paying big money. It appears that people are more interested in purchasing hope than getting rid of the problem.

From the discussion so far it is clear that professional Social Work is a big failure in India; it can neither provide you decent employment nor earn an independent living. Students of Social Work at the universities, colleges and departments are therefore heading for a disaster. The government should take steps to weed out such unnecessary disciplines from our education system or consider modifying these to suit our conditions. Employing trained social workers in rural areas where community organisation is a big challenge also appears to be an attractive option. Is any body listening?

## Nature of Social Work

Social work is a profession for those with a strong desire to help improve people's lives. *Social workers* assist people by helping them cope with and solve issues in their everyday lives, such as family and personal problems and dealing with relationships. Some social workers help clients who face a disability, life-threatening disease, social problem, such as inadequate housing, unemployment, or substance abuse. Social workers also assist families that have serious domestic conflicts, sometimes involving child or spousal abuse.

Additionally, they may conduct research, advocate for improved services, or become involved in planning or policy development. Many social workers specialize in serving a particular population or working in a specific setting. In all settings, these workers may also be called *licensed clinical social workers*, if they hold the appropriate State mandated license.

*Child, family, and school social workers* provide social services and assistance to improve the social and psychological functioning of children and their families. Workers in this field assess their client's needs and offer assistance to improve their situation.

This often includes coordinating available services to assist a child or family. They may assist single parents in finding day care, arrange adoptions, or help find foster homes for neglected, abandoned, or abused children. These workers may specialize in working with a particular problem, population or setting, such as child protective services, adoption, homelessness, domestic violence, or foster care.

In schools, social workers often serve as the link between students' families and the school, working with parents, guardians, teachers, and other school officials to ensure that students reach their academic and personal potential.

They also assist students in dealing with stress or emotional problems. Many school social workers work directly with children with disabilities and their families.

In addition, they address problems such as misbehaviour, truancy, teenage pregnancy, and drug and alcohol problems and advise teachers on how to cope with difficult students. School social workers may teach workshops to entire classes on topics like conflict resolution.

Child, family, and school social workers may be known as child welfare social workers, family services social workers, or child protective services social workers. These workers often work for individual and family services agencies, schools, or State or local governments.

*Medical and public health social workers* provide psychosocial support to individuals, families, or vulnerable populations so they can cope with chronic, acute, or terminal illnesses, such as Alzheimer's disease, cancer, or AIDS. They also advise family caregivers, counsel patients, and help plan for patients' needs after discharge from hospitals.

They may arrange for at-home services, such as meals-on-wheels or home care. Some work on interdisciplinary teams that evaluate certain kinds of patients, such as geriatric or organ transplant patients.

Some specialize in services for senior citizens and their families. These social workers may run support groups for the adult children of aging parents. Also, they may assess, coordinate, and monitor services such as housing, transportation, and long-term care. These workers may be known as gerontological social workers.

Medical and public health social workers may work for hospitals, nursing and personal care facilities, individual and family services agencies, or local governments.

*Mental health and substance abuse social workers* assess and treat individuals with mental illness or substance abuse problems. Such services include individual and group therapy, outreach, crisis intervention, social rehabilitation, and teaching skills needed for everyday living.

They also may help plan for supportive services to ease clients' return to the community when leaving inpatient facilities. They may provide services to assist family members of those who suffer from addiction or other mental health issues. These workers may work in outpatient facilities, where clients come in for treatment and then leave, or in inpatient programs, where patients reside at the facility.

Some mental health and substance social workers may work in employee-assistance programs. In this setting, they may help people cope with job-related pressures or with personal problems that affect the quality of their work. Other social workers work in private practice, where they are employed directly by the client. These social workers may be known as *clinical social workers, occupational social workers,* or *substance abuse social workers.*

Other types of social workers include *social work administrators, researchers, planners* and *policymakers,* who develop and implement programs to address issues such as child abuse, homelessness, substance abuse, poverty, and violence. These workers research and analyse policies, programs, and regulations. They identify social problems and suggest legislative and other solutions. They may help raise funds or write grants to support these programs.

Work environment. Social workers usually spend most of their time in an office or residential facility, but they also may travel locally to visit clients, meet with service providers, or attend meetings.

Some may meet with clients in one of several offices within a local area. Social work, while satisfying, can be challenging. Understaffing and large caseloads add to the pressure in some agencies. Full-time social workers usually work a standard 40-hour week, but some occasionally work evenings and weekends to meet with clients, attend community meetings, and handle emergencies. Some work part time, particularly in voluntary nonprofit agencies.

## Training, other Qualifications, and Advancement

A bachelor's degree is the minimum requirement for entry into the occupation, but some positions require an advanced degree. All States and the District of Columbia have some licensure, certification, or registration requirement; but these regulations vary.

Education and training. A bachelor's degree in social work (BSW) is the most common minimum requirement to qualify for a job as a social worker; however, majors in psychology, sociology, and related fields may qualify for some entry-level jobs, especially in small community agencies.

Although a bachelor's degree is sufficient for entry into the field, an advanced degree is required for some positions. A master's degree in social work (MSW) is typically required for positions in health and school settings and is required for clinical work, as well. Some jobs in public and private agencies may require an advanced degree, such as an MSW with a concentration in social services policy or administration. Supervisory, administrative, and staff training positions usually require an advanced degree. College and university teaching positions and most research appointments normally require a doctorate in social work (DSW or Ph.D.).

As of June 2009, the Council on Social Work Education accredited 468 bachelor's programs and 196 master's programs. The Group for the Advancement of Doctoral Education listed 74 doctoral programs in social work (DSW or Ph.D.) in the United States.

Bachelor degree programs prepare graduates for direct service positions, such as caseworker, mental health assistant, group home worker and residential counsellor. These programs include courses in social work values and ethics, dealing with a culturally diverse clientele and at-risk populations, promotion of social and economic justice, human behaviour and the social environment, social welfare policy and services, social work practice, social research methods, and field education. Accredited programs require a minimum of 400 hours of supervised field experience.

Master's degree programs prepare graduates for work in their chosen field of concentration and continue to develop the skills required to perform clinical assessments, manage large caseloads, take on supervisory roles, and explore new ways of drawing upon social services to meet the needs of clients.

Master's programs usually last 2 years and include a minimum of 900 hours of supervised field instruction or internship. A part-time program may take 4 years.

Entry into a master's program does not require a bachelor's degree in social work, but courses in psychology, biology, sociology, economics, political science, and social work are recommended. In addition, a second language can be very helpful. Most master's programs offer advanced standing for those with a bachelor's degree from an accredited social work program.

Licensure. All States and the District of Columbia have licensing, certification, or registration requirements regarding social work practice and the use of professional titles. Most States require 2 years or 3,000 hours of supervised clinical experience for licensure of clinical social workers. Due to some limitations on what settings unlicensed social workers may work and some variation in the requirements to obtain a license, those interested in becoming a social worker should research requirements in their State.

Other qualifications. Social workers should be emotionally mature, objective, and sensitive to people and their problems. They must be able to handle responsibility, work independently, and maintain good working relationships with clients and coworkers. Volunteer or paid jobs as a social work aide can help people test their interest in this field.

Certification and advancement. Advancement to supervisor, program manager, assistant director, or executive director of a social service agency or department usually requires an advanced degree and related work experience.

Other career options for social workers include teaching, research, and consulting. Some of these workers help formulate government policies, by analysing and advocating policy positions in government agencies, in research institutions, and on legislators' staffs.

Some social workers go into private practice. Most private practitioners are clinical social workers who provide psychotherapy, usually paid for through health insurance or by the client themselves. Private practitioners must have at least a master's degree and a period of supervised work experience. A network of contacts for referrals also is essential.

Social work is a responsible and demanding job. Practitioners work in social settings characterised by enormous diversity, and they perform a range of roles, requiring different skills. Public expectations, agency requirements and resources and the needs of service users all create pressures for social workers.

The public receives only a snapshot of a social worker's responsibilities and, against a background of media concentration on the sensational, the thousands of successful outcomes and years of hard work in child care and with vulnerable adults are never considered (Hardy and Hannibal, 1997).

In intervening in people's lives, social workers face practice dilemmas arising from the relationship between social work values and the law (for example, working to promote the rights and self-determination of service users and having to balance this with the need to protect them and to protect the rights of others).

The relationship between social work and the law is part of an ongoing debate. There are those who adopt a legalistic model and argue that the law, reflected through court orders, is central to social work practice (for example, Blom-Cooper, 1985). Others have argued that over-reliance on the law fails to address the problems people face and may even exacerbate them. This seems to present a dilemma for practice.

The growing importance of the law in social work practice and decision making is reflected in the training requirements for professionals working in the field of social work (Department of Health, 2002). Yet it is essential that alongside this there is a value base with an emphasis on principles, such as partnership, equality and empowerment, which must inform good practice.

Over the past two decades there have been a number of events that raised serious questions regarding social work practice. There has been fierce debate in relation to child protection issues, the changes within the criminal justice system (for example the introduction, by the Crime and Disorder Act 1998, of antisocial behaviour orders) and the effectiveness of community care.

There have been well-documented tragedies and errors of judgement (Blom-Cooper, 1985), apparent over-zealousness such as in the Cleveland affair (Butler-Sloss, 1988) and the misuse of power in residential care in the 'pindown' affair (Levy and Kahan, 1991).

For many professionals in the field of social work, the publicity surrounding these and other events has led to a feeling of crisis. Social work as a profession has frequently been under attack since the mid-1980s, and this has undermined the public's awareness of social work's successes.

For example, one of the observations about the Children Act 1989 was that it was based on current best practice within social work at the time, though such practice was not sufficiently widespread. The Act represented a new start for children and families and other professionals working with children by radically changing the legal framework regulating the care and upbringing of children (Hardy and Hannibal, 1997). No legislation or legal framework can remain static, however, and as a result of reviews and enquiries such as the Victoria Climbie Inquiry Report (Department of Health and Home Office, 2003), the Children Act 1989 has been significantly updated, and the way in which it is interpreted, resourced and implemented has been strengthened.

## The Nature and Scope of Social Work

As new problems are generated in the complex urban lifestyles the need for social and welfare workers has increased. These workers attempt to alleviate and prevent social problems or suffering caused by illness, poverty, maladjustment, crisis in family or at work, antisocial behaviour, constricted lifestyle etc. In India this is an emerging profession, multinational influences, complexities of every day life, neo nuclear families have generated complex day to day problems.

The growing incidence of handicaps both physical and mental and psychological stress, delinquency all call for persons who can work on the front line to alleviate and relieve tensions and sufferings.

The study of social work is a broad one. It encompasses subjects such as sociology, psychology, human growth and development, marriage and family, economics, education, biology, criminology etc. Social work then is a practical application of this knowledge to such problems as mentioned earlier.

There's much more to social work than charity. It's another exciting field which is showing signs of steady growth. Hundreds of voluntary organisations have mushroomed in the past few years and are offering a vast job market. The whole concept of social service has undergone a sea change. It is no longer a matter of charity or compassion.

The growing awareness that it is a professional discipline is drawing young people to it. There are specialist social work professionals who deal with cases pertaining to AIDS, Leprosy awareness, drug abuse, care for the elderly, disability, skill development etc. More than 200 societies are registered every day, a large percentage being NGOs.

## *Nature of Work*

Social work goes on at three major levels. These are the individual level, also known as case work, group work and community or organization work.

Social workers are generally engaged in activities undertaken by agencies in any of these areas. Working with individual client on a case involves face to face contact with the individual or family, joint meetings in the office, home visits, work in a hospital or work with children at home, school or special institutions. Group work goals are generally rehabilitative in nature or at times aim at recreation.

Generally group work involves working with special groups e.g the old, handicapped, people from similar socio economic groups, workers, delinquents etc.

Community work involves analysing problems of the whole community and finding possible solutions. It may involve community education or soliciting cooperation from the whole community. Generally a social worker has to work at almost all the 3 levels. The agency or organization with which the social worker is working generally determines the nature of work.

## *School Social Work*

Social workers who work with schools work with students, teachers and parents. The major role a social worker plays is to bridge the gap between the school and the home with an effort to get the best for the child.

Education, counselling and advocacy are important aspects of school, social work. They educate school students for the prevention of drug and alcohol abuse, sex related problems and diseases etc. and provide family life education.

Social workers counsel students facing problems of disabilities, addiction, emotional deprivation and abuse. They manage truancy and maladjustment among children. School social workers organize community programmes for students to develop in them the qualities of helpfulness and care. Sometimes social workers make referrals to other agencies particularly to help children and parents facing critical problems.

### *Medical Social Work*

Medical social workers are found in cancer hospitals and in departments where critically ill are admitted. While in the West most hospitals employ social workers, in India this concept has to catch on yet. Coming to terms with a permanent disability or restricted mobility is difficult. A social worker is trained to work with seriously ill and with bereaved families. Counselling and practical assistance is given to the patients and their family.

### *Psychiatric Social Work*

There are two main work settings for psychiatric social work: child guidance clinics and psychiatric units or hospitals. In child guidance clinics a team consisting of social workers, psychiatrists and clinical psychologists work with disturbed children and adolescents.

Most of the referrals come from medical practitioners and generally include those with behavioural problems, phobia, maladjusted teenagers, withdrawal cases and children with learning problems causing them to lag behind in school work or to play truant. The social worker makes an assessment of the social factors contributing to the problem by getting involved with the whole family to offer family therapy and other kinds of intervention. In some cases they liaise with teachers, and educational psychologists.

In a psychiatric hospital, social workers meet various different client groups. Patients could be old people suffering from senile dementia or depression or those suffering from psychological problems. They help the psychiatrist assess a new re feral, work out what the problem is and what has led up to it, while doing the case sheet writing. They also continue to work as facilitators in the treatment process.

### *Community Social Work*

Community social workers specialise in working with groups who have a common problem, e.g., those facing problems of bad housing, unemployment, lack of local facilities, or minority group issues within the community.

Community social workers initiate or support remedial action and use their knowledge, professional contacts and the resources they can summon to help a group, tackle problems. Social workers work towards influencing social policy at times and towards resources for the underprivileged. They can work in urban and rural areas and even with international or national organizations.

### *Child Care/Family Services*

Child care services include day care centres and child care homes. Social workers handle situations related to children from infancy to adulthood. With families they are equipped to handle problems related to different cultures and services for children with congenital disabilities.

### *Gerontological Social Work*

This branch deals with care of old people. Old peoples homes requires gerontological social workers. In the area of AIDS also care of old people is becoming a growing problem.

### *Criminology and Correctional Social Work*

Prisons, reformatories, remand homes, crime and delinquent prevention programmes exist in every country. Crime and delinquency needs to be prevented. Social workers are trained to work in these areas largely to create a positive social climate for prevention of antisocial behaviours.

### *Labour Welfare and Industrial Relations*

Social workers, today, form an integral part of the labour welfare section of personnel departments in industries and commercial organizations. In private as well as public sector enterprises employee's welfare is a major concern for maintaining a healthy industrial climate. Social workers work with personnel managers to achieve this goal.

### *Research*

Social workers carry on social research. Social workers in India are researching for tribal welfare, for investigating human suffering after Bhopal gas tragedy or following the Latur earthquake etc.

### *Social Entrepreneurship*

Social Entrepreneurship is a comparatively new concept in India. Harvard, Stanford, John F Kennedy School of Government introduced formal programmes in Social Entrepreneurship. In London, School of Social Entrepreneurs offers an 8 week course in fund raising, marketing and accounting. In US 6 alumni of Stanford Graduate School floated a non profit organisation ' Start Up"

In India, the newly-established National Foundation for Innovation in Ahmedabad (under the Department of Science & Technology) is being projected as a breeding ground for the 'unsung heroes'. The foundation rewards grass root innovators; trains them in principles of marketing; looks for commercial/non-commercial outlets for these small projects and generally helps them move-up the value-chain.

The Ashoka Programme-Drayton, developed the 'venture capital' approach to social problems. He established 'Ashoka; Innovators for the Public', a non-profit foundation based in Arlington, VA. The foundation has backed more than 1,000 Ashoka Fellows in 34 countries, running its longest programme in India with 170 Fellows over the last two decades.

# 2

# Social Welfare Management

## Introduction to Management and Organizations

The 21st century has brought with it a new work place, one in which everyone must adapt to a rapidly hanging society with constantly shifting demands and opportunities. The economy has become global and is driven by innovations and technology and organizations have to transform themselves to serve new customer expectations. Today's economy presents challenging opportunities as well as dramatic uncertainty. The new economy has become knowledge based and is performance driven.

The themes in the present context area 'respect', participation, empowerment, teamwork and self management. In the light of the above challenges a new kind of leader is needed to guide business through turbulence. Managers in organizations do this task.

A manager is someone who coordinates and oversees the work of other people so that organizational goals can be accomplished. It is not about personal achievement but helping others do their job. Managers may also have additional work duties not related to coordinating the work of others. Managers can be classified by their level in the organization, particularly in traditionally structured organizations—those shaped like a pyramid:

1) First-line managers (often called supervisors) are located on the lowest level of management.
2) Middle managers include all levels of management between the first-line level and the top level of the organization.

3) Top managers include managers at or near the top of the organization who are responsible for making organization-wide decisions and establishing plans and goals that affect the entire organization.

The changing nature of organizations and work often requires employees in formerly nonmanagerial jobs to perform managerial activities. Non managerial jobs are those where one works directly on a job and had no one reporting to him.

Mary Parker Follet defines management as, "The art of getting things done through people" Management involves coordinating and overseeing the work activities of others so that their activities are completed efficiently and effectively.

1) Coordinating and overseeing the work of others is what distinguishes a managerial position from a nonmanagerial one.
2) Efficiency is getting the most output from the least amount of inputs in order to minimize resource costs. Efficiency is often referred to as "doing things right" Effectiveness is completing activities so that organizational goals are attained and is often described as "doing the right things" No two managers' jobs are exactly alike. All managers perform certain function, enact certain roles and display a set of skills in their jobs.

## Management Functions

According to the functions approach managers perform certain activities to efficiently and effectively coordinate the work of others. They can be classified as :

1) Planning involves defining goals, establishing strategies for achieving those goals, and developing plans to integrate and coordinate activities.
2) Organizing involves arranging and structuring work to accomplish the organization's goals.
3) Leading involves working with and through people to accomplish organizational goals.
4) Controlling involves monitoring, comparing, and correcting work performance.

Since these four management functions are integrated into the activities of managers throughout the workday, they should be viewed as an ongoing process and they need not the done in the above sequence.

### *Management Roles*

In the late 1960s, Henry Mintzberg conducted a precise study of managers at work. He concluded that managers perform 10 different roles, which are highly interrelated.

Management roles refer to specific categories of managerial behaviour. Overall there are ten specific roles performed by managers which are included in the following three categories :

1) Interpersonal roles include figurehead, leadership, and liaison activities.

2) Informational roles include monitoring, disseminating, and spokesperson activities.

3) Decisional roles include entrepreneur, disturbance handler, resource allocator, and negotiator.

Although the functions approach represents the most useful way to describe the manager's job, Mintzberg's roles give additional insight into managers' work. Some of the ten roles do not fall clearly into one of the four functions, since all managers do some work that is not purely managerial.

### *Management Skills*

Managers need certain skills to perform the challenging duties and activities associated with being a manager. Robert L. Katz found through his research in the early 1970s that managers need three essential skills

1) Technical skills are job-specific knowledge and techniques needed to proficiently perform specific tasks.

2) Human skills are the ability to work well with other people individually and in a group.

3) Conceptual skills are the ability to think and to conceptualize about abstract and complex situations.

These skills reflect a broad cross-section of the important managerial activities that are elements of the four management functions Significant changes in the internal and external environments have a measurable impact on management. Security threats, corporate ethics scandals, global economic and political uncertainties, and technological advancements have had a great impact on the manager's job. Two significant changes facing today's managers are importance of customers to the manager's job and Importance of innovation to the manager's job Organizations need managers. An organization is a deliberate arrangement of people to accomplish some specific purpose.

Organizations share three common characteristics:

(1) Each has a distinct purpose.

(2) Each is composed of people.

(3) Each develops some deliberate structure so members can do their work.

Although these three characteristics are important in defining *what* an organization is, the concept of an organization is changing.

The characteristic of new organizations of today include: flexible work arrangements, employee work teams, open communication systems, and supplier alliances. Organizations are becoming more open, flexible, and responsive to changes. Organizations are changing because the world around them has changed and is continuing to change. These societal, economic, global, and technological changes have created an environment in which successful organizations must embrace new ways of getting their work done. The importance of studying management in today's dynamic global environment can be explained by looking at the universality of management, the reality of work, and the rewards and challenges of being a manager.

***The Universality of Management:*** Management is needed in all types and sizes of organizations, at all organizational levels, and in all organizational work areas throughout the world.

***The Reality of Work:*** All employees of an organization either manage or are managed.

***Rewards and Challenges of Being a Manager Challenges***

a) Managers may have difficulty in effectively blending the knowledge, skills, ambitions, and experiences of a diverse group of employees.

b) A manager's success typically is dependent on others' work performance.

*Rewards*

a) MaRewards and Challenges of Being a Managernagers have an opportunity to create a work environment in which organizational members can do their work to the best of their ability and help the organization achieve its goals.

b) Managers often receive recognition and status in the organization and in the larger community; influence organizational outcomes; and receive appropriate compensation.

c) Knowing that their efforts, skills, and abilities are needed by the organization gives many managers great satisfaction.

The manager of today must integrate management skills with new approaches that emphasize the human touch, enhance flexibility, and involve employees.

## Management Yesterday and Today

Organizations and managers have existed for thousands of years. The Egyptian pyramids and the Great Wall of China were projects of tremendous scope and magnitude, and required good management. Regardless of the titles given to managers throughout history, someone has always had to plan what needs to be accomplished, organize people and materials, lead and direct workers, and impose controls to ensure that goals were attained as planned.

Two historical events significant to the study of management are work of Adam Smith, in his book,' *The Wealth of Nations'*, in which he argued brilliantly for the economic advantages of division of labour (the breakdown of jobs into narrow, repetitive tasks).

The Industrial Revolution is second important pre-twentieth-century influence on management. The introduction of machine powers combined with the division of labour made large, efficient factories possible. Planning, organizing, leading, and controlling became necessary activities. There are six major approaches to management. They are explained as follows :

### *Scientific Management*

Scientific management is defined as the use of the scientific method to determine the "one best way" for a job to be done. The most important contributor in this field was Frederick W. Taylor who is known as the "father" of scientific management. Using his principles of scientific management, Taylor was able to define the "one best way" for doing each job. Frank and Lillian Gilbreth were inspired by Taylor's work and proceeded to study and develop their own methods of scientific management. They devised a classification scheme to label 17 basic hand motions called therbligs in order to eliminate wasteful motions Guidelines devised by Taylor and others to improve production efficiency are still used in today's organizations. However, current management practice is not restricted to scientific management practices alone.

Elements of Scientific Management Still Used Include:

1. Using time and motion studies.
2. Hiring best qualified workers.
3. Designing incentive systems based on output.

### *General Administrative Theorists*

This group of writers, who focused on the entire organization, developed more general theories of what managers do and what constitutes good management practice. Henri Fayol and Max Weber were the two most prominent proponents of the general administrative approach. Fayol focused on activities common to all managers. He described the practice of management as distinct from other typical business functions.

He Stated 14 Principles of Management which are as Follows:

1. Division of Work.
2. Authority.
3. Discipline.
4. Unity of Command.
5. Unity of Direction.
6. Subordination of individual interest to group interest.
7. Remuneration.
8. Centralization.

9. Scalar Chain.
10. Order.
11. Equity.
12. Stability.
13. Initiative.
14. Espirit de corps.

Max Weber was a German sociologist who developed a theory of authority structures and described organizational activity based on authority relations. He described the ideal form of organization as a bureaucracy marked by division of labour, a clearly defined hierarchy, detailed rules and regulations, and impersonal relationships Some current management concepts and theories can be traced to the work of the general administrative theorists.

The functional view of a manager's job relates to Henri Fayol's concept of management. Weber's bureaucratic characteristics are evident in many of today's large organizations—even in highly flexible organizations that employ talented professionals. Some bureaucratic mechanisms are necessary in highly innovative organizations to ensure that resources are used efficiently and effectively.

### *Quantitative Approach to Management*

The quantitative approach to management, sometimes known as *operations research* or *management science,* uses quantitative techniques to improve decision making. This approach includes applications of statistics, optimization models, information models, and computer simulations. The quantitative approach originated during World War II as mathematical and statistical solutions to military problems were developed for wartime use.

The relevance of quantitative approach today is that it has contributed most directly to managerial decision making, particularly in planning and controlling. The availability of sophisticated computer software programs has made the use of quantitative techniques more feasible for managers.

## Organizational Behaviour

The field of study concerned with the actions (behaviours) of people at work is organizational behaviour. Organizational behaviour (OB) research has contributed much of what we know about human resources management and contemporary views of motivation, leadership, trust, teamwork, and conflict management. The early advocates of OB approach were Robert Owen, Hugo Munsterberg, Mary Parker Follett, and Chester Barnard. Their ideas served as the foundation for employee selection procedures, motivation programs, work teams, and organization-environment management techniques.

The Hawthorne Studies were the most important contribution to the development of organizational behaviour. This series of experiments conducted from 1924 to the early 1930s at Western Electric Company's Hawthorne Works in Cicero, Illinois, were initially devised as a scientific management experiment to assess the impact of changes in various physical environment variables on employee productivity.

After Harvard professor Elton Mayo and his associates joined the study as consultants, other experiments were included to look at redesigning jobs, make changes in workday and work week length, introduce rest periods, and introduce individual versus group wage plans. The researchers concluded that social norms or group standards were key determinants of individual work behaviour.

Although not without criticism (concerning procedures, analyses of findings, and the conclusions), the Hawthorne Studies stimulated interest in human behaviour in organizational settings. In the present day context behavioural approach assists managers in designing jobs that motivate workers, in working with employee teams, and in facilitating the flow of communication within organizations. The behavioural approach provides the foundation for current theories of motivation, leadership, and group behaviour and development.

### *The Systems Approach*

During the 1960s researchers began to analyse organizations from a systems perspective based on the physical sciences. A system is a set of interrelated and interdependent parts arranged in a manner that produces a unified whole. The two basic types of systems are open and closed. A closed system is not influenced by and does not interact with its environment. An open system interacts with its environment. Using the systems approach, managers envision an organization as a body with many interdependent parts, each of which is important to the well-being of the organization as a whole. Managers coordinate the work activities of the various parts of the organization, realizing that decisions and actions taken in one organizational area will affect other areas. The systems approach recognizes that organizations are not self-contained; they rely on and are affected by factors in their external environment.

### *The Contingency Approach*

The contingency approach recognizes that different organizations require different ways of managing. The contingency approach to management is a view that the organization recognizes and responds to situational variables as they arise.

## Current Trends and Issues

The following are the current concepts and practices are changing the way managers do their jobs today.

*Globalization:* Organizational operations are no longer limited by national borders. Managers throughout the world must deal with new opportunities and challenges inherent in the globalization of business.

*Ethics:* Cases of corporate lying, misrepresentations, and financial manipulations have been widespread in recent years. Managers of firms such as Enron, ImClone, Global Crossing, and Tyco International have placed their own self-interest ahead of other stockholders' welfare. While most managers continue to behave in a highly ethical manner, abuses suggest a need to " upgrade" ethical standards. Organizations are taking a more active role in creating and using codes of ethics, ethics training programs, and ethical hiring procedures.

*Work force diversity:* It refers to a work force that is heterogeneous in terms of gender, race, ethnicity, age, and other characteristics that reflect differences. Accommodating diverse groups of people by addressing different lifestyles, family needs, and work styles is a major challenge for today's managers.

*Entrepreneurship:* It is the process whereby an individual or group of individuals use organized efforts to pursue opportunities to create value and grow by fulfilling wants and needs through innovation and uniqueness, no matter what resources the entrepreneur currently has.

Three important themes stand out in this definition:

a. The pursuit of opportunities.
b. Innovation.
c. Growth.

Entrepreneurship will continue to be important to societies around the world.

*Managing in an E-Business World:* E-business (electronic business) is a comprehensive term describing the way an organization does its work by using electronic (Internet-based) linkages with its key constituencies in order to efficiently and effectively achieve its goals.

*Knowledge Management and Learning Organizations:* Change is occurring at an unprecedented rate. To be successful, today's organization must become a learning organization—one that has developed the capacity to continuously learn, adapt, and change. Knowledge management involves cultivating a learning culture where organizational members systematically gather knowledge and share it with others in the organization so as to achieve better performance.

*Quality Management:* Quality management is a philosophy of management that is driven by continual improvement and response to customer needs and expectations. The objective of quality management is to create an organization committed to continuous improvement in work.

## Organization Culture and Environment: The Constraints

The components of an organization's culture are as complex as the different aspects of an individual's personality. Today's managers must understand how the forces of an organization's internal and external environment influence, and sometimes constrain, its productivity. Managers must realize that organizational culture and organizational environment have important implications for the way an organization is managed.

Two perspectives concerning the role that managers play in

an organization's success or failure have been proposed. The omnipotent view of management maintains that managers are directly responsible for the success or failure of an organization. This view of managers as being omnipotent is consistent with the stereotypical picture of the "take-charge" executive who can overcome any obstacle in carrying out the organization's objectives. When organizations perform poorly, someone must be held accountable and according to the omnipotent view, that "someone" is management.

The symbolic view of management upholds the view that much of an organization's success or failure is due to external forces outside managers' control. The influence that managers do have is seen mainly as a symbolic outcome. Organizational results are influenced by factors outside of the control of managers, including the economy, market changes, governmental policies, competitors' actions, the state of the particular industry, the control of proprietary technology, and decisions made by previous managers in the organization.

The manager's role is to create meaning out of randomness, confusion, and ambiguity. According to the symbolic view, the actual part that management plays in the success or failure of an organization is minimal.

Reality suggests a synthesis; managers are neither helpless nor all powerful. Instead, the more logical approach is to see the manager as operating within constraints imposed by the organization's culture and environment.

## The Organization's Culture

Just as individuals have a personality, so, too, do organizations. We refer to an organization's personality as its culture. Organizational culture is the shared values, principles, traditions, and ways of doing things that influence the way organizational members act.

This Definition Implies :

- Individuals perceive organizational culture based on what they see, hear, or experience within the organization.
- Organizational culture is shared by individuals within the organization.

- Organizational culture is a descriptive term. It describes, rather than evaluates.

Seven dimensions of an organization's culture have been proposed :

a. Innovation and risk taking (the degree to which employees are encouraged to be innovative and take risks).
b. Attention to detail (the degree to which employees are expected to exhibit precision, analysis, and attention to detail).
c. Outcome orientation (the degree to which managers focus on results or outcomes rather than on the techniques and processes used to achieve those outcomes).
d. People orientation (the degree to which management decisions take into consideration the effect on people within the organization).
e. Team orientation (the degree to which work activities are organized around teams rather than individuals).
f. Aggressiveness (the degree to which people are aggressive and competitive rather than easy going and cooperative).
g. Stability (the degree to which organizational activities emphasize maintaining the status quo in contrast to growth).

### *Strong Versus Weak Cultures*

Strong cultures are found in organizations where key values are intensely held and widely shared. Whether a company's culture is strong, weak, or somewhere in between depends on organizational factors such as size, age, employee turnover rate, and intensity of original culture. A culture has increasing impact on what managers do as the culture becomes stronger.

Most organizations have moderate-to-strong cultures. In these organizations, high agreement exists about what is important and what defines "good" employee behaviour. Culture is transmitted and learned by employees principally through stories, rituals, material symbols, and language.

An innovative culture should have these characteristics:

- Challenge and involvement.

- Freedom.
- Trust and openness.
- Idea time.
- Playfulness/humour.
- Conflict resolution.
- Debates.
- Risk taking.

### *The Organization's Environment*

The general environment includes these broad external conditions that may affect the organization: economic, political/ legal, sociocultural, demographic, technological, and global conditions.

- Economic conditions include interest rates, inflation rates, changes in disposable income, stock market fluctuations, and the general business cycle.
- Political/legal conditions include the general political stability of countries in which an organization does business and the specific attitudes that elected officials have toward business.
- Sociocultural conditions include the changing expectations of society. Societal values, customs, and tastes can change, and managers must be aware of these changes.
- Demographic conditions, including physical characteristics of a population (e.g., gender, age, level of education, geographic location, income, composition of family) can change, and managers must adapt to these changes.
- Technological conditions, which have changed more rapidly than any other element of the general environment.
- Global factors include global competitors and global consumer markets.

Environments differ in their amount of environmental uncertainty, which relates to :

(1) the degree of change in an organization's environment and

(2) the degree of complexity in that environment Degree of change is characterized as being dynamic or stable.

In a dynamic environment, components of the environment change frequently. If change is minimal, the environment is called a stable environment.

The degree of environmental complexity is the number of components in an organization's environment and the extent of an organization's knowledge about those components. If the number of components and the need for sophisticated knowledge is minimal, the environment is classified as simple.

If a number of dissimilar components and a high need for sophisticated knowledge exist, the environment is complex.

As uncertainty is a threat to organizational effectiveness, managers try to minimize environmental uncertainty.

### *Managing in a Global Environment*

Managers in all types and sizes of organizations must constantly monitor changes and consider the particular characteristics of their own location as they plan, organize, lead, and control in this dynamic environment.

Managers might have one of three perspectives or attitudes toward international business :

1. An ethnocentric attitude is the parochialistic belief that the best work approaches and practices are those of the home country (the country in which the company's headquarters are located).
2. A polycentric attitude is the view that the managers in the host country (the foreign country where the organization is doing business) know the best work approaches and practices for running their business.
3. A geocentric attitude is a world-oriented view that focuses on using the best approaches and people from around the globe. To be a successful global manager, an individual needs to be sensitive to differences in national customs and practices Several significant forces are reshaping today's global environment.

Important features of the global environment include regional trading alliances and different types of global organizations.

## Regional Trading Alliances

Regional trading alliances are reshaping global competition. Competition is no longer limited to country versus country, but region versus region. The European Union (EU) is a union of 25 European nations created as a unified economic and trade entity:

a. The primary motivation for the creation of the EU in February 1992 was to allow member nations to reassert their position against the industrial strength of the United States and Japan.

b. All member states of the EU participate in the EMU (Economic and Monetary Union). The EMU consists of three stages for coordinating economic policy. Twelve member states of the European Union have entered the third stage of the EMU, in which participating countries share a single currency, the euro.

c. In 2004 the EU added 10 new members (Cyprus, Malta, the Czech Republic, Estonia, Hungary, Latvia, Lithuania, Poland, Slovakia, and Slovenia. Two additional counties may join the EU by the year 2007.

The North American Free Trade Agreement (NAFTA) is an agreement among the Mexican, Canadian, and U.S. governments in which barriers to trade have been eliminated.

a. NAFTA went into effect on January 1, 1994.

b. The signing of NAFTA was both criticized and supported.

c. Eliminating barriers to free trade (tariffs, import licensing requirements, customs user fees) has resulted in a strengthening of the economic power of all three countries.

d. Colombia, Mexico, and Venezuela signed an economic pact eliminating import duties and tariffs in 1994.

e. Thirty-four countries in the Western Hemisphere continue to negotiate a Free Trade Area of the Americas (FTAA) agreement.

FTAA was to have been in effect no later than 2005, but has not yet become operational; its future is still undetermined. The Association of Southeast Asian Nations (ASEAN) is a trading alliance of 10 Asian nations:

a. In the future, the Southeast Asian region promises to be one of the fastest-growing and increasingly influential economic regions of the world.
b. The future economic impact of the Southeast Asian region could rival that of both NAFTA and the EU.

### *Other Trade Alliances*

The 53-nation African Union came into existence in July 2002. Members plan to achieve greater economic development and unity among Africa's nations.

The World Trade Organization (WTO) Formed in 1995 and evolving from GATT, the WTO is the only global organization dealing with the rules of trade among nations.

1. Membership consists of 149 countries and 32 observer governments as of January 2006.
2. The WTO appears to play an important role even though critics are vocal and highly visible.

### *Different Types of Global Organizations*

Business has been conducted internationally for many years Multinational corporations did not become popular until the mid-1960s. Global organizations can be classified in the following categories:

1. The term multinational corporation (MNC) is a broad term that refers to any and all types of international companies that maintain operations in multiple countries.
2. A transnational corporation (TNC), sometimes called a borderless organization, is a type of international company in which artificial geographical barriers are eliminated.

### *Stages of Internationalization*

An organization that goes international typically progresses through three stages. Companies that go international may begin by using global sourcing (also called global out sourcing). In this stage of going international, companies purchase materials or labour from around the world, wherever the materials or labour are least expensive. Beyond the stage of global sourcing, each successive stage to become more international involves more investment and risk.

In the next stage, companies may go international by exporting (making products domestically and selling them abroad) or importing (acquiring products made abroad and selling the products domestically). Both exporting and importing require minimal investment and risk.

In the early stages of going international, managers may also use licensing (giving another organization the right to make or sell its products using its technology or product specifications) or franchises (giving another organization the right to use its name and operating methods After an organization has done international business for a period of time, managers may decide to make more of a direct investment in international markets by forming a strategic alliance, which is a partnership between an organization and a foreign company partner(s). In a strategic alliance, partners share resources and knowledge in developing new products or building production facilities.

A joint venture (a specific type of strategic alliance) may be undertaken to allow partners to form a separate, independent organization for some business purpose.

Managers may decide to make a direct investment in a foreign country by establishing a foreign subsidiary, in which a company sets up a separate and independent production facility or office. Establishing a foreign subsidiary involves the greatest commitment of resources and the greatest risk of all of the stages in going international.

Managing in a global environment entails the following challenges :

*The Legal-Political Environment:* The legal-political environment does not have tó be unstable or revolutionary to be a challenge to managers. The fact that a country's political system differs from that of the United States is important to recognize.

*The Economic Environment:* The economic environment also presents many challenges to foreign-based managers, including fluctuations in currency rates, inflation, and diverse tax policies. In a market economy, resources are primarily owned by the private sector. In a command economy, all economic decisions are planned by a central government.

*The Cultural Environment:* Countries have different cultures, just as organizations do.

National culture is the values and attitudes shared by individuals from a specific country that shape their behaviour and their beliefs about what is important.

A framework developed by Geert Hofstede serves as a valuable framework for understanding differences between national cultures.

1. Hofstede studied individualism versus collectivism. Individualism is the degree to which people in a country prefer to act as individuals rather than as members of groups. Collectivism is characterized by a social framework in which people prefer to act as members of groups and expect others in groups of which they are a part (such as a family or an organization) to look after them and to protect them.
2. Another cultural dimension is power distance, which describes the extent to which a society accepts the fact that power in institutions and organizations is distributed unequally.
3. Uncertainty avoidance describes a cultural measure of the degree to which people tolerate risk and unconventional behaviour.
4. Hofstede identified the dimension of achievement versus nurturing. Achievement is the degree to which values such as assertiveness, the acquisition of money and material goods, and competition prevail. Nurturing emphasizes sensitivity in relationships and concern for the welfare of others.
5. Long-term and short-term orientation. People in countries having long-term orientation cultures look to the future and value thrift and persistence. Short-term orientation values the past and present and emphasizes a respect for tradition and social obligations.
6. Countries have different rankings on Hofstede's cultural dimensions, and managers should be aware of the cultural differences present in countries in which they do business.

The Global Leadership and Organizational Behaviour Effectiveness (GLOBE) research program is an assessment that updates Hofstede's studies. GLOBE began in 1993 and identified nine dimensions on which *National Cultures Differ:* Assertiveness, future orientation, gender differentiation, uncertainty avoidance, power distance, individualism collectivism, in-group collectivism, performance orientation, and humane orientation.

In today's world the openness that is necessary to conduct business successfully in a global environment poses great challenges. The increased threat of terrorism, economic interdependence of trading countries, and significant cultural create a complicated environment in which to manage. Successful global managers need to have great sensitivity and understanding. Managers must adjust leadership styles and management approaches to accommodate culturally diverse views.

## Social Responsibility and Managerial Ethics

This chapter discusses issues involving social responsibility and managerial ethics and their effect on managerial decision making. Both social responsibility and ethics are responses to a changing environment and are influenced by organizational culture Managers regularly face decisions that have dimensions of social responsibility.

Examples include employee relations, philanthropy, pricing, resource conservation, product quality, and doing business in countries that violate human rights

### *Social Responsibility*

Two opposing views of social responsibility are presented:

- The classical view is the view that management's only social responsibility is to maximize profits.
- The socioeconomic view is the view that management's social responsibility goes beyond the making of profits to include protecting and improving society's welfare.

A four stage model shows how social responsibility progresses in organizations Social responsibility may progress from the stance of obeying all laws and regulations while caring for stockholders' interests to the point of demonstrating responsibility to society as a whole which characterizes the highest socioeconomic commitment.

*Social Obligations to Responsiveness to Responsibility:* Social obligation occurs when a firm engages in social actions because of its obligation to meet certain economic and legal responsibilities. Social responsiveness is seen when a firm engages in social actions in response to some popular social need. Social responsibility is a business's intention, beyond its legal and economic obligations, to do the right things and act in ways that are good for society.

### *The Greening of Management*

A number of highly visible ecological problems and environmental disasters (e.g., Exxon *Valdez* oil spill, mercury poisoning in Japan, Three Mile Island, Chernobyl) brought about a new spirit of environmentalism. Recognizing the close link between an organization's decisions and activities and its impact on the natural environment is called the greening of management.

Values-based management is an approach to managing in which managers are guided by the organization's shared values in their management practices.

Purposes of Shared Values are:

1) They act as guideposts for managerial decisions and actions.
2) Shared values serve to shape employee behaviour and to communicate what the organization expects of its members.
3) Shared corporate values can influence an organization's marketing efforts.
4) Shared values are a way to build team spirit in organizations.

## Managerial Ethics

The term ethics refers to principles, values, and beliefs that define what is right and wrong behaviour.

### *Factors That Affect Employee Ethics*

Stages of Moral Development. Research confirms three levels of moral development. Each level has two stages.

a) The first level is called *preconventional*. At this level, the individual's choice between right or wrong is based on personal consequences involved.

b) At the second stage, which is labelled *conventional*, moral values reside in maintaining expected standards and living up to the expectations of others.

c) The third level—the *principled* level—the individual makes a clear effort to define moral principles apart from the authority of the groups to which the person belongs.

d) Research on the stages of moral development indicates that people proceed sequentially through the six stages of these three levels, with no guarantee of continued development at any stage. The majority of adults are at Stage.

The higher the stage an employee reaches, the more likelihood that he or she will behave ethically.

***Individual Characteristics:*** A person joins an organization with a relatively entrenched set of values.

a. Values are basic convictions about what is right and wrong. Values are broad and cover a wide variety of issues.

b. Ego strength is a personality measure of the strength of a person's convictions. Individuals who score high on ego strength are likely to resist impulses to act unethically and are likely do what they think is right.

c. Locus of control is a personality attribute that measures the degree to which people believe they control their own fate. Individuals with an internal locus of control think that they control their destiny, while persons with an external locus of control are less likely to take personal responsibility for the consequences of their behaviour and are more likely to rely on external forces. Externals believe that what happens to them is due to luck or chance.

A third factor influencing managerial ethics is structural variables.

The existence of structural variables such as formal rules and regulations, job descriptions, written codes of ethics, performance appraisal systems, and reward systems can strongly influence ethical behaviour.

The content and strength of an organization's culture influences ethical behaviour.

a. An organizational culture most likely to encourage high ethical stand cards is one that is high in risk tolerance, control, and conflict tolerance.
b. A strong culture exerts more influence on managers than does a weak one.
c. However, in organizations with weak cultures, work groups and departmental standards strongly influence ethical behaviour.

Finally, the intensity of an issue can affect ethical decisions. Six characteristics determine issue intensity;

a. Greatness of harm.
b. Consensus of wrong.
c. Probability of harm.
d. Immediacy of consequences.
e. Proximity to victim.
f. Concentration of effect.

*Improving Ethical Behaviour*

Organizations can take a number of actions to cultivate ethical behaviour among members. Some of those are"

1) The selection process for bringing new employees into organizations should be viewed as an opportunity to learn about an individual's level of moral development, personal values, ego strength, and locus of control.
2) A code of ethics is a formal statement of an organization's primary values and the ethical rules it expects employees to follow. In addition, decision rules can be developed to guide managers in handling ethical dilemmas in decision making.
3) Top management's leadership and commitment to ethical behaviour is extremely important since the cultural tone for an organization is established by its top managers.

4) Employees' job goals should be tangible and realistic, because clear and realistic goals reduce ambiguity and motivate rather than punish. Job goals are usually a key issue in the performance appraisal process.
5) If an organization wants employees to uphold high ethical standards, this dimension must be included in the appraisal process. Performance appraisals should include this dimension, rather than focusing solely on economic outcomes.
6) Ethics training should be used to help teach ethical problem solving and to present simulations of ethical situations that could arise. At the least, ethics training should increase awareness of ethical issues.
7) Independent social audits evaluate decisions and management practices in terms of the organization's code of ethics and can be used to deter unethical behaviour.
8) Organizations can provide formal protective mechanisms so that employees with ethical dilemmas can do what is right without fear of reprisal.

Social Entrepreneurship: A social entrepreneur is an individual or organization who seeks out opportunities to improve society by using practical, innovative, and sustainable approaches.

Social impact management: Managers are increasingly expected to act responsibly in the way they conduct business.

Managers using a social impact management approach examine the social impacts of their decisions and actions.

When they consider how their actions in planning, organizing, leading and controlling will work in light of the social context within which business operates, managers become more aware of whether they are leading in a responsible manner.

## Decision Making: The Essence of the Manager's Job

Everyone in an organization makes decisions, but decision making is particularly important in a manager's job. Decision making is such an important part of all four managerial functions that decision making is said to be synonymous with managing.

### *The Decision-Making Process*

A decision is a choice made from two or more alternatives. The decision-making process is a set of eight steps that include the following:

- Identifying a problem: A problem is a discrepancy between an existing state and a desired state of affairs. In order to identify a problem, a manager should be able to differentiate the problem from its symptom; he should be under pressure to taken action and must have the authority and resources to take action.
- Identifying decision criteria: Decision criteria are criteria that define what is relevant in a decision.
- Allocating weights to the criteria: The criteria identified in the previous step of the decision-making process may not have equal importance. So he decision maker must assign a weight to each of the items in order to give each item accurate priority in the decision.
- Developing alternatives: The decision maker should then identify viable alternatives that could resolve the problem.
- Analysing alternatives: Each of the alternatives are then critically analysed by evaluating it against the criteria established in Steps 2 and 3.
- Selecting an alternative: The next step is to select the best alternative from among those identified and assessed. If criteria weights have been used, the decision maker would select the alternative that received the highest score in Step 5.
- Implementing the alternative: The selected alternative is implemented by effectively communicating the decision to the individuals who would be affected by it and their commitment to the decision is acquired.
- Evaluating decision effectiveness: The last step in the decision-making process is to assess the result of the decision in order to determine whether or not the problem has been resolved.

Managers can make decisions on the basis of rationality, bounded rationality, or intuition.

1. Rational decision making. Managerial decision making is assumed to be rational—that is, making choices that are consistent and value-maximizing within specified constraints. A rational manager would be *completely* logical and objective. Rational decision making assumes that the manager is making decisions in the best interests of the *organization*, not in his/her own interests. The assumptions of rationality can be met if the manager is faced with a simple problem in which (1) goals are clear and alternatives limited, (2) time pressures are minimal and the cost of finding and evaluating alternatives is low, (3) the organizational culture supports innovation and risk taking, and (4) outcomes are concrete and measurable.
2. Bounded rationality. As the *perfectly* rational model of decision making isn't realistic, managers tend to operate under assumptions of bounded rationality, which is decision-making behaviour that is rational, but limited (bounded) by an individual's ability to process information. Under bounded rationality, managers make satisfaction decisions, in which they accept solutions that are "good enough." Managers' decision making may be strongly influenced by the organization's culture, internal politics, power considerations, and by a phenomenon called escalation of commitment—an increased commitment to a previous decision despite evidence that it may have been wrong.
3. Intuitive decision making. Managers also regularly use their intuition. Intuitive decision making is a subconscious process of making decisions on the basis of experience and accumulated judgment. Although intuitive decision making will not replace the rational decision-making process, it does play an important role in managerial decision making.

### *Types of Problems and Decisions*

Managers encounter different types of problems and use different types of ecisions to resolve them. Problems can be structured problems or unstructured problems and decisions can be programmed decisions or non-programmed decisions.

Structured problems are straightforward, familiar, and easily defined. In dealing with structured problems, a manager may use a programmed decision, which is a repetitive decision that can be handled by a routine approach.

Managers rely on three types of programmed decisions:

a. A procedure is a series of interrelated sequential steps that can be used to respond to a structured problem.

b. A rule is an explicit statement that tells managers what they can or cannot do.

c. A policy is a guideline for making decisions.

Unstructured problems are problems that are new or unusual and for which information is ambiguous or incomplete. These problems are best handled by a non-programmed decision that is a unique decision that requires a custommade solution.

At higher levels in the organizational hierarchy, managers deal more often with difficult, unstructured problems and make non-programmed decisions in attempting to resolve these problems and challenges. Lower-level managers handle routine decisions, using programmed decisions.

## Decision-Making Conditions

Decision can be made under conditions of certainty, uncertainty and risk. Certainty is a situation in which a manager can make accurate decisions because all outcomes are known. Few managerial decisions are made under the condition of certainty.

More common is the situation of risk, in which the decision maker is able to estimate the likelihood of certain outcomes. Uncertainty is a situation in which the decision maker is not certain and cannot even make reasonable probability estimates concerning outcomes of alternatives. In such a situation, the choice of alternative is influenced by the limited amount of information available to the decision maker. It's also influenced by the psychological orientation of the decision maker.

1) An optimistic manager will follow a *maximax* choice, maximizing the maximum possible payoff.

2) A pessimistic manager will pursue a *maximin* choice, maximizing the minimum possible payoff.

3) The manager who desires to minimize the maximum regret will opt for a *minimax* choice.

Decision-Making Styles: Managers have different styles in making decisions and solving problems. One perspective proposes that people differ along two dimensions in the way they approach decision making. One dimension is an individual's *way of thinking*—rational or intuitive. The other is the individual's *tolerance for ambiguity*—low or high. Diagramming these two dimensions lead to a matrix showing four different decision-making styles.

a. The directive style is characterized by low tolerance for ambiguity and a rational way of thinking.
b. The analytic style is one characterized by a high tolerance for ambiguity and a rational way of thinking.
c. The conceptual style is characterized by a high tolerance for ambiguity and an intuitive way of thinking.
d. The behavioural style is characterized by a low tolerance for ambiguity and an intuitive way of thinking.

In reality, most managers have both a dominant style and alternate styles, with some managers relying almost exclusively on their dominant style and others being more flexible, depending on the particular situation.

Decision-Making Biases and Errors: Managers use different styles and "rules of thumb" (heuristics) to simply their decision making. Some of decision making biases and errors are:

1. *Overconfidence bias* occurs when decision makers tend to think that they know more than they do or hold unrealistically positive views of themselves and their performance.
2. *Immediate gratification bias* describes decision makers who tend to want immediate rewards and avoid immediate costs.
3. The *anchoring effect* describes when decision makers fixate on initial information as a starting point and then, once set, fail to adequately adjust for subsequent information.
4. *Selective perception bias* occurs when decision makers selectively organize and interpret events based on their biased perceptions.

5. *Confirmation bias* occurs when decision makers seek out information that reaffirms their past choices and discount information that contradicts their past judgments.
6. *Framing bias* occurs when decision makers select and highlight certain aspects of a situation while excluding others.
7. *Availability bias* is seen when decision makers tend to remember events that are the most recent and vivid in their memory.
8. Decision makers who show *representation bias* assess the likelihood of an event based on how closely it resembles other events or sets of events.
9. *Randomness bias* describes the effect when decision makers try to create meaning out of random events.
10. The *sunk costs error* is when a decision maker forgets that current choices cannot correct the past. Instead of ignoring sunk costs, the decision maker cannot forget them. In assessing choices, the individual fixates on past expenditures rather than on future consequences.
11. *Self-serving bias* is exhibited by decision makers who are quick to take credit for their successes and blame failure on outside factors.
12. *Hindsight bias* is the tendency for decision makers to falsely believe, once the outcome is known, that they would have accurately predicted the outcome.

## Foundations of Planning

Planning is one of the four functions of management. Planning involves defining the organization's goals, establishing an overall strategy for achieving these goals, and developing plans for organizational work activities. The term *planning* as used in this chapter refers to *formal* planning.

### *Purposes of Planning*

Planning serves a number of significant purposes.

1. Planning gives direction to managers and non-managers of an organization.
2. Planning reduces uncertainty.

3. Planning minimizes waste and uncertainty.
4. Planning establishes goals or standards used in controlling.

### *Planning and Performance*

Although organizations that use formal planning do not *always* outperform those that do not plan, most studies show positive relationships between planning and performance. Effective planning and implementation play a greater part in high performance than does the amount of planning done. Studies have shown that when formal planning has *not* led to higher performance, the external environment is often the reason.

### *The Role of Goals and Plans in Planning*

Planning is often called the primary management function because it establishes the basis for all other functions. Planning involves two important elements: goals and plans.

Goals (often called objectives) are desired outcomes for individuals, groups, or entire organizations.

### *Types of Goals*

a. Financial goals versus strategic goals Financial goals related to the financial performance of the organization while strategic goals are related to other areas of an organizations performance.
b. Stated goals versus real goals Stated goals are official statements of what an organization *says* and what it wants its various stockholders to believe its goals are. Real goals are those that an organization actually pursues, as defined by the *actions* of its members.

### *Types of Plans*

Plans can be described by their breadth, time frame, specificity, and frequency of use:

- On the basis of Breadth plans can be Strategic or operational plans. Strategic plans (long-term plans) are plans that apply to the entire organization, establish the organization's overall goals, and seek to position the organization in terms of its environment. Operational plans (short-term plans) are plans that specify the details of how the overall goals are to be achieved.

- On the basis of Time frame plans can be Short-term or long-term plans. Shortterm plans are plans that cover one year or less. Long-term plans are plans with a time frame beyond three years.
- On the basis of Specificity plans can be Specific or directional plans. Specific plans are plans that are clearly defined and leave no room for interpretation. Directional plans are flexible plans that set out general guidelines.
- On the basis of Frequency of use plans can be Single-use or standing plans. A single-use plan is a one-time plan specifically designed to meet the needs of a unique situation. Standing plans are ongoing plans that provide guidance for activities performed repeatedly.

### *Approaches to Establishing Goals*

Goals can be established through the process of traditional goal setting or through MBO (management by objectives). Traditional goal setting is an approach to setting goals in which goals are set at the top level of the organization and then broken into subgoals for each level of the organization. Traditional goal setting assumes that top managers know what is best because of their ability to see the "big picture." Employees are to work to meet the goals for their particular area of responsibility.

This traditional approach requires that goals must be made more specific as they flow down to lower levels in the organization. In striving to achieve specificity, however, objectives sometimes lose clarity and unity with goals set at a higher level in the When the hierarchy of organizational goals *is* clearly defined, it forms an integrated meansend chain—an integrated network of goals in which the accomplishment of goals at one level serves as the means for achieving the goals, or ends, at the next level.

Management by objectives (MBO) is a process of setting mutually agreed-upon goals and using those goals to evaluate employee performance. Studies of actual MBO programs confirm that MBO can increase employee performance and organizational productivity. However, top management commitment and involvement are important contributions to the success of an MBO program.

The following steps are involved in a typical MBO program:

- The organizations overall objectives and strategies are formulated.
- Major objectives are allocated among divisional and departmental units.
- Unit managers collabouratively set specific objectives for their units with their managers.
- Specific objectives are collabouratively set with all department members.
- Action plans, defining how objectives are to be achieved, are specified and agreed upon by managers and employee.
- The action plans are implemented.
- Progress toward objectives is periodically reviewed, and feedback is provided.
- Successful achievement of objectives is reinforced by performance based rewards.

Whether an organization uses a more traditional approach to establishing objectives, uses some form of MBO, or has its own approach, managers must define objectives before they can effectively and efficiently complete other planning activities.

### *Characteristics of Well-Designed Goals*

1. Written in terms of outcomes.
2. Measurable and quantifiable.
3. Clear as to a time frame.
4. Challenging, but attainable.
5. Written down.
6. Communicated to all organizational members.

### *Five Steps in Goals Setting*

1. Review the organization's mission (the purpose of the organization).
2. Evaluate available resources.
3. Determine the goals individually or with input from others.
4. Write down the goals and communicate them to all who need to know.

5. Review results and whether goals are being met. Make changes as needed.

### *Developing Plans*

The process of developing plans is influenced by three contingency factors and by the particular planning approach used by the organization.

Three Contingency Factors in Planning are;

- Manager's level in the organization: *Operational* planning usually dominates the planning activities of *lower*-level managers. As managers move up through the levels of the organization, their planning becomes more strategy oriented.
- Degree of environmental uncertainty: The greater the environmental uncertainty, the more directional plans should be, with emphasis placed on the short term. When uncertainty is high, plans should be specific, but flexible. Managers must be prepared to rework and amend plans, or even to abandon their plans if necessary.
- Length of future commitments: According to the commitment concept, plans should extend far enough to meet those commitments made today. Planning for too long or for too short a time period is inefficient and ineffective.

### *Approaches to Planning*

In the traditional approach, planning was done entirely by top-level managers who were often assisted by a formal planning department. Another approach to planning is to involve more members of the organization in the planning process. In this approach, plans are not handed down from one level to the next, but are developed by organizational members at various levels to meet their specific needs.

### *Criticisms of Planning*

Although planning is an important managerial function with widespread use, five major arguments have been directed against planning:

- Planning may create rigidity.

- Plans can't be developed for a dynamic environment.
- Formal plans can't replace intuition and creativity.
- Planning focuses managers' attention on today's competition, not on tomorrow's survival.
- Formal planning reinforces success, which may lead to failure.

The external environment is constantly changing. Therefore managers should develop plans that are specific, but flexible. Managers must also recognize that planning is an *ongoing* process, and they should be willing to change directions if environmental conditions warrant. Flexibility is particularly important. Managers must remain alert to environmental changes that could impact the effective implementation of plans, and they must be prepared to make changes as needed.

## Strategic Management

The present day news is filled with examples of changing organizational strategies like Mergers, Strategic alliances, Downsizing, Spin-offs and Global expansion.

This chapter examines the strategic management process as it relates to the planning function. Managers must carefully consider their organization's internal and external environments as they develop strategic plans. They should have a systematic means of analyzing the environment, assessing their organization's strengths and weaknesses, identifying opportunities that would give the organization a competitive advantage, and incorporating these findings into their planning. The value of *thinking strategically* has an important impact on organization performance.

Strategic management is what managers do to develop the organization's strategies. Strategic management involves all four of the basic management functions—planning, organizing, leading, and controlling.

Strategic management has a is important for organizations as it has a significant impact on how well an organization performs. In today's business world, organizations of all types and sizes must manage constantly changing situations. Today's companies are composed of diverse divisions, units, functions, and work activities that must be coordinated. Strategic management is involved in many of the decisions that managers make. The strategic management process is a six-step process that encompasses strategic planning, implementation, and evaluation.

- Identifying the Organization's Current Mission, Objectives, and Strategies: Every organization needs a mission, which is a statement of the purpose of an organization. The mission statement addresses the question: What is the organization's reason for being in business? The organization must identify its current objectives and strategies, as well.
- External Analysis: Managers in every organization need to conduct an external analysis. Influential factors such as competition, pending legislation, and labour supply are included in the external environment. After analyzing the external environment, managers must assess what they have learned in terms of opportunities and threats. Opportunities are positive trends in external environmental factors; threats are negative trends in environmental factors. Because of different resources and capabilities, the same external environment can present opportunities to one organization and pose threats to another.
- Internal Analysis: Internal analysis should lead to a clear assessment of the organization's resources and capabilities. Any activities the organization does well or any unique resources that it has are called strengths. Weaknesses are activities the organization does not do well or resources it needs but does not possess.

The organization's major value-creating skills and capabilities that determine its competitive weapons are the organization's core competencies. Organizational culture is important in internal analysis; the company's culture can promote or hinder its strategic actions. SWOT analysis is an analysis of the organization's strengths, weaknesses, opportunities, and threats.

- Formulating Strategies: After the SWOT, managers develop and evaluate strategic alternatives and select strategies that are appropriate. Strategies need to be established for corporate, business, and functional levels.
- Implementing Strategies

- Evaluating Results to know how effective the strategies have been and if any adjustments are necessary.

## Types of Organizational Strategies

Strategic planning takes place on three different and distinct levels:

### *Corporate Strategy*

It is an organizational strategy that determines what businesses a company is in, should be in, or wants to be in, and what it wants to do with those businesses.

There are three main types of corporate strategies:

a. A growth strategy is a corporate strategy that is used when an organization wants to grow and does so by expanding the number of products offered or markets served, either through its current business) or through new businesses.

b. A stability strategy is a corporate strategy characterized by an absence of significant change in what the organization is currently doing.

c. A renewal strategy is a corporate strategy designed to address organizational weaknesses that are leading to performance declines. Two such strategies are retrenchment strategy and turnaround strategy.

Corporate Portfolio Analysis is used when an organization's corporate strategy involves a number of businesses. Managers can manage this portfolio of businesses using a corporate portfolio matrix, such as the BCG matrix. The BCG matrix is a strategy tool that guides resource allocation decisions on the basis of market share and growth rate of Strategic Business Units (SBUs).

### *Business (Competitive) Strategy*

A business strategy (also known as a competitive strategy) is an organizational strategy focused on how the organization will compete in each of its businesses. Competitive advantage plays an important role in formulating the business strategy. A competitive advantage is what sets an organization apart, that is, its distinctive edge. An organization's competitive advantage can come from its core competencies. If implemented properly, quality can be one way for an organization to create a sustainable competitive advantage. An organization must be able to sustain its competitive advantage; it must keep its edge despite competitors' action and regardless of major changes in the organization's industry.

Michael Porter's work explains how managers can create and sustain a competitive advantage that will give a company above-average profitability. Industry analysis is an important step in Porter's framework.

He says there are five competitive forces at work in an industry; together, these five forces determine industry attractiveness and profitability. Porter proposes that the following five factors can be used to assess an industry's attractiveness:

i. *Threat of new entrants.* How likely it is that new competitors will come into the industry? Managers should assess barriers to entry, which are factors that determine how easy or difficult it would be for new competitors to enter the industry.
ii. *Threat of substitutes.* How likely is it that products of other industries could be substituted for a company's products?
iii. *Bargaining power of buyers.* How much bargaining power do buyers (customers) have?
iv. *Bargaining power of suppliers.* How much bargaining power do a company's suppliers have?
v. *Current rivalry.* How intense is the competition among firms that are currently in the industry?

According to Porter, managers must choose a strategy that will give their organization a competitive advantage. Porter identifies three generic competitive strategies. Which strategy managers select depends on the organization's strengths and core competencies and the particular weaknesses of its competitor(s). Based on the above analysis, only three types of generic strategies are available to organizations to choose from.

They are:

a. A cost leadership strategy is a business or competitive strategy in which the organization competes on the basis of having the *lowest costs* in its industry.

b. A differentiation strategy is a business or competitive strategy in which a company offers *unique products* that are widely valued by customers.

c. A focus strategy is a business or competitive strategy in which a company pursues a cost or differentiation advantage in a *narrow industry segment.*

An organization that has been not been able to develop either a low cost or a differentiation competitive advantage is said to be "stuck in the middle."

### *Functional Strategy*

These are strategies used by an organization's various functional departments to support the business or competitive strategy.

### *New Directions in Organizational Strategies*

- E-Business Strategies. Using the Internet, companies have created knowledge bases that employees can tap into any time, anywhere. E-business as a strategy can be used to develop a sustainable competitive advantage; it can also be used to establish a basis for differentiation or focus.
- Customer Service Strategies. These strategies give customers what they want, communicate effectively with them, and provide employees with customer service training.
- Innovation Strategies. These strategies focus on breakthrough products and can include the application of existing technology to new uses.

## Project Management –An Overview

Project is a perfect blend of human and non-human resources pulled together in an organization to achieve a specified purpose. A project has a single set of objectives and when these objectives are achieved, the project is termed to be completed. Therefore, a project has a finite and well-defined life span.

Project management is an important managerial activity for any organization. Wherever there is a need for a specified time-bound work, project management is called for-whether it is a specified time-bound work, project management is called for-whether it is an educational institution, a hospital, a publishing house, a business house, a financial institution, an agricultural and rural development work, a social work or an industrial construction project. Project management envisages meticulous planning, effective implementation and professional organization to achieve the management of cost, time and performance.

Therefore, the traditional form of organization with functional divisions, hierarchical relationship and continuous flow of repetitive work is not suitable for project management. Project management calls for sharper tools of planning and control and improved ways of coping with human problems as a project has certain distinctive features of a non-routine and non-repetitive undertaking plagued with uncertainties, a co-ordinated effort of persons drawn from different divisions, disciplines and also from external agencies; and a dynamic, temporary and flexible relationships.

These characteristic features make management of a project different from management of operations and involve issues like from of project organization, project planning, project implementation, project control and human aspects of project management. Therefore, in the undertaking of project management, following aspects are important:

- The objectives, scope and type of management.
- The project phase concept.
- The feasibility study involving preparation of detailed project report and project selection.
- Financial evaluation, cost and time over runs.
- Implementation phase in project management.
- Other aspects like contracts and specifications, foreign exchange and import controls, power shortage, labour and tax incentives etc.

Project management is the application of a collection of tools and techniques to direct the use of diverse resources towards the accomplishment of a unique, complex, one-time task within time, cost and quality constraints. Each task requires a particular mix of these tools and techniques structured to fit a project environment an life cycle of the project. Thus, project management means dedicating organizational resources to the end objective and keeping the totality in focus all the time. The emphasis in project management is on results with the holistic approach. A good project management seeks to remove, among other things, delays in execution, avoid cause of delays and identification of technical flaws in executing projects.

Project management is the planning, organizing, directing and controlling of company resources for a relatively short-term objective that has been established to complete specific goals and objectives. Furthermore, project management utilizes the system approach to management by having functional personnel (the vertical hierarchy) assigned to a specific project (the horizontal hierarchy).

In a project management, all work has inter-dependence and inter-relationship with others. This approach of project management differs from functional management in that the latter does not hold responsible to any one individual for a work from start end or from A to Z.

This create problems of communication, co-ordination, commitment and control. No good decision could be taken without considering all inter-related things and no use ful result can be achieved without completing the whole work.

The importance of any work depends on how it stands in relation to others and to the whole. The inter-relationship and even the work to be performed is liable to be changed, but the objective does not change. In project management environment, the future is uncertain unlike in an ordinary functional management, and therefore, it is necessary to keep an eye on the future and to adopt very fast changed needs of the further. Quick responses and flexibility are essential for dealing with ever-changing dynamic situations which pervade the project management. Thus, the aims and objectives of project management are:

- Timely completion of the project.
- Avoidance of delay, technical flaws and drawings defects.
- Proper flow of funds.
- Proper tooling and techniques.
- Proper control over chain reaction activities.

Project 'National Initiative on Care for Elderly':

The project 'NICE', a National Initiative on Care for Elderly is developed by the National Institute of Social Defence (NISD) to enhance the delivery of care to the elderly in de-institutionalised settings. The focus of the project is on creating awareness, identification of the needs, targeted intervention and optimising capabilities to improve the quality of life of the elderly.

### *The Need*

The demographic trend in India has been towards an increasing number of elderly due to the increased life span of the population, in general. The demographic change has been accompanied with a fast changing family structure due to forces like urbanization and migration which are not quite conducive to the welfare of the elderly. The trend clearly reveals that ageing will become a major social challenge in the future and vast resources will be required towards support, care and treatment of the older persons. In order to cope with the problems faced by the aged, it is necessary to educate & import training to persons concerned with the welfare of the older persons and to develop trained manpower, which can take care of older persons within the community setting.

### *The Mandate*

With an overall objective of ensuring active, healthy and dignified ageing, NICE aims at the well being of the older persons. Thus, it is involved in (i) identifying the specific needs of the elderly (ii) capacity building of service providers and cadre of professional care givers and (iii) creating enabling social environment and attitude.

### *Areas of Intervention*

Lifestyles : Enhanced independence;

- Self-Care.
- Independent functioning.
- Transportation & Mobility.
- Attitudes & Perceptions.
- Overcome marginalisation/diminishing self-confidence.
- Issue of emotional dependence.
- Communication skill.

- Environmental/Cultural factors.
- Encourage realistic perception of self.
- Enhance copying mechanism for problem solving.
- Causes of ageing.

### *Problem Solving*

- Issue of elderly abuse.
- Crisis intervention.
- Adjustment Problems.
- Dealing with Stress.
- Older persons affected by conflicts/disasters.
- Self-help groups.
- Pressure groups.
- Networking of formal & informal organization.

### *Three Components of the Project*

- Prevention.
- Control.
- Care.

### *Courses Profile*

Most aged people need special care. They also require trained caretakers who can perceive their needs and address them appropriately. Realizing the dearth of trained Geriatric care givers, the NISD has conceptualised & initiated a unique programme under the project 'NICE' to educate those concerned with care of the elderly through master trainers trained by them.

### *Eligibility/Selection Criterion*

Candidates having Matriculation and attained 18 years are eligible for these courses. Preference is given to candidates having an experience(s) of working in Age Care Organisations. The training courses are meant for sponsored candidates. Selection for admission in the 6-month certificate course is made through Common Aptitude Test (CAT) held on all India basis followed by a personal interview.

Career Opportunities:

- Home Care.

- Social Worker.
- Emergency Relief Worker.
- Health Worker.
- Nursing Assistant.
- Home Nursing Attendant.
- Assistant-Mobile Medicare Unit.
- Project Assistant.
- Physiotherapy assistant.

*Approach :* All aspects of old age related activities, problems, expectations, behaviour and performance have been taken into account while developing a comprehensive course curriculum, which is broadly classified into major subjects. Each subject is further classified into various learning units, including classroom training, observation visits/field visits. Each learning unit covers topics consisting of lesson plan.

*Methodology :* The Courses are an appropriate mix of theoretical sessions with field exposure and practical training to build up knowledge, attitude and skills in the field of Geriatric Care. To maximize learning, the methodology includes a variety of methods like small group activities, case studies, role-play, participatory activities, presentations, lectures, hospital/ institutional visit, individual assignments and panel discussions. Inputs of the best practices of working with elderly are also provided to the students by national level experts in Geriatrics.

*Internship :* The internship includes placement of students with old age homes, age care institutions & some selected homes of the elderly besides an extensive door to door survey to collect data. The survey is basically meant to identify the realistic needs of the elderly perceived by the elderly themselves. Preparation & submission of a dissertation of their individual field surveys is an essential part of the course.

***Highlights of the Basic Curriculum***

- *Social Gerontology :* Introduction to ageing; Its basics, definition, demographic trends, processes, myths & stereotype of ageing and prejudice & discrimination against elderly; Sociology & Social Work; Knowledge about effects of culture, tradition and customs on older persons, position of the older persons within the community; Understanding the merits & demerits of nuclear and joint family systems; Social security measures, social work methods; Psychology & Human Behaviour; Understanding the concept of mental health and the emotional status in old age; Dementia and attending to their safety needs; Knowledge of mental ability and behaviour of the aged; Knowledge about social psychology-interpersonal relationships, group behaviour and comfort, counselling, rehabilitation, family and social adjustment.

- *Basic Geriatrics* : Community Health and Environmental Hygiene; knowledge about promotion of environmental health through safe water supply, sanitation programmes, control of communicable diseases; Ways of imparting the same through home visits and health education; Coping up with problems of elderly by counselling, referrals, identification and productive engagement of older persons; Knowing about good communication skills-verbal and nonverbal with older persons; Understanding the nutritional needs of the older persons specially during sickness and diet management; Anatomy & Physiology; Basic terms, organization of body, different body parts and their systems.
- *Applied Geriatrics* : Fundamental of Ageing Care: Understanding the concept of the basic care, basic needs, first aid, terminal care for the elderly; Social Welfare Activities; Ability to organize Old Age Homes and Day Care Centres; free health check up; Club for the Aged; cultural events; Economic support from Government and non-Government Sector, etc.
- *Geriatric Nursing* : Special Care of the Elderly. Understanding old age-related diseases and the ability to attend to the needs of older persons during sickness such as cardio-vascular problems, hypertension, respiratory problems, gastro-intestinal changes, disorders of urinary system, nervous system disorder, cataract, glaucoma and hearing problems; Physiotherapy and Rehabilitation; Understanding the techniques for restoring normal life

for older persons as far as possible; Knowledge of the types of exercises-active/passive/therapeutic, heat application-types of heat, radiation and heat modalities; rehabilitation devices and their uses; Healthy Ageing: How to lead an active and healthy life in old age.

### *Post Graduate Diploma : An Overview*

The concept of 'Geriatric Care' in India seeks an adequate attention to provide positive interventions for strengthening social support systems for the older persons.

The support services in existing system require boosting to cater to the needs of increasing number of the older persons, both in urban as well as rural settings.

Accordingly, a specialized one year Post Graduate Diploma Course in 'Integrated geriatric care' is instituted under the Project 'NICE', with a specific aim to develop a team of quality geriatric care personnel at managerial level. The course is open to on-job volunteers as well as regular graduates to meet the demand for providing skill based, field oriented, trained personnel in the Geriatric care.

### *Eligibility/Selection Criterion*

Candidates possessing Bachelor's Degree, preferably in Sociology, Social Work, Anthropology, Psychology, Nursing, Home Science or equivalent from a recognized University or Institute and minimum of 20 years of age are eligible for the Course. Working in Age Care Organizations and/or holding a certificate(s) in the field of Old Age Care have an advantage. Final selection for admission is made through Common Aptitude Test (CAT) held in all India basis followed by group discussion & interview.

## Career Prospects NGOs

### *National*

- Project Director and Programme Managers.
- Human Resource Development Professionals & Managers.
- Counselors & Consultants in Community Based Organisations.
- Associates with Residents Welfare Associations (RWA).

*International*

- Programme Officers/Associates.
- Social Development Divisions of International Organisations.
- Foreign assisted Programmes/Projects run by various International Bodies/Countries.

*Government Sector*

- Professionals in Hospital Settings Middle level Professionals/Welfare Officers.
- Academic Institutes.
- Prospective Faculty Members and Instructors/Trainers.

*Course Contents*

*Geriatrics :* Fundamentals of Gerontology, Myths & Misconceptions about Aged, Population Ageing, Theories of Ageing, Epidemiology of Ageing, Family and the Aged, Aged and Community, Aspects of Elder Care, Minimum Standards of Elderly Care, Rehabilitation, Geriatric Career: An Emerging Issue.

*Geriatrics Health :* Basics of Geriatrics, Principles of Clinical Geriatrics, Geriatric Physical Disorders, Geriatric Mental Disorder, Common Geriatric Diseases: Prevention & Care, Approach to Elderly, Health Education, Physical Activity and Fitness, Nutrition & Diet of Elderly, Poly-pharmacy, Health Care Services, Long Term Care in Geriatric Rehabilitation, Community Geriatrics.

*Geriatrics Management :* Managament Processes, HRD-Concept & Sub-Systems, Role, Stress and Conflict Management, Management-Specific Situation, Project Management and MIS, Managing Age Care, Budgeting & Accounting, Feedback and Evaluation, Communications and Public Relations.

*Social Policy and Planning :* Social Change, Law & Justice; Government, Social, Economic Support & Security; Specialised Schemes and Services; Social Work Methods; Advocacy; Empowerment & Policy Intervention; Role of Media & Issues of Elderly.

*Geriatrics Counselling :* Counselling: Conceptual Framework; Principles of Care; Counselling: Skill, Techniques and Methods; Counselling Process; Counselling & its Types; Crisis Intervention

& Counselling; Preventive Intervention for Problems of Older Persons; Social Support & Networking; Roles, Responsibility & Contribution of Older Persons; Life Style Dynamics.

***Geriatrics Research :*** Meaning and Types of Research; Methods of Research; Research Design; Meaning and Types; Data Collection; Statistical Applications in Research; Interpretation Techniques and Report Writing; Information & Communication Techniques (ICT) in Research; Action Oriented Research; Specialized Research Intervention Strategies.

***Project/Seminar Presentation :*** Team project is a joint venture of a group of four students each. These students would work as a team and prepare a 'project' based on the secondary data with reference to field of their choice. Besides, each student has to present an individual seminar based on the subject 'Geriatrics'.

***Internship and Dissertation :*** Students are placed at different Age Care Institutions as part of their internship/pre-job training after the completion of classroom teaching. Concurrently, they are carrying out fieldwork (household survey) for these two months and submit a dissertation report based on the specific topic assigned to an individual student under the vigilance of the supervisor.

# 3

# Social Work : Values and Ethics

## Preamble

The primary mission of the social work profession is to enhance human well-being and help meet the basic human needs of all people, with particular attention to the needs and empowerment of people who are vulnerable, oppressed, and living in poverty. A historic and defining feature of social work is the profession's focus on individual well-being in a social context and the well-being of society. Fundamental to social work is attention to the environmental forces that create, contribute to, and address problems in living.

Social workers promote social justice and social change with and on behalf of clients. "Clients" is used inclusively to refer to individuals, families, groups, organizations, and communities. Social workers are sensitive to cultural and ethnic diversity and strive to end discrimination, oppression, poverty, and other forms of social injustice.

These activities may be in the form of direct practice, community organizing, supervision, consultation administration, advocacy, social and political action, policy development and implementation, education, and research and evaluation. Social workers seek to enhance the capacity of people to address their own needs. Social workers also seek to promote the responsiveness of organizations, communities, and other social institutions to individuals' needs and social problems.

The mission of the social work profession is rooted in a set of core values. These core values, embraced by social workers throughout the profession's history, are the foundation of social work's unique purpose and perspective:

- service.
- social justice.
- dignity and worth of the person.
- importance of human relationships.
- integrity.
- competence.

This constellation of core values reflects what is unique to the social work profession. Core values, and the principles that flow from them, must be balanced within the context and complexity of the human experience.

## Purpose of the NASW Code of Ethics

Professional ethics are at the core of social work. The profession has an obligation to articulate its basic values, ethical principles, and ethical standards. The *NASW Code of Ethics* sets forth these values, principles, and standards to guide social workers' conduct. The *Code* is relevant to all social workers and social work students, regardless of their professional functions, the settings in which they work, or the populations they serve.

### *The NASW Code of Ethics Serves Six Purposes*

1. The Code identifies core values on which social work's mission is based.
2. The *Code* summarizes broad ethical principles that reflect the profession's core values and establishes a set of specific ethical standards that should be used to guide social work practice.
3. The *Code* is designed to help social workers identify relevant considerations when professional obligations conflict or ethical uncertainties arise.
4. The *Code* provides ethical standards to which the general public can hold the social work profession accountable.
5. The *Code* socializes practitioners new to the field to social work's mission, values, ethical principles, and ethical standards.

6. The *Code* articulates standards that the social work profession itself can use to assess whether social workers have engaged in unethical conduct. NASW has formal procedures to adjudicate ethics complaints filed against its members.

In subscribing to this *Code,* social workers are required to cooperate in its implementation, participate in NASW adjudication proceedings, and abide by any NASW disciplinary rulings or sanctions based on it.

The *Code* offers a set of values, principles, and standards to guide decision making and conduct when ethical issues arise. It does not provide a set of rules that prescribe how social workers should act in all situations. Specific applications of the *Code* must take into account the context in which it is being considered and the possibility of conflicts among the *Code's* values, principles, and standards. Ethical responsibilities flow from all human relationships, from the personal and familial to the social and professional.

Further, the *NASW Code of Ethics* does not specify which values, principles, and standards are most important and ought to outweigh others in instances when they conflict. Reasonable differences of opinion can and do exist among social workers with respect to the ways in which values, ethical principles, and ethical standards should be rank ordered when they conflict. Ethical decision making in a given situation must apply the informed judgment of the individual social worker and should also consider how the issues would be judged in a peer review process where the ethical standards of the profession would be applied.

Ethical decision making is a process. There are many instances in social work where simple answers are not available to resolve complex ethical issues. Social workers should take into consideration all the values, principles, and standards in this *Code* that are relevant to any situation in which ethical judgment is warranted. Social workers' decisions and actions should be consistent with the spirit as well as the letter of this *Code.*

In addition to this *Code,* there are many other sources of information about ethical thinking that may be useful. Social workers should consider ethical theory and principles generally, social work theory and research, laws, regulations, agency policies, and other relevant codes of ethics, recognizing that among codes of ethics social workers should consider the *NASW Code of Ethics* as their primary source. Social workers also should be aware of the impact on ethical decision making of their clients' and their own personal values and cultural and religious beliefs and practices.

They should be aware of any conflicts between personal and professional values and deal with them responsibly. For additional guidance social workers should consult the relevant literature on professional ethics and ethical decision making and seek appropriate consultation when faced with ethical dilemmas. This may involve consultation with an agency-based or social work organization's ethics committee, a regulatory body, knowledgeable colleagues, supervisors, or legal counsel.

Instances may arise when social workers' ethical obligations conflict with agency policies or relevant laws or regulations. When such con-flicts occur, social workers must make a responsible effort to resolve the conflict in a manner that is consistent with the values, principles, and standards expressed in this Code. If a reasonable resolution of the conflict does not appear possible, social workers should seek proper consultation before making a decision.

The *NASW Code of Ethics* is to be used by NASW and by individuals, agencies, organizations, and bodies (such as licensing and regulatory boards, professional liability insurance providers, courts of law, agency boards of directors, government agencies, and other professional groups) that choose to adopt it or use it as a frame of reference. Violation of standards in this *Code* does not automatically imply legal liability or violation of the law. Such determination can only be made in the context of legal and judicial proceedings. Alleged violations of the *Code* would be subject to a peer review process. Such processes are generally separate from legal or administrative procedures and insulated from legal review or proceedings to allow the profession to counsel and discipline its own members.

A code of ethics cannot guarantee ethical behaviour. Moreover, a code of ethics cannot resolve all ethical issues or disputes or capture the richness and complexity involved in striving to make responsible choices within a moral community. Rather, a code of ethics sets forth values, ethical principles, and ethical standards to which professionals aspire and by which their actions can be judged. Social workers' ethical behaviour should result from their personal commitment to engage in ethical practice. The *NASW Code of Ethics* reflects the commitment of all social workers to uphold the profession's values and to act ethically. Principles and standards must be applied by individuals of good character who discern moral questions and, in good faith, seek to make reliable ethical judgments.

## Ethical Principles

The following broad ethical principles are based on social work's core values of service, social justice, dignity and worth of the person, importance of human relationships, integrity, and competence. These principles set forth ideals to which all social workers should aspire.

***Value:*** Service

***Ethical Principle:*** Social workers' primary goal is to help people in need and to address social problems.

Social workers elevate service to others above self-interest. Social workers draw on their knowledge, values, and skills to help people in need and to address social problems. Social workers are encouraged to volunteer some portion of their professional skills with no expectation of significant financial return (pro bono service).

***Value:*** Social Justice

***Ethical Principle:*** Social workers challenge social injustice.

Social workers pursue social change, particularly with and on behalf of vulnerable and oppressed individuals and groups of people. Social workers' social change efforts are focused primarily on issues of poverty, unemployment, discrimination, and other forms of social injustice. These activities seek to promote sensitivity to and knowledge about oppression and cultural and ethnic diversity. Social workers strive to ensure access to needed information, services, and resources; equality of opportunity; and meaningful participation in decision making for all people.

*Value:* Dignity and Worth of the Person

*Ethical Principle:* Social workers respect the inherent dignity and worth of the person.

Social workers treat each person in a caring and respectful fashion, mindful of individual differences and cultural and ethnic diversity. Social workers promote clients' socially responsible self-determination. Social workers seek to enhance clients' capacity and opportunity to change and to address their own needs. Social workers are cognizant of their dual responsibility to clients and to the broader society. They seek to resolve conflicts between clients' interests and the broader society's interests in a socially responsible manner consistent with the values, ethical principles, and ethical standards of the profession.

**Value**: Importance of Human Relationships

*Ethical Principle:* Social workers recognize the central importance of human relationships.

Social workers understand that relationships between and among people are an important vehicle for change. Social workers engage people as partners in the helping process. Social workers seek to strengthen relationships among people in a purposeful effort to promote, restore, maintain, and enhance the well-being of individuals, families, social groups, organizations, and communities.

*Value:* Integrity

*Ethical Principle:* Social workers behave in a trustworthy manner.

Social workers are continually aware of the profession's mission, values, ethical principles, and ethical standards and practice in a manner consistent with them. Social workers act honestly and responsibly and promote ethical practices on the part of the organizations with which they are affiliated.

*Value:* Competence

*Ethical Principle:* Social workers practice within their areas of competence and develop and enhance their professional expertise.

Social workers continually strive to increase their professional knowledge and skills and to apply them in practice. Social workers should aspire to contribute to the knowledge base of the profession.

## Ethical Standards

The following ethical standards are relevant to the professional activities of all social workers. These standards concern (1) social workers' ethical responsibilities to clients, (2) social workers' ethical responsibilities to colleagues, (3) social workers' ethical responsibilities in practice settings, (4) social workers' ethical responsibilities as professionals, (5) social workers' ethical responsibilities to the social work profession, and (6) social workers' ethical responsibilities to the broader society.

Some of the standards that follow are enforceable guidelines for professional conduct, and some are aspirational. The extent to which each standard is enforceable is a matter of professional judgment to be exercised by those responsible for reviewing alleged violations of ethical standards.

## Social Workers' Ethical Responsibilities to Clients

### *Commitment to Clients*

Social workers' primary responsibility is to promote the well-being of clients. In general, clients' interests are primary. However, social workers' responsibility to the larger society or specific legal obligations may on limited occasions supersede the loyalty owed clients, and clients should be so advised. (Examples include when a social worker is required by law to report that a client has abused a child or has threatened to harm self or others.)

### *Self- Determination*

Social workers respect and promote the right of clients to self-determination and assist clients in their efforts to identify and clarify their goals. Social workers may limit clients' right to self-determination when, in the social workers' professional judgment, clients' actions or potential actions pose a serious, foreseeable, and imminent risk to themselves or others.

### *Informed Consent*

(a) Social workers should provide services to clients only in the context of a professional relationship based, when appropriate, on valid informed consent. Social workers should use clear and understandable language to inform clients of the purpose of the services, risks related to the services, limits to services because of the requirements of a third-party payer, relevant costs, reasonable alternatives, clients' right to refuse or withdraw consent, and the time frame covered by the consent. Social workers should provide clients with an opportunity to ask questions.

(b) In instances when clients are not literate or have difficulty understanding the primary language used in the practice setting, social workers should take steps to ensure clients' comprehension. This may include providing clients with a detailed verbal explanation or arranging for a qualified interpreter or translator whenever possible.

(c) In instances when clients lack the capacity to provide informed consent, social workers should protect clients' interests by seeking permission from an appropriate third party, informing clients consistent with the clients' level of understanding. In such instances social workers should seek to ensure that the third party acts in a manner consistent with clients' wishes and interests. Social workers should take reasonable steps to enhance such clients' ability to give informed consent.

(d) In instances when clients are receiving services involuntarily, social workers should provide information about the nature and extent of services and about the extent of clients' right to refuse service.

(e) Social workers who provide services via electronic media (such as computer, telephone, radio, and television) should inform recipients of the limitations and risks associated with such services.

(f) Social workers should obtain clients' informed consent before audiotaping or video taping clients or permitting observation of services to clients by a third party.

*Competence*

(a) Social workers should provide services and represent themselves as competent only within the boundaries of their education, training, license, certification, consultation received, supervised experience, or other relevant professional experience.

(b) Social workers should provide services in substantive areas or use intervention techniques or approaches that are new to them only after engaging in appropriate study, training, consultation, and supervision from people who are competent in those interventions or techniques.

(c) When generally recognized standards do not exist with respect to an emerging area of practice, social workers should exercise careful judgment and take responsible steps (including appropriate education, research, training, consultation, and supervision) to ensure the competence of their work and to protect clients from harm.

### *Cultural Competence and Social Diversity*

(a) Social workers should understand culture and its function in human behaviour and society, recognizing the strengths that exist in all cultures.

(b) Social workers should have a knowledge base of their clients' cultures and be able to demonstrate competence in the provision of services that are sensitive to clients' cultures and to differences among people and cultural groups.

(c) Social workers should obtain education about and seek to understand the nature of social diversity and oppression with respect to race, ethnicity, national origin, colour, sex, sexual orientation, gender identity or expression, age, marital status, political belief, religion, immigration status, and mental or physical disability.

### *Conflicts of Interest*

(a) Social workers should be alert to and avoid conflicts of interest that interfere with the exercise of professional discretion and impartial judgment. Social workers should inform clients when a real or potential conflict of interest arises and take reasonable steps to resolve the issue in a manner that makes the clients' interests primary and protects clients' interests to the greatest extent possible. In some cases, protecting clients' interests may require termination of the professional relationship with proper referral of the client.

(b) Social workers should not take unfair advantage of any professional relationship or exploit others to further their personal, religious, political, or business interests.

(c) Social workers should not engage in dual or multiple relationships with clients or former clients in which there is a risk of exploitation or potential harm to the client. In instances when dual or multiple relationships are unavoidable, social workers should take steps to protect clients and are responsible for setting clear, appropriate, and culturally sensitive boundaries. (Dual or multiple relationships occur when social workers relate to clients in more than one relationship, whether professional, social, or business. Dual or multiple relationships can occur simultaneously or consecutively.)

(d) When social workers provide services to two or more people who have a relationship with each other (for example, couples, family members), social workers should clarify with all parties which individuals will be considered clients and the nature of social workers' professional obligations to the various individuals who are receiving services. Social workers who anticipate a conflict of interest among the individuals receiving services or who anticipate having to perform in potentially conflicting roles (for example, when a social worker is asked to testify in a child custody dispute or divorce proceedings involving clients) should clarify their role with the parties involved and take appropriate action to minimize any conflict of interest.

*Privacy and Confidentiality*

(a) Social workers should respect clients' right to privacy. Social workers should not solicit private information from clients unless it is essential to providing services or conducting social work evaluation or research. Once private information is shared, standards of confidentiality apply.

(b) Social workers may disclose confidential information when appropriate with valid consent from a client or a person legally authorized to consent on behalf of a client.

(c) Social workers should protect the confidentiality of all information obtained in the course of professional service, except for compelling professional reasons. The general expectation that social workers will keep information confidential does not apply when disclosure is necessary to prevent serious, foreseeable, and imminent harm to a client or other identifiable person. In all instances, social workers should disclose the least amount of confidential information necessary to achieve the desired purpose; only information that is directly relevant to the purpose for which the disclosure is made should be revealed.

(d) Social workers should inform clients, to the extent possible, about the disclosure of confidential information and the potential consequences, when feasible before the disclosure is made. This applies whether social workers disclose confidential information on the basis of a legal requirement or client consent.

(e) Social workers should discuss with clients and other interested parties the nature of confidentiality and limitations of clients' right to confidentiality. Social workers should review with clients circumstances where confidential information may be requested and where disclosure of confidential information may be legally required. This discussion should occur as soon as possible in the social worker-client relationship and as needed throughout the course of the relationship.

(f) When social workers provide counselling services to families, couples, or groups, social workers should seek agreement among the parties involved concerning each individual's right to confidentiality and obligation to preserve the confidentiality of information shared by others. Social workers should inform participants in family, couples, or group counselling that social workers cannot guarantee that all participants will honour such agreements.

(g) Social workers should inform clients involved in family, couples, marital, or group counselling of the social worker's, employer's, and agency's policy concerning the social worker's disclosure of confidential information among the parties involved in the counselling.

(h) Social workers should not disclose confidential information to third-party payers unless clients have authorized such disclosure.

(i) Social workers should not discuss confidential information in any setting unless privacy can be ensured. Social workers should not discuss confidential information in public or semipublic areas such as hallways, waiting rooms, elevators, and restaurants.

(j) Social workers should protect the confidentiality of clients during legal proceedings to the extent permitted by law. When a court of law or other legally authorized body orders social workers to disclose confidential or privileged information without a client's consent and such disclosure could cause harm to the client, social workers should request that the court withdraw the order or limit the order as narrowly as possible or maintain the records under seal, unavailable for public inspection.

(k) Social workers should protect the confidentiality of clients when responding to requests from members of the media.

(l) Social workers should protect the confidentiality of clients' written and electronic records and other sensitive information. Social workers should take reasonable steps to ensure that clients' records are stored in a secure location and that clients' records are not available to others who are not authorized to have access.

(m) Social workers should take precautions to ensure and maintain the confidentiality of information transmitted to other parties through the use of computers, electronic mail, facsimile machines, telephones and telephone answering machines, and other electronic or computer technology. Disclosure of identifying information should be avoided whenever possible.

(n) Social workers should transfer or dispose of clients' records in a manner that protects clients' confidentiality and is consistent with state statutes governing records and social work licensure.

(o) Social workers should take reasonable precautions to protect client confidentiality in the event of the social worker's termination of practice, incapacitation, or death.

(p) Social workers should not disclose identifying information when discussing clients for teaching or training purposes unless the client has consented to disclosure of confidential information.

(q) Social workers should not disclose identifying information when discussing clients with consultants unless the client has consented to disclosure of confidential information or there is a compelling need for such disclosure.

(r) Social workers should protect the confidentiality of deceased clients consistent with the preceding standards.

### *Access to Records*

(a) Social workers should provide clients with reasonable access to records concerning the clients. Social workers who are concerned that clients' access to their records could cause serious misunderstanding or harm to the client should provide assistance in interpreting the records and consultation with the client regarding the records. Social workers should limit clients' access to their records, or portions of their records, only in exceptional circumstances when there is compelling evidence that such access would cause serious harm to the client. Both clients' requests and the rationale for withholding some or all of the record should be documented in clients' files.

(b) When providing clients with access to their records, social workers should take steps to protect the confidentiality of other individuals identified or discussed in such records.

### *Sexual Relationships*

(a) Social workers should under no circumstances engage in sexual activities or sexual contact with current clients, whether such contact is consensual or forced.

(b) Social workers should not engage in sexual activities or sexual contact with clients' relatives or other individuals with whom clients maintain a close personal relationship when there is a risk of exploitation or potential harm to the client. Sexual activity or sexual contact with clients' relatives or other individuals with whom clients maintain a personal relationship has the potential to be harmful to the client and may make it difficult for the social worker and client to maintain appropriate professional boundaries. Social workers—not their clients, their clients' relatives, or other individuals with whom the client maintains a personal relationship—assume the full burden for setting clear, appropriate, and culturally sensitive boundaries.

(c) Social workers should not engage in sexual activities or sexual contact with former clients because of the potential for harm to the client. If social workers engage in conduct contrary to this prohibition or claim that an exception to this prohibition is warranted because of extraordinary circumstances, it is social workers—not their clients—who assume the full burden of demonstrating that the former client has not been exploited, coerced, or manipulated, intentionally or unintentionally.

(d) Social workers should not provide clinical services to individuals with whom they have had a prior sexual relationship. Providing clinical services to a former sexual partner has the potential to be harmful to the individual and is likely to make it difficult for the social worker and individual to maintain appropriate professional boundaries.

### *Physical Contact*

Social workers should not engage in physical contact with clients when there is a possibility of psychological harm to the client as a result of the contact (such as cradling or caressing clients). Social workers who engage in appropriate physical contact with clients are responsible for setting clear, appropriate, and culturally sensitive boundaries that govern such physical contact.

### *Sexual Harassment*

Social workers should not sexually harass clients. Sexual harassment includes sexual advances, sexual solicitation, requests for sexual favours, and other verbal or physical conduct of a sexual nature.

### *Derogatory Language*

Social workers should not use derogatory language in their written or verbal communications to or about clients. Social workers should use accurate and respectful language in all communications to and about clients.

### *Payment for Services*

(a) When setting fees, social workers should ensure that the fees are fair, reasonable, and commensurate with the services performed. Consideration should be given to clients' ability to pay.

(b) Social workers should avoid accepting goods or services from clients as payment for professional services. Bartering arrangements, particularly involving services, create the potential for conflicts of interest, exploitation, and inappropriate boundaries in social workers' relationships with clients. Social workers should explore and may participate in bartering only in very limited circumstances when it can be demonstrated that such arrangements are an accepted practice among professionals in the local community, considered to be essential for the provision of services, negotiated without coercion, and entered into at the client's initiative and with the client's informed consent. Social workers who accept goods or services from clients as payment for professional services assume the full burden of demonstrating that this arrangement will not be detrimental to the client or the professional relationship.

(c) Social workers should not solicit a private fee or other remuneration for providing services to clients who are entitled to such available services through the social workers' employer or agency.

## Clients Who Lack Decision-Making Capacity

When social workers act on behalf of clients who lack the capacity to make informed decisions, social workers should take reasonable steps to safeguard the interests and rights of those clients.

### *Interruption of Services*

Social workers should make reasonable efforts to ensure continuity of services in the event that services are interrupted by factors such as unavailability, relocation, illness, disability, or death.

### *Termination of Services*

(a) Social workers should terminate services to clients and professional relationships with them when such services and relationships are no longer required or no longer serve the clients' needs or interests.

(b) Social workers should take reasonable steps to avoid abandoning clients who are still in need of services. Social workers should withdraw services precipitously only under unusual circumstances, giving careful consideration to all factors in the situation and taking care to minimize possible adverse effects. Social workers should assist in making appropriate arrangements for continuation of services when necessary.

(c) Social workers in fee-for-service settings may terminate services to clients who are not paying an overdue balance if the financial contractual arrangements have been made clear to the client, if the client does not pose an imminent danger to self or others, and if the clinical and other consequences of the current nonpayment have been addressed and discussed with the client.

(d) Social workers should not terminate services to pursue a social, financial, or sexual relationship with a client.

(e) Social workers who anticipate the termination or interruption of services to clients should notify clients promptly and seek the transfer, referral, or continuation of services in relation to the clients' needs and preferences.

(f) Social workers who are leaving an employment setting should inform clients of appropriate options for the continuation of services and of the benefits and risks of the options.

## Social Workers' Ethical Responsibilities to Colleagues

### *Respect*

(a) Social workers should treat colleagues with respect and

should represent accurately and fairly the qualifications, views, and obligations of colleagues.

(b) Social workers should avoid unwarranted negative criticism of colleagues in communications with clients or with other professionals. Unwarranted negative criticism may include demeaning comments that refer to colleagues' level of competence or to individuals' attributes such as race, ethnicity, national origin, colour, sex, sexual orientation, gender identity or expression, age, marital status, political belief, religion, immigration status, and mental or physical disability.

(c) Social workers should cooperate with social work colleagues and with colleagues of other professions when such cooperation serves the well-being of clients.

*Confidentiality*

Social workers should respect confidential information shared by colleagues in the course of their professional relationships and transactions. Social workers should ensure that such colleagues understand social workers' obligation to respect confidentiality and any exceptions related to it.

*Interdisciplinary Collaborating*

(a) Social workers who are members of an interdisciplinary team should participate in and contribute to decisions that affect the well-being of clients by drawing on the perspectives, values, and experiences of the social work profession. Professional and ethical obligations of the interdisciplinary team as a whole and of its individual members should be clearly established.

(b) Social workers for whom a team decision raises ethical concerns should attempt to resolve the disagreement through appropriate channels. If the disagreement cannot be resolved, social workers should pursue other avenues to address their concerns consistent with client well-being.

## Disputes Involving Colleagues

(a) Social workers should not take advantage of a dispute between a colleague and an employer to obtain a position or otherwise advance the social workers' own interests.

(b) Social workers should not exploit clients in disputes with colleagues or engage clients in any inappropriate discussion of conflicts between social workers and their colleagues.

*Consultation*

(a) Social workers should seek the advice and counsel of colleagues whenever such consultation is in the best interests of clients.

(b) Social workers should keep themselves informed about colleagues' areas of expertise and competencies. Social workers should seek consultation only from colleagues who have demonstrated knowledge, expertise, and competence related to the subject of the consultation.

(c) When consulting with colleagues about clients, social workers should disclose the least amount of information necessary to achieve the purposes of the consultation.

*Referral for Services*

(a) Social workers should refer clients to other professionals when the other professionals' specialized knowledge or expertise is needed to serve clients fully or when social workers believe that they are not being effective or making reasonable progress with clients and that additional service is required.

(b) Social workers who refer clients to other professionals should take appropriate steps to facilitate an orderly transfer of responsibility. Social workers who refer clients to other professionals should disclose, with clients' consent, all pertinent information to the new service providers.

(c) Social workers are prohibited from giving or receiving payment for a referral when no professional service is provided by the referring social worker.

*Sexual Relationships*

(a) Social workers who function as supervisors or educators should not engage in sexual activities or contact with supervises, students, trainees, or other colleagues over whom they exercise professional authority.

(b) Social workers should avoid engaging in sexual relationships with colleagues when there is potential for a conflict of interest. Social workers who become involved in, or anticipate becoming involved in, a sexual relationship with a colleague have a duty to transfer professional responsibilities, when necessary, to avoid a conflict of interest.

## Sexual Harassment

Social workers should not sexually harass supervises, students, trainees, or colleagues. Sexual harassment includes sexual advances, sexual solicitation, requests for sexual favors, and other verbal or physical conduct of a sexual nature.

### *Impairment of Colleagues*

(a) Social workers who have direct knowledge of a social work colleague's impairment that is due to personal problems, psychosocial distress, substance abuse, or mental health difficulties and that interferes with practice effectiveness should consult with that colleague when feasible and assist the colleague in taking remedial action.

(b) Social workers who believe that a social work colleague's impairment interferes with practice effectiveness and that the colleague has not taken adequate steps to address the impairment should take action through appropriate channels established by employers, agencies, NASW, licensing and regulatory bodies, and other professional organizations.

### *Incompetence of Colleagues*

(a) Social workers who have direct knowledge of a social work colleague's incompetence should consult with that colleague when feasible and assist the colleague in taking remedial action.

(b) Social workers who believe that a social work colleague is incompetent and has not taken adequate steps to address the incompetence should take action through appropriate channels established by employers, agencies, NASW, licensing and regulatory bodies, and other professional organizations.

*Unethical Conduct of Colleagues*

(a) Social workers should take adequate measures to discourage, prevent, expose, and correct the unethical conduct of colleagues.

(b) Social workers should be knowledgeable about established policies and procedures for handling concerns about colleagues' unethical behaviour. Social workers should be familiar with national, state, and local procedures for handling ethics complaints. These include policies and procedures created by NASW, licensing and regulatory bodies, employers, agencies, and other professional organizations.

(c) Social workers who believe that a colleague has acted unethically should seek resolution by discussing their concerns with the colleague when feasible and when such discussion is likely to be productive.

(d) When necessary, social workers who believe that a colleague has acted unethically should take action through appropriate formal channels (such as contacting a state licensing board or regulatory body, an NASW committee on inquiry, or other professional ethics committees).

(e) Social workers should defend and assist colleagues who are unjustly charged with unethical conduct.

## Social Workers' Ethical Responsibilities in Practice Settings

*Supervision and Consultation*

(a) Social workers who provide supervision or consultation should have the necessary knowledge and skill to supervise or consult appropriately and should do so only within their areas of knowledge and competence.

(b) Social workers who provide supervision or consultation are responsible for setting clear, appropriate, and culturally sensitive boundaries.

(c) Social workers should not engage in any dual or multiple relationships with supervises in which there is a risk of exploitation of or potential harm to the supervisee.

(d) Social workers who provide supervision should evaluate supervises' performance in a manner that is fair and respectful.

### *Education and Training*

(a) Social workers who function as educators, field instructors for students, or trainers should provide instruction only within their areas of knowledge and competence and should provide instruction based on the most current information and knowledge available in the profession.

(b) Social workers who function as educators or field instructors for students should evaluate students' performance in a manner that is fair and respectful.

(c) Social workers who function as educators or field instructors for students should take reasonable steps to ensure that clients are routinely informed when services are being provided by students.

(d) Social workers who function as educators or field instructors for students should not engage in any dual or multiple relationships with students in which there is a risk of exploitation or potential harm to the student. Social work educators and field instructors are responsible for setting clear, appropriate, and culturally sensitive boundaries.

### Performance Evaluation

Social workers who have responsibility for evaluating the performance of others should fulfil such responsibility in a fair and considerate manner and on the basis of clearly stated criteria.

### *Client Records*

(a) Social workers should take reasonable steps to ensure that documentation in records is accurate and reflects the services provided.

(b) Social workers should include sufficient and timely documentation in records to facilitate the delivery of services and to ensure continuity of services provided to clients in the future.

(c) Social workers' documentation should protect clients' privacy to the extent that is possible and appropriate and should include only information that is directly relevant to the delivery of services.

(d) Social workers should store records following the termination of services to ensure reasonable future access. Records should be maintained for the number of years required by state statutes or relevant contracts.

***Billing***

Social workers should establish and maintain billing practices that accurately reflect the nature and extent of services provided and that identify who provided the service in the practice setting.

***Client Transfer***

(a) When an individual who is receiving services from another agency or colleague contacts a social worker for services, the social worker should carefully consider the client's needs before agreeing to provide services. To minimize possible confusion and conflict, social workers should discuss with potential clients the nature of the clients' current relationship with other service providers and the implications, including possible benefits or risks, of entering into a relationship with a new service provider.

(b) If a new client has been served by another agency or colleague, social workers should discuss with the client whether consultation with the previous service provider is in the client's best interest.

***Administration***

(a) Social work administrators should advocate within and outside their agencies for adequate resources to meet clients' needs.

(b) Social workers should advocate for resource allocation procedures that are open and fair. When not all clients' needs can be met, an allocation procedure should be developed that is nondiscriminatory and based on appropriate and consistently applied principles.

(c) Social workers who are administrators should take reasonable steps to ensure that adequate agency or organizational resources are available to provide appropriate staff supervision.

(d) Social work administrators should take reasonable steps to ensure that the working environment for which they are responsible is consistent with and encourages compliance with the *NASW Code of Ethics*. Social work administrators should take reasonable steps to eliminate any conditions in their organizations that violate, interfere with, or discourage compliance with the *Code*.

### *Continuing Education and Staff Development*

Social work administrators and supervisors should take reasonable steps to provide or arrange for continuing education and staff development for all staff for whom they are responsible. Continuing education and staff development should address current knowledge and emerging developments related to social work practice and ethics.

### *Commitments to Employers*

(a) Social workers generally should adhere to commitments made to employers and employing organizations.

(b) Social workers should work to improve employing agencies' policies and procedures and the efficiency and effectiveness of their services.

(c) Social workers should take reasonable steps to ensure that employers are aware of social workers' ethical obligations as set forth in the *NASW Code of Ethics* and of the implications of those obligations for social work practice.

(d) Social workers should not allow an employing organization's policies, procedures, regulations, or administrative orders to interfere with their ethical practice of social work. Social workers should take reasonable steps to ensure that their employing organizations' practices are consistent with the *NASW Code of Ethics*.

(e) Social workers should act to prevent and eliminate discrimination in the employing organization's work assignments and in its employment policies and practices.

(f) Social workers should accept employment or arrange student field placements only in organizations that exercise fair personnel practices.

(g) Social workers should be diligent stewards of the resources of their employing organizations, wisely conserving funds where appropriate and never misappropriating funds or using them for unintended purposes.

*Labour-Management Disputes*

(a) Social workers may engage in organized action, including the formation of and participation in labour unions, to improve services to clients and working conditions.

(b) The actions of social workers who are involved in labour-management disputes, job actions, or labour strikes should be guided by the profession's values, ethical principles, and ethical standards. Reasonable differences of opinion exist among social workers concerning their primary obligation as professionals during an actual or threatened labour strike or job action. Social workers should carefully examine relevant issues and their possible impact on clients before deciding on a course of action.

## Social Workers' Ethical Responsibilities as Professionals

*Competence*

(a) Social workers should accept responsibility or employment only on the basis of existing competence or the intention to acquire the necessary competence.

(b) Social workers should strive to become and remain proficient in professional practice and the performance of professional functions. Social workers should critically examine and keep current with emerging knowledge relevant to social work. Social workers should routinely review the professional literature and participate in continuing education relevant to social work practice and social work ethics.

(c) Social workers should base practice on recognized knowledge, including empirically based knowledge, relevant to social work and social work ethics.

*Discrimination*

Social workers should not practice, condone, facilitate, or collaborate with any form of discrimination on the basis of race, ethnicity, national origin, colour, sex, sexual orientation, gender identity or expression, age, marital status, political belief, religion, immigration status, or mental or physical disability.

### *Private Conduct*

Social workers should not permit their private conduct to interfere with their ability to fulfil their professional responsibilities.

## Dishonesty, Fraud, and Deception

Social workers should not participate in, condone, or be associated with dishonesty, fraud, or deception.

### *Impairment*

(a) Social workers should not allow their own personal problems, psychosocial distress, legal problems, substance abuse, or mental health difficulties to interfere with their professional judgment and performance or to jeopardize the best interests of people for whom they have a professional responsibility.

(b) Social workers whose personal problems, psychosocial distress, legal problems, substance abuse, or mental health difficulties interfere with their professional judgment and performance should immediately seek consultation and take appropriate remedial action by seeking professional help, making adjustments in workload, terminating practice, or taking any other steps necessary to protect clients and others.

### *Misrepresentation*

(a) Social workers should make clear distinctions between statements made and actions engaged in as a private individual and as a representative of the social work profession, a professional social work organization, or the social worker's employing agency.

(b) Social workers who speak on behalf of professional social work organizations should accurately represent the official and authorized positions of the organizations.

(c) Social workers should ensure that their representations to clients, agencies, and the public of professional qualifications, credentials, education, competence, affiliations, services provided, or results to be achieved are accurate. Social workers should claim only those relevant professional credentials they actually possess and take steps to correct any inaccuracies or misrepresentations of their credentials by others.

### *Solicitations*

(a) Social workers should not engage in uninvited solicitation of potential clients who, because of their circumstances, are vulnerable to undue influence, manipulation, or coercion.

(b) Social workers should not engage in solicitation of testimonial endorsements (including solicitation of consent to use a client's prior statement as a testimonial endorsement) from current clients or from other people who, because of their particular circumstances, are vulnerable to undue influence.

### *Acknowledging Credit*

(a) Social workers should take responsibility and credit, including authorship credit, only for work they have actually performed and to which they have contributed.

(b) Social workers should honestly acknowledge the work of and the contributions made by others.

## Social Workers' Ethical Responsibilities to the Social Work Profession

### *Integrity of the Profession*

(a) Social workers should work toward the maintenance and promotion of high standards of practice.

(b) Social workers should uphold and advance the values, ethics, knowledge, and mission of the profession. Social workers should protect, enhance, and improve the integrity of the profession through appropriate study and research, active discussion, and responsible criticism of the profession.

(c) Social workers should contribute time and professional expertise to activities that promote respect for the value, integrity, and competence of the social work profession.

These activities may include teaching, research, consultation, service, legislative testimony, presentations in the community, and participation in their professional organizations.

(d) Social workers should contribute to the knowledge base of social work and share with colleagues their knowledge related to practice, research, and ethics. Social workers should seek to contribute to the profession's literature and to share their knowledge at professional meetings and conferences.

(e) Social workers should act to prevent the unauthorized and unqualified practice of social work.

### *Evaluation and Research*

(a) Social workers should monitor and evaluate policies, the implementation of programs, and practice interventions.

(b) Social workers should promote and facilitate evaluation and research to contribute to the development of knowledge.

(c) Social workers should critically examine and keep current with emerging knowledge relevant to social work and fully use evaluation and research evidence in their professional practice.

(d) Social workers engaged in evaluation or research should carefully consider possible consequences and should follow guidelines developed for the protection of evaluation and research participants. Appropriate institutional review boards should be consulted.

(e) Social workers engaged in evaluation or research should obtain voluntary and written informed consent from participants, when appropriate, without any implied or actual deprivation or penalty for refusal to participate; without undue inducement to participate; and with due regard for participants' well-being, privacy, and dignity. Informed consent should include information about the nature, extent, and duration of the participation requested and disclosure of the risks and benefits of participation in the research.

(f) When evaluation or research participants are incapable of giving informed consent, social workers should provide an appropriate explanation to the participants, obtain the participants' assent to the extent they are able, and obtain written consent from an appropriate proxy.

(g) Social workers should never design or conduct evaluation or research that does not use consent procedures, such as certain forms of naturalistic observation and archival research, unless rigorous and responsible review of the research has found it to be justified because of its prospective scientific, educational, or applied value and unless equally effective alternative procedures that do not involve waiver of consent are not feasible.

(h) Social workers should inform participants of their right to withdraw from evaluation and research at any time without penalty.

(i) Social workers should take appropriate steps to ensure that participants in evaluation and research have access to appropriate supportive services.

(j) Social workers engaged in evaluation or research should protect participants from unwarranted physical or mental distress, harm, danger, or deprivation.

(k) Social workers engaged in the evaluation of services should discuss collected information only for professional purposes and only with people professionally concerned with this information.

(l) Social workers engaged in evaluation or research should ensure the anonymity or confidentiality of participants and of the data obtained from them. Social workers should inform participants of any limits of confidentiality, the measures that will be taken to ensure confidentiality, and when any records containing research data will be destroyed.

(m) Social workers who report evaluation and research results should protect participants' confidentiality by omitting identifying information unless proper consent has been obtained authorizing disclosure.

(n) Social workers should report evaluation and research findings accurately. They should not fabricate or falsify results and should take steps to correct any errors later found in published data using standard publication methods.

(o) Social workers engaged in evaluation or research should be alert to and avoid conflicts of interest and dual relationships with participants, should inform participants when a real or potential conflict of interest arises, and should take steps to resolve the issue in a manner that makes participants' interests primary.

(p) Social workers should educate themselves, their students, and their colleagues about responsible research practices.

## Social Workers' Ethical Responsibilities to the Broader Society

### *Social Welfare*

Social workers should promote the general welfare of society, from local to global levels, and the development of people, their communities, and their environments. Social workers should advocate for living conditions conducive to the fulfillment of basic human needs and should promote social, economic, political, and cultural values and institutions that are compatible with the realization of social justice.

### *Public Participation*

Social workers should facilitate informed participation by the public in shaping social policies and institutions.

### *Public Emergencies*

Social workers should provide appropriate professional services in public emergencies to the greatest extent possible.

### *Social and Political Action*

(a) Social workers should engage in social and political action that seeks to ensure that all people have equal access to the resources, employment, services, and opportunities they require to meet their basic human needs and to develop fully. Social workers should be aware of the impact of the political arena on practice and should advocate for changes in policy and legislation to improve social conditions in order to meet basic human needs and promote social justice.

(b) Social workers should act to expand choice and opportunity for all people, with special regard for vulnerable, disadvantaged, oppressed, and exploited people and groups.

(c) Social workers should promote conditions that encourage respect for cultural and social diversity within the United States and globally. Social workers should promote policies and practices that demonstrate respect for difference, support the expansion of cultural knowledge and resources, advocate for programs and institutions that demonstrate cultural competence, and promote policies that safeguard the rights of and confirm equity and social justice for all people.

(d) Social workers should act to prevent and eliminate domination of, exploitation of, and discrimination against any person, group, or class on the basis of race, ethnicity, national origin, colour, sex, sexual orientation, gender identity or expression, age, marital status, political belief, religion, immigration status, or mental or physical disability.

# 4

# Some Aspects of Field Work Supervision

## The Function of Supervision

Examining the different functions of supervision throws up various questions and issues. These questions include asking 'in whose interest does supervision work?' Confusion also arises concerning notions such as 'mentoring', 'practice teaching' and 'clinical supervision'. Here we explore Alfred Kadushin's model of supervision and the in sights it brings to these questions.

The immediate roots of what we have come to know as supervision in the human services lie in the development of social work and casework. We see this, for example, in the concern for the needs of clients; and the taking up of ideas and practices that owe much to the emergence of psychoanalysis. However, to make sense of supervision it is necessary to look to the various forms of apprenticeship that have existed in different societies.

In ancient China, Africa and Europe (feudal and otherwise), for example, there are numerous examples of people new to a craft or activity having to reveal their work to, and explore it with, masters or mistresses i.e. those recognized as skilled and wise. This process of being attached to an expert, of 'learning through doing' allows the novice to gain knowledge, skill and commitment. It also enables them to enter into a particular 'community of practice' such as tailoring or midwifery. By spending time with practitioners, by 'looking over their shoulders', taking part in the routines and practices associated with the trade or activity, and having them explore our work, we become full members of the community of practice.

### *Overseeing*

Supervision can be found in the growth of charitable social agencies in Europe and North America during the nineteenth century. It involved the recruitment, organization and oversight of a large number of volunteers and, later, paid workers. The volunteers were commonly known as 'visitors'. Their task was to call on a small number of families to offer advice and support. The main concern was to foster self help, and the adoption of 'healthy' habits and behaviours. In addition, visitors were also often in a position to access limited funds via their agencies, although such monies were only given after a careful investigation of the family's circumstances. In other words, a decision had to be made as to whether they were 'deserving'.

The person assigning cases, organizing work and taking decisions on behalf of the agency was basically an 'overseer'-and hence the growing use of the term 'supervisor'. (In Latin *super* means 'over', and *videre*, 'to watch, or see'). As Petes has pointed out, traditionally, part of the overseer's job was to ensure that work was done well and to standard. This can be viewed as an administrative task. However, overseers also had to be teachers and innovators. These were new forms of organization and intervention: 'standards were being set, new methods developed'.

In these early forms-and especially in the work of the Charity Organization Society in the USA and UK-the present functions and approaches of supervision were signalled. As thinking and practice around casework became more sophisticated, especially through the work of pioneers such as Mary Richmond, and demands for more paid workers grew, so supervision became more of an identified process. For example, books on the subject began to appear-e.g. Jeffrey R. Brackett's *Supervision and Education in Charity* (1904).

Also, the hierarchical position of the supervisor (or paid agent) was revealed:

While the 'paid agent' acted as supervisor to the volunteer visitor, the paid agent 'supervisor' was himself supervised by the district committee, which had ultimate authority for case decisions...

The paid agent supervisor was then in a middle-management position, as is true of supervisors today-supervising the direct service worker but themselves under the authority of the agency administrators.

It is this hierarchical and managerial idea of supervision that tends to permeate much of the literature in social work.

## Kadushin's Model of Supervision

It is at this point that Alfred Kadushin's discussion of supervision in social work becomes helpful. He goes back to earlier commentators such as John Dawson (1926) who stated the functions of supervision in the following terms:

*Administrative*-the promotion and maintenance of good standards of work, co-ordination of practice with policies of administration, the assurance of an efficient and smooth-running office;

*Educational*-the educational development of each individual worker on the staff in a manner calculated to evoke her fully to realize her possibilities of usefulness; and

*Supportive*-the maintenance of harmonious working relationships, the cultivation of esprit de corps.

It is a short step to translate these concerns into the current language of the 'learning organization'. As Salaman (1995) argues, managers must have a concern for both performance and learning.

The essentially *managerial* aspects of managers' work is their responsibility for monitoring and improving the work of others; their *managerial* effectiveness is determined by their capacity to improve the work of others. if managers are not able to make this contribution, then what value are they adding? The only ultimate justification of managers' existence is the improvement of the work of their subordinates. If managers fail in this way they fail as managers.

In this way managers are expect to develop relationships and environments that enable people to work together and respond to change. Such 'joint performance' involves having common goals, common values, the right structures, and continuing training and development (Drucker 1988).

I want to concentrate on how managers approach supervision-later I will suggest that the threefold education/administration/support model also works for 'non-managerial' supervision. In our experience of management some of us will have found that all three elements were present-and were acknowledged by the parties involved.

As managers we may well express a concern for the well being of those we are responsible for; we may also attend to gaining clarity around the tasks to be achieved (and how they are to be undertaken). In addition, we may have a care for staff development. We may well explore particular incidents and situations and seeing how they could be handled in different ways.

There may also be situations where these elements are not all present. For example, we may have slipped into a strong task orientation with a particular worker. Or, and this is quite common, we may focus rather too strongly on the support side. In voluntary and not-for-profit organizations it is not uncommon to find that staff require a good deal of 'working with'!

I find it helpful to think of the three elements as inter linked (or as overlapping). They flow one into another. If we are to remove one element than the process becomes potentially less satisfying to both the immediate parties-and less effective. It is easy to simply identify managerial supervision with administrative supervision.

### *Administration*

Kadushin tightens up on Dawson's formulation and presents his understanding of the three elements in terms of the primary problem and the primary goal. In administrative supervision the primary problem is concerned with the correct, effective and appropriate implementation of agency policies and procedures. The primary goal is to ensure adherence to policy and procedure. The supervisor has been given authority by the agency to oversee the work of the supervisee. This carries the responsibility:

> ... Both to *ensure* that agency policy is implemented-which implies a controlling function-and a parallel responsibility to *enable* supervises to work to the best of their ability.

It also entails a responsibility not to lose touch with the rationale for the agency-'to provide a first-class service for people who need it (or in some cases are required to have it, in order that they or others may be protected from harm)'.

### *Education*

In educational supervision the primary problem for Kadushin (1990: 20) is worker ignorance and/or ineptitude regarding the knowledge, attitude and skills required to do the job. The primary goal is to dispel ignorance and upgrade skill. The classic process involved with this task is to encourage reflection on, and exploration of the work. Supervises may be helped to:

- Understand the client better;
- Become more aware of their own reactions and responses to the client;
- Understand the dynamics of how they and their client are interacting;
- Look at how they intervened and the consequences of their interventions;

### *Support*

In supportive supervision the primary problem is worker morale and job satisfaction. The primary goal is to improve morale and job satisfaction (Kadushin 1992). Workers are seen as facing a variety of job-related stresses which, unless they have help to deal with them, could seriously affect their work and lead to a less than satisfactory service to clients. For the worker there is ultimately the problem of 'burnout'.

Kadushin argues that the other two forms of supervision focus on instrumental needs, whereas supportive supervision is concerned with expressive needs (ibid.: 292).

The supervisor seeks to prevent the development of potentially stressful situations, removes the worker from stress, reduces stress impinging on the worker, and helps her adjust to stress. The supervisor is available and approachable, communicates confidence in the worker, provides perspective, excuses failure when appropriate, sanctions and shares responsibility for different decisions, provides opportunities for independent functioning and for probable success in task achievement.

### *Some Issues*

This way of representing the functions of supervision does leave me with a number of questions. First, the way these functions are depicted tends towards seeing supervises in deficit. They are lacking in certain ways-and it is the job of the supervisor to help them put things right.

The problem is that supervisors can easily slip into acting *on*, or upon behalf of, supervises. Kadushin is primarily concerned with organizational or managerial supervision. Such supervisor-managers have responsibility to the organization or agency for the actions of their staff and so such a deficit orientation may not be surprising.

However, there will be a number of us who would argue for a different approach to management-one that stresses conversation and a concern for fostering an environment in which workers can take responsibility for their own actions. I do not think that this criticism undermines the shape of the model, i.e. the splitting into administrative, educative and supportive functions, but it does remind us to take great care when approaching it.

Second, I am always a bit wary of fuzzy notions such as 'support'. At one level I could argue that having a concern for the management and development of the worker (i.e. looking to administrative and educational supervision) is support in itself. I suppose this is where the various functions could be seen as overlapping or feeding into each other. On the other hand, separating out 'support' does have the virtue of making explicit the need to have a concern for the emotions of supervises. I guess that it is in this area that the real danger of slippage into a counselling framework appears. We make the *main* focus the person of the supervisee rather than the work. By incorporating support into the model we are at least able to frame the concern for the person of the supervisee within the larger concern for the service to the client.

Third, there is always the question of what may have been left out from the model. Approaching it from a managerial perspective, especially where you are concerned with the operation of teams, there might be the temptation to add in mediation as a function.

Then there may be issues around the naming of the separate functions. For example, is it helpful to separate administration from management, would management be a better overall title and so on?

Fourth, there is the question of how tied this model is to managerial supervision. Proctor (1987) uses the same basic split but uses different terms-formative (education), normative (administration) and restorative (support). This has the virtue of lifting the administrative category out of line-management and thus, allowing the model to be approached from a 'non-managerial' standpoint. We will return to this later.

Even given these questions, the Kadushin framework remains helpful. It has found a consistent echo in the social work field, and in the English language literature of supervision. Perhaps the main reason for this is that by naming the categories in this way Kadushin and others are able to highlight a number of key issues and tensions around the performance of supervision.

## Putting the Functions Together

Having mapped out Kadushin's model it is now possible to look at some of the different foci that can be attributed to supervision. For example, Hawkins and Shohet (1989) list 10 different foci and then categorize them in relation to Kadushin's elements.

Hawkins and Shohet (1989) suggest that foci one and two could be seen as educational; foci three and four as educational/ supportive; foci five and six as supportive; foci seven to nine as administative/supportive and ten as administrative. I know that when I attempted to put categories against the foci-I ended up with some differences. For example, I could argue that foci 8 can be approached as an educative element.

I know some people will have problems with the language and the basic conceptual position that these writers have taken up. For example, to what extent can a supervisor/manager ensure that things happen when they are working in conjunction with others? They can work for conditions that will foster good quality work-but they then have to leave matters to their team members.

## 'Non-Managerial', 'Consultative' or 'Professional' Supervision

At this point I want to return to the idea of 'non-managerial supervision-sometimes described as consultant (e.g. Brown 1984) or professional supervision in the literature. The most common distinction I hear made is that the manager's first point of reference has to be the interest of the organization or agency (it is on their authority that she or he is acting), while the non-managerial supervisor looks to the development of the worker. Sometimes this is reduced to the difference between administrative and educational supervision.

That is to say, one version argues that managers should not be concerned with educational supervision; and consultant supervisors should only focus on education and support. There is some truth in portraying the primary responsibilities in this way-but it would be very misleading to leave it there. As we have seen, Kadushin argues that management supervision involves all three categories. I want to suggest that both 'managerial' and 'non-managerial' supervisors share larger responsibilities-to the client group and to other professionals; and that both look to the development of the worker.

### *Supervision and the Emergence of Psychoanalysis and Counselling*

Some of the confusion around supposed differences arises from the roots of consultant, non-managerial or professional supervision. Its development has, arguably, owed much to the emergence of psychoanalysis and counselling. In the case of the former, practice, supervision, teaching and personal analysis have formed the central elements of training since the 1920s. If we consider current approaches to training social workers, teachers or informal and community educators, then we can see similar elements. For example, with regard to this programme there are various 'teaching' moments (perhaps most obviously seen in the form of lectures, study materials, seminars and study groups); self-assessment (as against self-analysis), practice (whether in the form of our day-to-day work, any placements we undertake, and our engagement with other students) and supervision.

Student or trainee supervision can be contrasted with practitioner supervision. The latter is addressed to established workers. Some writers, such as Page and Wosket (1994), claim that there are many differences between the focus in supervision of students or trainees, and that of established practitioners. The former are more likely to be concerned with issues of technique, boundary, understanding the material clients' bring, and dealing with personal feelings of anxiety. 'The experienced practitioner is more likely to be concerned with teasing out relationship dynamics, choosing intervention options and perhaps dealing with feelings of frustration and boredom towards clients' (op cit.). This is something that you may like to think about. My own experience of supervision is that the degree of difference in these respects can easily be overstated. Experienced practitioners may have a greater repertoire of experiences and models to draw upon, and may have grown jaded. But the supervisor who fails to attend to the extent to which experienced practitioners face new situations and different clients, can overlook the chance of practitioners feeling like novices again. Similarly, those labelled as student workers may well be experiencing frustration and boredom toward their clients.

However, the demand for 'practitioner supervision' in counselling can be seen as a key factor in the spread of non-managerial or consultant supervision. By the early 1950s, with the 'coming of age' of the profession, there was a substantial growth 'in the proportion of practitioners with significant experience', many of whom valued, 'having a fellow practitioner to act in a consultative capacity'. This linking of consultant supervision with the development of counselling is significant. The form that supervision takes may well mirror or adopt ways of working from the host profession. Thus, a counsellor supervisor may draw heavily on the theory and practice of a counselling model and apply this to supervision.

A psycho-dynamic supervisor would interpret the material being presented and use an awareness of the relationship dynamics between himself and the counsellor in supervision as a means of supervising. A client-centred supervisor would be concerned to communicate the core conditions of acceptance, respect and genuiness to her supervisee.

We now can begin to appreciate why many of the arguments and questions around supervision can become confusing. Contrasts between managerial and consultant supervision, for example, inevitably focus on the managerial element. Yet those involved may well be drawing on very different models and sets of under standings. The debate may be between a psycho-dynamic and a task orientation!

This drawing upon from psycho-dynamic and counselling can also add to the common slippage from supervision into therapy or 'working with'. We have already noted problems around this area with regard to the management of staff-and it applies with great force in consultant supervision.

The first thing to say here is that it may well be appropriate for us as supervisors to change the focus of the session from 'supervision' to 'counselling'.

The situation may demand it-and we have what may be described as a 'counselling interlude'. However, there are two particular dangers: we may slip into a different framework without being aware of it; and, further, even where the shift is conscious, it may not be appropriate. That is to say we should have held our boundaries as supervisors.

There can also be confusion between *shifting* our frame of reference and *drawing upon* in sights from a particular field. It may be that to properly approach a question that has arisen in workers' practice we need to attend to their emotional and psychological lives.

Here we may draw upon, for example, psycho-dynamic in sights, to work with supervises to enhance the quality of their interactions with clients. This does not entail moving beyond a supervisor's frame of reference. Our focus remains on the enhancement of practice.

However, where our primary concern is no longer the work, but the well-being of the supervisee, this is a different situation. When the worker becomes the primary focus (rather than the work), I think there is a significant shift-we move into the realm of counselling or 'working with' proper. We should not make the mistake of describing this as supervision.

## *Responsibilities to Clients, other Professionals and the Community*

This last discussion highlights something fundamental about supervision. While the manager may have in mind the needs of the agency; and the practice teacher or college supervisor the needs of the student-worker, their fundamental concern in supervision lies with the quality of service offered by the supervisee to their clients. In other words, supervision focuses on the work of the practitioner.

Clients at the centre. It is easy to fall into the trap of viewing changes in the individual supervisee as the central goal of the process. It is not difficult to understand how this happens. As we have seen, in supervision we draw on under standings and ways of working that we have developed in other settings. The most obvious of these are 'counselling' and other one-to-one relationships.

Yet, as Kadushin (1992) puts it in relation to managerial supervision, 'The supervisor's ultimate objective is to deliver to agency clients the best possible service, both quantitatively and qualitatively, in accordance with agency policies and procedures'. The same applies to consultant or non-managerial supervision:

> The responsibility of the supervisor to protect the interests of the client emerges as a central component of trainee supervision. Attention to client welfare is equally important... in practitioner supervision.

The British Association of Counselling makes the point unambiguously: 'The primary purpose of supervision is to protect the best interests of the client'. Change in supervises is fostered for a purpose-the enhancement of the service they provide for their clients. However, in considering this we also have to take into account what may be in the interests of the community as a whole.

Accountability to the wider community. In the well known phrase of C. Wright Mills-there are considerable dangers in seeing private troubles merely as troubles-and not as public issues (and vice versa). There is always the danger that we 'slip past structure to focus on isolated situations..., a tendency for problems to be considered as the problems of individuals'. As practitioners and supervisors we have to balance the needs and wishes of the individual with considerations of those of others in the community. There will be times when what may be identified as being in the interest of the client seriously affects the rights and lives of others. The tensions can be quickly seen if we examine the four basic or first order principles identified by Sarah Banks as central to social work (and, indeed, informal and community education):

1. Respect for and promotion of individuals' rights to self determination.
2. Promotion of welfare or well-being
3. Equality
4. Distributive justice.

As supervisors we may have to remind supervises of the requirement to consider the extent to which a course of action they are pursuing leads to human flourishing, promotes equality or whether they are 'distributing public resources (whether they be counselling, care or money) according to certain criteria based variously on rights, dessert and need' ? In a similar fashion we have to reflect on our actions as supervisors.

Being part of a community of practice. There are likely to be endless arguments about considerations such as these-especially when they are thought about in relation to specific cases and situations. We may have our individual ideas, but as members of a community of practice we need also to consider the views of others. That is to say we need to appeal to collective wisdom. Within professional groupings a key port of call here is a code of ethics.

I want to suggest here that while managerial supervisors, as members of the profession or community of practice, have a duty to consider the appropriate standards and codes, the main way that they do this is via the policies and practices of the agency. On the other hand, while non-managerial or consultant supervisors may be contracted by the supervisee (or the College in the case of student workers), their authority comes from their membership of the community of practice. Their concern for the service offered to clients is fed through a set of shared under standings concerning what constitutes 'good practice'. In other words, at certain points in the supervision process they may be required to represent that constitutes acceptable behaviour or good practice.

Professional supervisors act on behalf of the community of practice of which they are members. They should have a concern with the quality of service offered and the needs of the wider community. This links back to the way that Proctor (1987) redefined Kadushin's administrative category as 'normative'. If we were to adjust Kadushin's (1992) definition it would read something like the following:

The primary problem in administrative supervision is concerned with the quality of the supervisee's practice in respect of professional standard and ethics. The primary goal is to ensure adherence to these standards.

In other words, so called 'non-managerial' supervisors have an administrative responsibility. Where workers consistently fail to live up to these standards or present a danger to clients they have a responsibility to act.

This could take the form of them discouraging the supervisee from practice, or of reporting matters to the appropriate professional body. Managerial supervisors also look to professional concerns and to the interests of clients and the wider community, but they do so through the framework of agency policies and procedures.

## A Question of Power

We can see in all this that there are questions concerning power relationships within supervision. There are issues arising from position in agency hierarchies; and the extent to which dynamics around gender, 'race', age and class intersect with the roles of supervisor and supervisee. Turner (1996-in this unit) explores some issues and problems around this area. Here I just need to make three points.

First, because one person may be seen as more powerful (perhaps in the sense that they occupy a particular position, or are experts in their field) this should not encourage us to fall into the trap of seeing the other party as powerless. For example, Erving Goffman has provided us with numerous examples of how the performance of one party in an encounter depends on getting the right sorts of cues and responses from other participants. When these are denied or subverted in some way then the performance becomes problematic.

Thus managers, for example, require information from their subordinates in order to function. The subordinate, by managing the flow and character of information is in a position to affect how a manager sees an issue or situation.

Second, it is not possible to eliminate power differentials in supervision. Some writers have argued strongly for more dialogical approaches to supervision in order to 'flatten' unequal relations and to allow interaction across 'difference' (e.g. Waite 1995). Yet even in such forms there are power relationships-e.g. the supervisor is responsible to the community of practice.

However, this need not be a one-way relationship. Here it is useful to think of supervises also as members of the professional community. They may already be 'full' members (recognized and qualified) or apprentices. As such supervisors can be held accountable for the quality of the service they provide; and supervises for their practice with clients. Both have a responsibility to participate appropriately in the professional community of which they are a part.

Third, and linked to the above, we need to bear in mind questions of authority. Power is often discussed alongside questions of authority. When we talk of the authority of the supervisor, for example, what we can mean is that the supervisor has some sort of right or entitlement to act in relation to the supervisee. Managers occupy a certain position in the agency and with this is associated the ability to direct the labours of their staff.

There are various formal and informal 'rules' within which this may take place. Some activities may be seen as legitimate, others as not. The same applies to supervisors undertaking their work to meet the requirements of professional training programmes. To operate, the actions of supervisors must be seen as legitimate-by the supervisee and by significant others. Thus, in certain situations supervisors may be in a position to effectively impose their requirements on supervises. This they may do through the threat of sanctions such as a 'bad' assessment, or the allocation of unrewarding work. However, such actions may not be viewed as legitimate by the supervisee or other interested parties. In other words, their authority is questioned.

## The College or Training Programme Supervisor

At this point it may be useful to reflect more fully on the role of the supervisor within professional training programmes such as those involved with informal and community education.

For the professional or non-managerial supervisor within a training programme the lines of their authority are fairly clear. They act on behalf of the profession or community of practice. Students within programmes are having to develop, and provide evidence concerning, their work so that they may be recognized as qualified to join the professional community. Supervisors agree to provide a certain number of sessions and an assessment of supervises' abilities for the training provider.

The training provider, in turn, is accredited act for the profession by a relevant professional body (in the case of the College's informal and community education programmes this is CeVe Scotland and the English National Youth Agency). A supervisor may also hold some form of line-managerial responsibility for the student-worker.

In their supervision of the student-worker they will, thus, want to represent the interests of the agency and safeguard the quality of service offered to the agency's clientele. At the same time their involvement within the training programme highlights their responsibility to the community of practice or profession. Perhaps the best way of representing this is as a dual line of authority-to the profession and to the agency.

Training programmes are one of the few areas within informal and community education in Britain and Ireland where there is something approaching a formal mechanism linking supervision and the community of practice. We do not have full professional associations, nor codes of ethics. However, with the development of the accreditation of fieldwork supervisors and of training programmes-especially in Scotland-we have the beginnings of a technical framework.

### *Mentoring and Clinical Supervision*

Talk of training brings me round to some variations or additions to the supervisors' role. In some settings, the supervisor is asked to become more of a practice teacher or mentor. Their task is not just to enable the supervisee to reflect on practice and to develop new under standings and ways of working, but also to teach in a more formal sense.

Mentors and practice teachers may well need to instruct a student-worker on how to proceed in a particular situation; or to provide theoretical in sights. This comes closer to the apprentice-master/mistress relationship with which we began this discussion. Mentors are skilled performers-they can be observed, consulted and their actions copied.

For my own part I know that I am apt to slip into a 'telling' mode more often than I ought within a supervision framework-so I have to attend to this area. The line I try to apply in this area runs something like the following:

1. Supervision is a space for the supervisee to explore their practice, to build theory, attend to feelings and values, and to examine how they may act.
2. The supervisor should only switch into a more instructional mode where they are reasonably certain that the supervision process will be enhanced by their doing so.
3. Such 'instructional interludes' should remain interludes i.e. they should as far as is possible be brief and oriented to resuming exploration.

I suppose the key idea underlying this is that we should not act to undermine supervises' ability and commitment to take responsibility for exploring their practice. All this is not to say that the supervisor, outside the supervision session, should not also have an instructional role.

However, where they do so there is always the danger that expectations in one setting (the instructional) may be carried across into another (supervision). Here supervisors will have to make clear the difference between the two forms-and mark the boundary in some way e.g. by sitting in a different way, or waiting for the supervisee to begin the session.

### *Clinical Supervision*

Instruction and supervision can get confused is in the arena of educational supervision. This form of supervision is sometimes described as 'clinical'. This way of describing or approaching supervision derives from medical experience. It has been popularized in teacher training-especially in North America. As Cogan one of the pioneers of the approach in education has commented, the use of the term 'clinical' has involved some resistance, but what he particularly wanted to highlight was use of direct observation in the approach. Apprentice surgeons learn their trade by first observing the skilled practitioner at work; then by undertaking surgery under close surveillance. In this way they begin to develop their 'professional artistry'.

A working definition of clinical supervision has been given by Goldhammer *et al* (1993) in what has become pretty much the set text on the field:

Clinical supervision is that aspect of instructional supervision which draws upon data from direct first hand observation of actual teaching, or other professional events, and involves face-to-face and other associated interactions between the observer(s) and the person(s) observed in the course of analysing the observed professional behaviours and activities and seeking to define and/ or develop next steps toward improved performance. I think it is helpful to think of clinical supervision as a subset of educational supervision rather than confusing the two.

Some approaches to supervision benefit directly from the fact that the supervisor has not observed practice. This is because supervises have to articulate what happened-and what they were thinking and feeling. It is much easier for us as supervisors to focus on what was happening for the practitioner if we are not encumbered by our own direct memories of the encounter or incident.

On the other hand, directly observed practice also has its benefits. As we have seen it allows for feedback and the facility for the supervisor to introduce other material from the situation. Managerial supervisors will often engage in this form of activity on a day-to-day basis.

### *Conclusion*

In this discussion particular questions have been highlighted. Some of the main points developed are as follows:

1. The central focus of supervision is the quality of practice offered by the supervisee to clients.
2. Supervision can be seen as having three aspects: administration (normative); education (formative) and support (restorative).
3. Supervisors' authority is derived from their positions in agencies and/or the appropriate community of practice (profession).
4. There are particular issues arising from the hierarchical position of supervisors.
5. In some forms of supervision direct observation of practice is a major obstacle to the exploration of practice; in others an aid.

I am conscious that I have left a number of important questions unasked or unanswered. The various issues discussed here have particular implications for what areas legitimately may be discussed within supervision; what supervisors themselves may put on the agenda, and so on.

# 5

# Public-Private Partnerships

## *Civil Society Defined*

First it will be helpful to clarify what we are interested in looking at in this chapter. Sometimes you will find a more all-encompassing definition of civil society (or occasionally the citizen sector), which might even be used to include the government sector as well. This broader definition is considered useful in that it avoids portraying the government as a competitor or even antagonist to the NGO sector and general populace. However, here we are going to use the narrower definition to include most actors in society, except for the government and its agencies, which are going to be the partners of the public and NGO sector in our analysis.

Thus, for our purposes, civil society can be said to be made up of individuals, community, business, and volunteer or NGO sector, which are so-called private as in not being of government (e.g., CARE International styles itself as a "private" international humanitarian organization to set itself apart from, for instance, UNICEF, a public specialized agency in the UN system).

## *Why Transfer Activities from the Government to Civil Society?*

Historically, this process fits in with minimizing the government's role and decentralizing activities, which was originally a common corporate tactic considered to be more efficient. In the European Union, there is a very important principle known as the concept of "*subsidiarity*," which simply means trying to do things, such as delivering social services and taking decisions that affect people, at the lowest level possible (i.e., closest to the people affected so they can more easily influence these acts and decisions). In poor countries, though, the government is often already too small and is barely able to handle its core functions.

Low-level activities also encourage more grassroots involvement, which is thought to be more efficient and democratic. However, this virtue needs to be weighed against the proven benefits of economy of scale issues for delivering social services. Of course, some social services may be best delivered in bulk, while others may be delivered in a more individual and idiosyncratic manner.

Federal systems believe that most health and education services are best done at the local state level, but sometimes a big new threat requires higher-level involvement (e.g., HIV/AIDS and bird flu responses). Importantly, the new *"philanthro capitalism"* movement led by the Bill and Melinda Gates Foundation (including the billion dollar Buffett bequest) will be particularly targeting the health and education sectors in partnerships with developing countries and big business.

***Time for a Reality Check***

It is frequently difficult for poorer and less sophisticated economies to use decentralization to local government, let alone out sourcing to NGOs.

Complaints from NGOs that have tried to make these service delivery programs work—to no avail—are fairly common across developing countries. Often the motivation for a government to try to involve new civil society actors is the realization that they have not been able to meet their objectives in a difficult service area. Many international NGOs already have their own field operations and existing staff set up in developing or crisis-affected countries. And sometimes these teams are more easily able to operate on both sides of a civil war zone, when the government is obviously restricted to its own area of influence.

It is also hard to obtain reliable reports or fair assessments of the types of problems that arise from the government side.

***Tip***

- During some of the recent massive disaster relief operations, friction has developed between experienced expatriate humanitarian NGO operators and the local government relief coordinators, who feel they have not been consulted enough. International NGOs and their staff would do well to remind themselves that they are guests in the host country and should try to show the appropriate level of respect to the local authorities even if they are critical of their performance. In the worst case the local government, backed up by their civil and military authorities, would be able to order the NGOs out of the area if they failed to comply with directions.

## Models of Partnerships that have Worked: Microfinance, Compacts etc.

Given the very real problems in execution of these partnerships, let us look at a few models that have met with varying degrees of success. The classic example given is the provision of microfinance, which consists of small loans to households and small business entrepreneurs, frequently led by women. For various reasons, however, microlending to the poor or isolated is an expensive and labour-intensive undertaking. In the original Grameen Bank (version 1) story, the success elements were considered to be due to local level collectors, *group guarantees* of each borrower, and demand-driven, pro-poor financial products. But in this model there was still a significant amount of government support, including state-subsidized low interest rates. The key elements of this model have been widely replicated in developing countries, and even in the some of the poorer regions of rich countries.

Grameen Bank version 2 is moving closer to a formal bank with new financial products for savings; it is trying to become self-sufficient. By the end of 2004, for the first time, this Nobel prize-winning bank had more savings deposited than it had outstanding loans. Nevertheless, it will still take them some time to be completely free of government support, in the sense that banks can ever be said to operate without the implicit support of their host governments, especially if they should run into troubles. The profitable Association for Social Advancement (ASA) of Bangladesh is again cited as providing a classic and robust "Model T" of microfinance, worthy of emulation.

More well-run NGO microfinance programs around the world are becoming able to transform themselves into successful microfinance commercial banks, which can continue to combine their original social mission with a more sustainable business proposition. For instance in the late 1990s the NGO Accion Comunitaria del Peru became Mibanco, a microfinance commercial bank. With more success stories, governments are starting to realize that they do not always have to maintain an equity share or intervene in the management of a microfinance bank in order to ensure that it will continue to lend to the poor.

*Compacts* (also known as *social contracts*) are more legalistic and contractual arrangements between governments and a group of civil society providers in a field of service, frequently health, education, credit intermediation, care and environment. The hallmarks are promises to provide and mutual commitments if certain benchmarks are achieved. Experience has shown that it is usually best to try to keep these arrangements flexible enough to adapt to changes and not to rely on an overly legalistic or adversarial approach in times of difficulties (i.e., strive to stay partners rather than blaming each other when things go wrong).

### *Notable Partnerships*

- In Hong Kong social services are run by NGOs that are well funded by government, some up to 70–80% of their operating budgets.
- In India there was a major government-NGO compact for poverty alleviation mainly to help organize those who could benefit.
- In the Philippines an NGO umbrella group can register other NGOs to certify them as being able to get funds from the government.
- In Sri Lanka a government and private trust fund pooled their resources to allocate to small projects and grassroots organizations.
- In Gujarat, India, the state's food and supplies department sponsors a phone helpline so hungry people can be directed to the nearest of over 30 participating civil society food charities.

- In Singapore, the government helps NGOs with their office logistics and operating costs for social welfare work, which allows them to spend more of their own money directly on the beneficiaries.
- In the PRC, the China Health Alliance brings NGOs, companies and UN agencies together with the government for a more effective, united fight against the spread of tuberculosis and AIDS.

*Tips*

- Governments in many of the least developed countries may come to see themselves as competitors with NGOs for receiving overseas development assistance from donor countries. And to some extent this is true and needs to be faced squarely and recognized as a potential friction point.
- In the PRC, there has developed an interesting model that is worth watching for other countries and NGOs. As the state wants to attract private donations for public purposes, it will set up a foundation and pay all of the salaries and overheads, leaving 100% of the public donations to be directly spent on the programs and projects, such as helping indigenous peoples.

## Participation in Policymaking, Procurement, Privatization and Partnerships

NGOs are often eligible for equal bidding for funds, including technical assistance grants, and for competing for work with government departments. There are three classic ways of becoming involved with governments and their projects:

1. Commercial level procurement and tendering for provision of goods and services. Here, be aware of too onerous tender requirements by way of capital and past experiences, and also too big lots that all but eliminate most small to medium scale competition to the commercial and government regulars.
2. Seeking grants for an NGO's own projects that match criteria wanted by government. The most interesting benefit here for NGOs is that there is frequently very little guidance or oversight, save for some tax accountability

and prudence in initial selections. For instance, when grants are solicited in rich countries the tax authorities usually require a minimal reference check to two other sources to vouch for the bona fides of the applicant and its project. Technical assistance grants have frequently been offered by international organizations and government aid agencies directly to NGOs.

3. Entering into some form of cooperative arrangement more as an equal partner but with financing coming from the government and usually with a little more guidance than for grants. This form is frequently seen when the government knows it needs some vague type of research work, but cannot be more precise before it begins, and thus needs to monitor the work as it progresses. This type of involvement can benefit NGOs.

*Tips*

- How can NGOs find out about these opportunities and start to compete for the money? Check first with your governments and, if they have them, small business or entrepreneurial agencies or the like to see if they offer help in how to bid and get qualified for government projects, etc. Useful training or workshops might be offered by the governments themselves or with the support of development finance institutions.
- Another useful way to break the ice and get exposure to the government departments that may be judging the tenders could be through first being invited into Policymaking procedures through comments from the public or giving evidence before hearings. In this way the NGO establishes its expertise in certain areas and begins to win the confidence of government bureaucrats responsible for the tenders.

## Consultation as Equal Partners? Potential Pitfalls for NGOs of close Involvement with Government

Are NGOs and governments, or international organizations for that matter, equal *partners?* If not, are they ever going to be? What can NGOs do to even the balance in their favour? On the other hand, what are the pitfalls for NGOs becoming successful and getting too close to the government and becoming involved commercially in many of its projects?

Most obviously, the risk in these situations will be for independent activists losing their prized possessions of political and financial autonomy and integrity. As that slips away, the tendency towards self-censorship by NGO management of itself and its members grows as an understandable way of keeping lucrative contracts and grants.

By their self-definition NGOs are supposed to be non-government, after all, and not a form of shadow or quasi government executing agencies. Getting too successful in government grants and contract awards may also make other members, other NGOs and general society become suspicious of the integrity of a "non-government" organization that mainly works on "government projects."

For instance many of the civil society organizations associated with the European Commission enjoy high levels of subsidies that have called into question their independence.

Sometimes, we have seen situations where government or the legislature has pretended to listen to civil society during a consultation and participation process, but does not really take account of the views expressed.

These situations are frustrating and wasteful of NGOs' time and resources. But it is often hard to know how a process with the government will eventually turn out when you first commence it. It goes without saying that NGOs need to avoid being co-opted and used by governments for their own purposes. But often in practice it becomes very hard, especially for smaller or less experienced NGOs, to recognize when they are fairly engaging with the government and when they are being taken advantage of for political purposes.

At the World Bank it has been recognized that there is still precious little real will to be equal partners; more often than not the input of NGOs or civil society has been thought of, if at all, as "window dressing" or an afterthought, which is often required to appease other governments in international financial institutions.

## Direct Funding, Aid Disbursement and Tax Incentives

### *Direct Funding Support and Grants*

Cash flows are the lifeblood of any organization. Non-profit are no exception. Staff and supplies must be maintained for the larger NPOs; the smaller ones will need community funds or facilities to stage their events.

The four traditional sources will always be from members' dues and additional contributions, fees and charges from quasi-commercial services provided, government direct financial and in-kind supports or legislative appropriations and general public donations, including those inspired by tax incentives organized by the government.

New sources, including unsecured loans and temporary bridging financing, are being tried out in the more developed countries, but reliable banking and access to capital markets are still a long way off for most NGOs.

Additionally, limited amounts of income may also be earned from a variety of sideline business-type sources: most often from sales of products or memorabilia, provision of other services, such as training and conference organizing, Christmas "charity gift" catalogues and the renting of facilities. (The foundation Google.org is even trying to apply profit-making principles to some of its public benefit activities as an experimental approach.)

Grants from the corporate sector are also becoming increasingly important. For instance, many multinational IT firms now offer charitable grants or support-in-kind to NGOs to help them better utilize ICT equipment and training techniques in their operations. Some companies will lend their name and resources to cool fund raising events, e.g., Gap's Charity Concerts for Japanese NPOs.

Many governments of major countries and most of the big funding foundations have fairly strict grant procedures that forbid them from financially supporting associations that are not legally incorporated or set up as a registered NGO. However, some international organizations are more flexible when it comes to the small-scale grants to help grassroot and local community groups that lack a formal legal personality.

### *Tip*

- By their very nature as one-sided gifts, there remains a risk that a promised donation or grant may not come through on time or be honoured as expected. Even after a public pledge has been made there is still some doubt unless the grant is clearly written down as a contractual promise. Therefore, NGOs and NPOs should be prudent in making financial commitments on the expectation of grant funding, especially if they involve large purchases or taking on paid staff through formal employment arrangements.

### *Foreign Funding Restrictions*

Certain countries remain concerned about real or perceived outside influence of foreign supporters for NGOs operating within their borders. One way to minimize this concern is for the government to specify that foreign interests may not make contributions to their local NGOs or can only do so with government approval. This type of concern comes from a long tradition of general foreign ownership restrictions over such things as media or armaments industries, which is still seen in even a number of developed countries. Although this is frequently bothersome to both foreign donors and local recipients, it is usually a stage that a country slowly grows out of as less industrial sectors are controlled and will be able to liberalize. Recommendations from sympathetic outside governments with influence can occasionally help hasten this process.

Qualifying to bid for aid disbursement funds If an NGO has programs that parallel the social or aid priorities of its government, it is logical for that NGO to bid to undertake such programs either as part of the government delivery or on its own, but with government backing or funding.

NGOs are generally required to register their interest in competing to carry out government programs or to receive funding. (Some countries may have a public lottery that shares funding among eligible claimants, including reliable NGOs.) Often the receipt of grant funds from a government entity will come with strict reporting and accounting requirements of how the money can be used.

*Tip*

- Writing good grant fund proposals and effective marketing of them are becoming an integral part of every NGO's repertoire. Make sure some of your staff or volunteers attend any free training programs being offered to help them prepare better proposals with a greater chance of being accepted.

### *Direct and Indirect Tax Incentives*

If the host government can be convinced, it is usually a very good idea to introduce laws or regulations that will inspire donors to give to qualified NPOs (usually in that host country) on the expectation of receiving comparable tax breaks, which can take a multitude of forms.

1. Obviously a qualified NPO should itself be exempt under its host country's income tax law, to the extent that it generates a sufficient amount of income that would ordinarily be taxable in the hands of individuals or commercial taxpayers.
2. As we have noted, limited moneymaking or subsidiary economic activities may sometimes be pursued by an NPO so long as they do not overtake the principle not-for-profit mission. The tax treatment of this income may be either simple exemption or subjection to taxation depending on its amount or whether the moneymaking activity is primarily related to the not-for-profit mission.
3. Donors to NPOs are frequently allowed by the tax authorities to receive tax deductions themselves when they are calculating their personal tax liability. These could also be given in the form of full or partial credits against taxes they would otherwise owe. In many jurisdictions it is common for gifts to charities and for certain political contributions to enjoy such tax credit treatment.
4. Often NPOs might have property interests and could be granted an exemption from any taxes they may incur on their real property. Another way to do this could be to set their taxation percentage rates at zero (i.e., no charges) for the purposes of calculating any value added tax.

5. Interest and other income received on an NPO's investments could similarly be exempt.

These tax preferences are thought to encourage greater levels of giving by donors and can be viewed as a kind of indirect funding support from the government. In other words, the government gives up collecting the taxes normally due in order to encourage others to make similar amounts of money available by way of gifts. There is merit in trying to keep the preference schemes as simple as possible in operation. Often tax authorities try to complicate the regulations by specifying that exemptions will only apply to certain activities of NPOs in preferred sectors (e.g., health or education) or that there is a waiting period during which they would not qualify. The specification of preferred activities is frequently too controlling or is open to abuse by government and waiting periods make little sense as fledgling NPOs most need state support during the difficult start-up phase.

In many jurisdictions, particularly in the European Union, there is a common concern about whether these tax preferences and privileges should also be extended in the case of gifts going abroad or to foreign-based NPOs. In theory, this should not matter as much as it does, but the foreign element often fans a suspicion that the purpose of the cross-border transaction may not always be completely bona fide. Opinion is split as to whether qualifying for tax exemptions should be automatic simply upon registration as an NPO, or if a further application and tax ruling needs to be separately made with the tax authorities. This could depend on whether that country has gone through a period of abuse of its taxation laws by private foundations, family trusts or criminal fronts Generally, though, tax authorities prefer to retain the power to make their own determinations on such matters. Some standard forms are described in the tax incentive references listed below in the Open Access Resources section.

### *Tips*

- The law and practice concerning the tax status of not-for-profit foundations and charities, particularly in continental Europe and parts of Asia, is extremely complicated. Many companies or family estates also structure themselves in similar positions to take advantage of the tax exemptions of these non-profit-making entities. Therefore, legitimate NPOs would need to be careful that they do not find themselves confused with tax shelters or misused for inappropriate evasion purposes.

- Umbrella organizations that certify the validity and good faith of NPOs and their operations are another effective way to convince tax authorities of the legitimacy of an NPO and that it is not being used as an unproductive or illegal tax shelter.

## Legal and Business Relations with International Organizations

Understanding international playing field and rules of game Despite the considerable complexities often involved, there is probably more that can be achieved by NGOs seeking ways to cooperate more closely with host governments and international organizations (IOs). This is especially so in complicated rehabilitation settings arising out of recoveries from disasters or post-conflict situations. Well-connected NGOs that know their host countries and project beneficiaries need to work better with IOs to head off problems before they become much more serious. Gradually the more experienced practitioners in development and civil society have come to accept the desirability of a wider field of actors contributing their differing expertise and advantages to international solutions. To help us set the scene it is instructive to recall a few landmark case studies demonstrating some of the various ways NGOs have engaged with international organizations (IOs) with varying degrees of success.

### *Case Studies of Narmada Dam Campaign and Banning Landmines*

The *Narmada Dam campaign* in India is remembered on two accounts. It was the first time that involuntarily moved people got the World Bank to set up an inspection function to hold itself accountable for its actions (and failings). Second, this successful movement evolved into a standing International Dams Commission (there is now also one for International Rivers, etc.).

Princess Dianalent her personal charisma to the campaign to achieve the political negotiation through the United Nations of an international convention banning the use of landmines, although some major countries have not yet ratified it. But not every cause succeeds this well on the international plane. For instance, notwithstanding a long and well-organized campaign going back to the 1970s, there is still only a simple UN recommendation for a code on the proper marketing and use of baby milk substitutes in less developed countries, especially those lacking clean water. The hoped-for, binding multilateral convention on this topic never eventuated.

### *Role of other Umbrella Organizations*

There is considerable scope in the myriad of dealings with IOs for the involvement of umbrella civil society organizations, which by rolling together like-minded NGOs, can usefully encourage group standards and ratings as conditions for membership. An umbrella grouping can also present a common and more powerful face to IOs, introduce partners online and comprehensively manage knowledge and portals, as on the Development Gateway.

There is now even the possibility of committed individuals or umbrellas quickly setting up online things such as global interest networks or communities of practice on fast-emerging particular issues. In a few weeks following the Indian Ocean tsunami many millions dollars in donations were received and coordinated from the general public through the Internet and online pledging sites.

Other notable examples in this burgeoning field for the blogosphere were the Howard Dean campaign fund raising drives in the last presidential nominee race and online political activists such as the Daily Kos, MoveOn.org and Citizen space. There are an estimated 10 million blogs in the United States alone.

### *Opportunities to Contract or Provide Services for Fees*

In some of the recent big humanitarian operations, what we have often seen is that a lead agency, usually from the UN family, will negotiate access (with or without security) to a troubled area and then act as an umbrella for an integrated aid program involving NGOs, who often come as affiliated with the UN or under contract to them.

### *Services NGOs Offer to International Organizations*

1. Providing observers for elections (various democracy NGOs).

2. Providing legal training for judges and lawyers (by non-profit American Bar Association and its programs).
3. Providing monitoring of treaties on the environment (e.g., *CITES* or *Montreal Protocol*) or humanitarian rights in war (e.g., Red Cross/Crescent has duties delegated to it under the Geneva Conventions). This can be done either by way of being parallel, independent, such as a watchdog, or as a formal part of the treaty regime. One way to accomplish this is getting involved in the treaty's secretariat, such as by writing reports for them.
4. Providing a missing synthesis of grassroots learning with scientific work and/or a mediated product for lay persons. Remember that a lot of IOs will readily give permission for non-profit use of their published materials with credit (or through a public commons licence, for instance).
5. More logistic types of involvement, such engineering, sanitation, transport services (frequently used by UN system in particular).
6. Traditional service package contracts for services or others for sale of goods.

### *Tips*

- Although it appears complicated when starting out, there are really only a couple of key variations on how NGOs are contracted and remunerated. Most common is just payment for your negotiated fees plus actual costs. Fees can be stated as being lump sum, fixed fees or at unit rates applied to multipliers, usually of time, but maybe of outputs produced.
- Another method not used so often for NGOs could be a retainer on a standing basis to provide things at preagreed rates. These are sometimes also known as period contract arrangements.
- Usually the legal format will be that of an independent contractor or supplier of services to the commissioning IO. Usually the staff of an independent contractor will not be covered by the insurance of the IO and so separate arrangements will need to be made for them by the contracting NGO.

- Remember to watch out that your NPO does not get into too much of a business operation and breach its public benefit status or lose tax privileges as a non-profit. This depends mainly on how you are set up and the form of the local tax breaks you enjoy.

### *Co-Financing and Parallel Financing*

Where there are shared interests, often co-financing or parallel financing alongside an IO is a possibility.

How this often arises is where an IO wants to do part of a project itself with either its own staff or consultants, but needs to collaborate with NGOs and civil society to make it a complete success and more inclusive.

In these situations they might enter into a *Memorandum of Understanding* and agree to either co-financing of a unified project budget (where one party clearly takes the lead) or more traditional parallel financing or paying each other's way themselves.

### *Consultation, Project Preparation and Advocacy Avenues*

These opportunities are more like traditional consultants' contracts on a time-basis or for producing outputs required by client IOs. A good model for NGOs to consider emulating could be the way some universities have set up their own consulting firms or arms to compete more commercially than they have before.

For years the Economic and Social Council (*ECOSOC*) of the United Nations has operated a procedure for NGOs to gain a formal consultative status with the committee. Many thousands of NGOs are registered in various capacities with the United Nations system of committees and specialized agencies.

Although NGOs are rarely allowed to appear formally before UN bodies or have access to bring cases to international tribunals, this consultative status can give them much better participation in practice to express their views or set the agenda (especially noticeable in the new Human Rights Council). Specialized dispute resolutions panels, such as those of the World Trade Organization, also on occasion may look at expert reports or unsolicited briefs prepared by NGOs on contentious matters. Today, the processing cycles of most IOs require many earlier stages of feasibility and research, and then consultation and participation, before their policies, projects and programs are allowed to proceed by managements and governing boards. If an NGO can gain the trust of IOs and provide what will be perceived to be suitably impartial advice, there is no reason why they could not compete in these avenues on equal footing with commercial or university firms.

IOs must also have public hearings for major changes in their business procedures, program policies or rules. In these areas they often value calling in NGOs to offer comments and even criticize their draft proposals either through traditional faceto-face meetings or electronic consultations. Sometimes comments from external NGOs and other stockholders are posted on a dedicated web page for others to view.

On occasions NGOs might even be invited to participatory "write shops" sponsored by IOs, where they can actively contribute to writing new policies or action plans that might affect them.

*Tips*

- Watch for announcements by the IOs in your field of their public hearings and apply to participate. Sometimes you will be allowed in, even if only on an observer basis to start with (usually you can ask questions). Later as you gain their trust you may be invited to formally offer comments.
- As your NGO gains greater acceptance and credibility with the target IO, opportunities to formally provide speeches or training courses for IO officials or their clients at conferences etc. may arise (often these come with honoraria or participation costs). A good way to break the ice and get known to an IO could be for the NGO to apply to some of the various awards and recognition contests held by the IO community, in particular the high-profile ones of the United Nations (e.g., UN Population Award).
- An independent NGO might also be appointed by an IO or government executing agency to monitor the implementation of a development program, for example to report on how successful the consultation and participation with affected people on that project has been.

- Other contractual opportunities well suited to NGOs might be the provision of community facilitation and empowerment services for a project (e.g., helping to identify local community leaders and enable them to take part in a consultation process with the government or IO proposing the project).

### *Ways to Inspect and Hold International Organizations Accountable*

*First*—know what they are doing. Start with the IO's web site and get on their e-alerts, notifications, RSS feeds or newsletters.

Most IOs have adopted Freedom and Disclosure of Information policies (also called information policy and strategy). The key features of these strategies are:

- Presumption in favour of disclosure, but subject to terms on which information was originally supplied, usually sourced from a member government.
- Now seen as an important part of public relations and affairs and a part of the process of showing good faith toward stockholders and the wider community.
- At the high end of the disclosure spectrum, the World Bank and other IOs now even publicly release summaries of minutes of their board meetings. In this fashion their proceedings can be closely checked by interested watchers, such as the Bank Information Centre (BIC), an NGO advocacy watchdog following international financial institutions in particular.

### *Tip*

- Don't forget the effectiveness of the old-fashioned approach of just writing to the resident office of an IO or right person at HQ to request information. Sometimes they will supply it willingly and you can receive it without having to go through formal requesting channels.

*Second*—evaluate results and unintended outcomes and ask the IOs to be accountable for what they said they would do and the actual results. IO web sites often post draft terms of reference or issue papers about upcoming evaluations or investigations, which invite public comments to contribute or change them. During evaluations, submissions from interested parties are invited and taken for study.

After the reports are finalized, they are made public, and then formal comments from interested stockholders are again invited within a specified period (sometimes easier summaries in local languages will be made and out reach conferences convened in selected locales).

Even comments on the evaluation process itself will be occasionally solicited, say every three to five years. Try to influence the contents of work programs of the evaluation offices themselves (sometimes they also invite comments). For instance, suggest new evaluation techniques or stockholders who need to be consulted during the formal evaluation process. At the same time, recognize that these new procedures are not without costs in time and money.

Formal evaluations are mainly of actual projects. Another avenue is reporting suspected abuse or waste to an Auditor General of an IO (an internal auditor is more interested in internal misdeeds or waste of the IO or its staff, rather than the projects themselves). Whist leblowers or concerned NGOs that have credible information could come forward to file reports.

### *Example of ADB's Improved Accountability Procedures*

In May 2003, as a result of external pressure and recognition of the need for reform, the ADB Board introduced new accountability steps to improve the operations of the Asian Development Bank's projects.

ADB's new accountability steps are primarily concerned with its projects' effects on people; the new procedures offer flexible and innovative ways to fi x things before a problem becomes entrenched. They include:

*Consultation phase:* This is comprised chiefly of consultative dialogues with an independent Special Project Facilitator. He or she may use their good offices or either formal or informal mediation tools between the complaining parties and the ADB.

During this phase there are lots of potential roles for representative grassroots organizations or supportive global NGOs. Well-connected and trusted local NGOs can frequently serve as facilitators, interpreters and cultural intermediaries with complaining villagers. And an international NGO, Bank Information Centre (BIC), often assists local complaining groups in their disputes with international financial institutions by giving them advice or helping prepare compliance and rehabilitation status reports.

*Compliance review:* Then at a second, separate phase, affected people (or occasionally the ADB Board) can air complaints about a project and management's handling of it. This is done by fi ling a formal request for compliance review, but only of the ADB's conduct. Such a review does not yet extend to the borrowing country or any involved private sector sponsors. Findings of these reviews are not adjudicative and are mainly into how projects were formulated, processed and implemented (n.b. but not complaints about hiring consultants).

Affected people can claim for a desired outcome or practical remedy (often called a course of action, which will be approved by the ADB Board), rather than money damages or declaratory awards.

*Tips*

- Complaint filers are defined as "any group of two or more people (such as an organization, association, society or other group of individuals) ...." and "a local or nonlocal representative of the affected group."
- Filers can submit their documents in a local language if they are unable to provide an English translation.
- Names will be kept confidential if requested; however, anonymous complaints cannot be accepted.

### *Power of Influencing Member Governments Back Home*

Most IOs are creatures of their owning governments. So if you can influence your government back home to support your ideas, they can then try to put them into practice in the IOs' boardrooms.

Use standard tactics to lobby governments and also try the embarrassment approach on IOs, which do not like to look bad in the eyes of their member governments, who set their programs and approve their budgets.

Constituencies in home governments interested in IOs are generally small, however, so often politicians simply leave the bureaucrats to set the tones and policies towards the IOs over which they exercise supervision. (On the other hand, some commentators have felt that the strong response from civil society in the aftermath of the Indian Ocean tsunami has demonstrated to national politicians that their people really do care deeply about international aid and humanitarian issues.)

Nevertheless, dramatic things do occasionally happen, such as when the United States and Britain pulled out of UNESCO in dissatisfaction for many years in the 80s and 90s (both have since returned). Certainly getting member governments to hold up, delay or abstain on budgets of IOs is most effective for sending a message.

It may even be possible to get parliament to pass legislation that directs agencies to refrain from supporting certain IOs until specified reforms or changes get implemented (e.g., the long-standing US congressional forays against the UN).

## Media and Advocacy Strategies

### *Legitimacy of NGOs in Public Debate*

NGOs are usually not approved by any traditional democratic or electoral processes (sometimes called legitimization or a public trust test), yet often they try to control or even make claims on public funds or subsidies just like elected governments. In this way it can be said that NGOs parallel the role of industry lobbyists or associations and their access to governments and attempts to influence political decision making. But the criticism that NGOs unfairly attempt to influence the public debate without proper legitimacy or accountability is often raised to try to silence them or balance the aggressive approach they may take.

The prudent use of a media out reach or broader marketing campaign can be helpful in trying to defuse these criticisms and convince wider society that a valid role in public debate remains for NGOs, just as much as it does for lobbyists, columnists, commentators and other public opinion shapers.

Therefore, formal or abridged statements of an NGO's philosophy, purpose or mission should appear frequently and forcefully in its own publications (often on the back cover), annual reports and certainly on its web site. If applicable, the NGO could also highlight the financial support it enjoys from the beneficiary community to buttress its legitimacy.

### *Understanding and Shaping the Public Debate: Think Globally—Act Locally*

Even NGOs with worldwide reputations are strongest in their local market. They can cultivate local journalists and follow the preferred story line and headline tactics of media based in their country. And usually, country media have a more immediate impact upon their compatriots in civil society or political power.

Transparency International's UK unit, for instance, smartly gained wide-scale awareness of the global problem of money laundering funds from corruption. They achieved this by highlighting for influential London-based media how much the

City is being used for this activity. Their media message was simple but effective: "If laundering is so bad in a well-regulated market such as London, then imagine how much worse the problem must be worldwide!"

If you achieve success in gaining publicity, do not be surprised if you also attract criticism from the government, IOs or media; they may challenge your arguments and report findings. And even other NGOs can on occasion be critical of some of your positions or activities. Be prepared to respond to such criticism with evidence in support of your position. Action Aid frequently posts on its web site the criticisms it receives from official sources; the organization accompanies these postings with its formal responses, including links to supporting documentation.

Using statistics or scientific research in an intellectually honest and responsible way can sometimes be hard for lay people who are not experts in the particular field. Within the limits of their technical expertise NGOs should be careful in how they present and interpret their data and research so as not to mislead or overstate their case. Basing your positions on sound facts and credible analysis is the best way to enhance your NGO's reputation. Take care about plagiarism and properly crediting the research work of others.

*Tips*

- Try to interest local media by finding the local or national aspect that will immediately appeal to their audience.
- Watch how your target media covers similar "human interest" stories and try to frame your issue in the same style. Look for the opposing interests and try to set up the story as a conflict between the good and bad or big and little guys.

### *NGOs as Agents for Change*

The secret to a successful campaign is to clearly envisage what you and your NGO are aiming to change and then to set about crafting strategies to fit that end. Some of the many things that NGOs seek to change are: institutional behaviour; laws, policies and attitudes of public or private sectors; engagement of stockholders; increasing public awareness and access to resources and information. They also seek to physically do projects or save things or people from destruction. You must then ask the hard question: What causes real change in the things you want to do? And what actions are you or your NGO able to take to bring about those changes?

Of course, this can never be answered universally for every cause or problem. Nevertheless, history seems to suggest that going after the money stream is usually the most successful tactic, particularly when it comes to changing corporate or political behaviour. For instance, industrial pollution was never-ending until the environmental movement caused the United States to introduce super fund clean-up liability before the sales of land on which former factories had operated. More recently, we have witnessed the progress made in gradually changing consumers' tastes and getting them to prefer different products (organic cotton, fair trade coffee); these changes influence the manufacturers' profit margins.

Although it is the traditional path, people are becoming less convinced about the effectiveness of working through the political process. Even so, a powerful politician can still shape the public debate and place an important item on the global agenda. If these leaders can be influenced by the campaigns of an NGO, there is a meeting of interests. Be aware that politicians and their staff are more impressed by personal approaches rather than mass mailings using form letters from their constituents.

***Pointers for Dealing Successfully with the Media***

- Generally speak to journalists "on the record" and allow your name and affiliation to be used.
- Do not ask to vet a draft of an article, but do check to ensure that your direct quotations are correct.
- Approach smaller or lesser-known specialist media outlets; they will appreciate the attention.
- Prepare a key message and repeat it often throughout an interview.
- Think and speak in short, memorable phrases (useful for TV sound bites).
- Vivid descriptions, anecdotes or human interest stories are naturally compelling and quotable.
- Play up the relevance and newsworthiness of your NGO's message.

***Tips***

- Bringing about real change is always hard; it is especially hard if your group does not have ready access to the opinion shapers or decision makers. The best advice for a successful advocacy strategy is to know who or what you most want to influence and then to frame messages specially directed to them. Even better is to show them why it is in their own self-interest to implement the changes you recommend. Give them some options of short-term or long-term changes to increase the chances that something might get implemented.
- Always go well prepared to meetings or interviews with your facts and figures. Try to maintain a businesslike demeanour even if you are being patronized, disregarded or insulted. If a politician or journalist asks for more details that you may not currently have, be sure to find those details out and remember to send them along later in a professional follow-up. Journalists will use again sources who meet their deadlines and are reliable. And don't forget to express gratitude for the meeting and follow-up for the next step.

## *Tactics for Media Impact: Those that Work and Pitfalls to Avoid*

In a number of countries the media strongly proclaim that freedom of speech and freedom of the press are fundamental human rights. In this regard they are natural allies of NGOs and civil society and therefore should be regularly engaged, through some of these methods:

1. *Open letters* to VIPs (most famously Amnesty International's clemency pleas), or to offending companies' CEOs and/ or politicians. Sometimes these pieces can be just through the letter pages or done as a paid advertisement. Although they are harder to get picked up, editorial leaders or opened pieces submitted to mass circulation media can have a similar impact.
2. Staged incidents with graphic or novel appeal: arrests for blocking traffic and smearing blood on fast-food windows in Paris; blocking bulldozers in Tasmania's Franklin dam site; sitting in trees; mothers camping outside cruise missile bases in Europe; refugee sit-ins or occupations in front of the UNHCR visitors' centre; street marches of all kinds.
3. If the media cannot be there at the time, do not forget to provide the images yourself (another form of transparency). Some memorable images have come from video tapes of Green peace anti-whaling and nuclear testing, asylum seeking at embassy gates and cruelty to donkeys in the Mediterranean. The simple power of video pictures dramatizes a complex or distant issue in many people's minds.
4. Start with letters to editors to lay out and highlight issues and then try to follow up with visiting them in person to make your case and put a face to the letter.
5. Web site sidebar ads in online newspapers are often cheaper than traditional print ads (e.g., the regular "Please no more fighting" sidebar from Save the Children in Sri Lanka on the online edition of the Sri Lankan Sunday Observer).
6. Enlisting celebrities for full-page ads or the Hip Hop Action Summit/Live 8 for Africa events, making statements at awards shows or just wearing pins and ribbons. "When

Russell Simmons speaks, millions and millions of people listen," claims PETA spokesperson Bruce Friedrich. Many media personalities are sympathetic to NGO causes and are often ready to donate their time and influence.

7. Communicate honestly, politely and accurately, both externally and internally, about your mission, goals, objectives and programs. If the people most personally affected by an issue want to make themselves available to the media for interviews, this can sharpen the appeal of the story. But as usual, be sensitive; do not turn your affected people into helpless victims or poster people. If an NGO's spokes people feel they must criticize other individuals or organizations to make an important point, they must think carefully about whether the statements can pass the general standards of fair comment on a matter of public interest. In most progressive jurisdictions truth and reasonable expressions of opinion will be sufficient to protect your statements.
8. Reasons to communicate include advocacy of values and goals, information required by constituencies, and creation of favourable attitudes towards an organization and its goals and purposes.

***Tips***

- Depending on the nature of the NGO, public relations should be directed locally, nationally, regionally and internationally and should be pitched to different audiences, including business and general public (at the very local level, for instance, street signs can complain about excessive building heights). To the extent possible, don't forget to think of ways of monitoring or measuring your success.
- Some other helpful tools to use and examples include: person to person contacts, phone, personal letters, mass or direct mails, faxes (n.b. sometimes busy media like old-fashioned hard copy faxes as opposed to e-mails, which they often delete, block with a filter, or don't bother to print out and read), electronic media, smooth looking promotional materials, and newsletters.

- Don't forget that cheap-to-produce and easy-to-walk-around-in message T-shirts often work very effectively Some successful messages have been "Do Care" (a Domiciliary Care and visitation program for elderly in their homes), "No Dams!", "Fair Trade," and legal rights on being arrested; the latter became so popular that it even made some money. Paper leaflets get thrown away too easily but most people are happy to become walking billboards in free T-shirts if they have a cool message.

### *Handling a Scandal or Crisis Sensibly*

When things do go wrong (and they will) NGOs need to adopt the smarter practices observed in the corporate world. For instance, if a managing director makes a personal mistake that is starting to impact upon the reputation of the NGO, the board of the NGO needs to be seen taking the matter seriously and respond publicly and appropriately but in a caring and open manner. Trying to duck the issue and not actively step up to the responsibility will usually result in negative publicity and press reports about the NGO as a whole, even when the fault lies more in the managing director's behaviour.

In situations of a major scandal or governance failures threatening the legitimacy and continued existence of an NGO, calling in a special outside investigator or supervisor with credibility to correct errant behaviour might be the only lasting solution that will be accepted by the outside world. If your advisers suggest this course of action, don't delay too long in accepting their advice. It always looks better if a troubled NGO responds quickly to complaints coming from the public or media rather than hoping they will go away eventually.

Where there is sector-wide skepticism, such as in the aftermath of a string of donation scandals, a collective approach taken by a majority of law-abiding NGOs might be the most effective antidote rather than each going alone (e.g., the Giving Scotland anti-scandal advertising and media campaigns in 2003).

### *Final Tip*

- Be guided in all public affairs activities by the principle of how best to retain the trust and confidence of the public.

## The Changing Roles and Tasks of Social Work

### *The Influence of Globalisation*

Changes in political ideology have also coincided with major changes in economics and economic policy. These have had profound implications for public services. During the 1970s there was a strong pressure to reduce public expenditure because of economic recession. Subsequently a new emphasis was placed on the 'Globalisation' of the economy. Dominant interpretations of Globalisation emphasised the limited capacity of nation states to influence this international development. It was increasingly argued that public expenditure had to be controlled if states were to be competitive. This was accompanied in the UK by a rising emphasis on the market playing a much greater role in the provision of public services, including social work and social care. This has been a key determinant of the policies and services that service users have received.

### *Policy Context for Social Work*

Before we look at roles and tasks in social work first with adults and then with children and families, it will be helpful to look at the implications such distinctions between groups may have from service users' perspectives. For service users the distinction is often associated with a continuing sense that services for children and families that are given greater priority than those with adults because there are particular political and public concerns over child care tragedies and abuse. These can be guaranteed to generate headlines, if not significant improvement. Historically less attention has generally been paid to cases of abuse and neglect in relation to adult services

### *Categorising Service Users*

The recent history of statutory social work is one which has reinforced the division of service users into separate 'user groups'. This has followed both from a strengthening shift to specialisation in social work over the last 25 years and also the increasing organisation of social work through separate structures for different groups of service users. This has been most evident in relation to developing divisions between work with adults and with children and families, culminating after the government White Paper 'Every

Child Matters' in the separation of the two in two different government departments: the Department of Health (DH) and the Department for Education and Skills (DfES) and the creation of 'children's trusts'. Service users have highlighted that such divisions have created significant problems for them, for example:

- Where the identity of service users crosses over administrative boundaries, for example, that of disabled children;
- Where people have multiple identities as service users, for example, as parents and people with learning difficulties;
- At times of transition, for example, when disabled children are growing into young adulthood.

There are similar problems with adult services where these are divided administratively, for example, into older people (people can also expect to lose services and benefits when they reach traditional retirement age), people with physical and sensory impairments, both when people move from one category to another and when they fill more than one category (Gibbs, 2004). The overall effect for service users is that they feel they are not treated as whole people, but divided into service led administrative categories. This results in fragmentation of the services and support available to them (Morris, 2004).

### *A Policy Context for Social Work with Adults*

People with long term experience of using social care services have been on the receiving end of massive changes in policy, provision and ideology over the last 25 years. In terms of access to social work services, however, the message that frequently comes across from service users is how *little* in some senses their experience of social work and social care has actually changed fundamentally. The continuing trend that service users report is of reduced access to social work and social care support, with eligibility criteria that continue to narrow and focus on people seen as having the greatest need, rather than on preventing problems getting worse. Emerging developments Having said that the policy context for social work with adults has changed significantly in recent years. Key expressions of this are:

- The shift to a market based model of service provision, where the commercial sector has come to play the predominant role in the provision of social care services (domiciliary and institutional) and where services are means tested and service users are expected to pay for support, unless they cannot afford to and are included as eligible (Means and others, 2003).
- The shift to the market has placed an increasing importance on arrangements for allocating and rationing support. The 'care manager' approach was adopted to do this. This has fundamentally altered and limited the role of professional statutory social worker in the context of adult service users. It also resulted in professional assessment procedures coming to have fundamental significance for service users and playing a key gate keeping role for access to resources.
- The emergence from the 1980s of new organisations (national, regional, local and international) of service users as well as of new service user movements. This was a development beyond policy, but it was supported by parallel policy developments and spread to a growing range of service user groups, starting with the disabled people's movement. Service users and their organisations have been committed to having a greater say in social work and social care services and have argued and worked for their democratisation. One expression of this development has been the establishment of local democratically structured disabled people's and service users' organisations, providing opportunities for collective action and campaigning, as well as providing support for independent living, direct payments schemes and user-led services.
- The emergence of a new rhetoric of participation, partnership and empowerment, linked with the shift to consumerist market welfare approaches from the 1980s (White and others, 1988). Provisions for such participation were built into legislation and guidance of the community care reforms, for example. Service users and their organisations remain uncertain what this new consumerist

rhetoric means and achieves in practice and frequently express concerns about 'consultation overload', 'tick box exercises' and 'tokenism'-in participation particularly. Concepts of participation and empowerment have been particularly central among service users, their organisations and movements. Empowerment for them includes both personal and political empowerment and takes account of the complex relations between the two. As people become more personally empowered they are able to make a more effective political impact. Similarly through collective action, people can become more empowered personally Participation or user involvement, is concerned with increasing the say and control that service users can have over their lives and services they use or which impact upon them.

- The Valuing People initiative (Department of Health, 2001) represents a break with traditional approaches to policy and practice with people with learning difficulties. Significantly based on principles of normalization (Race, 1999, 2002), the aim was to raise standards of support for people with learning difficulties and enable them to participate more actively in mainstream society. It has offered a powerful central impetus for positive practice, but service users argue that its impact at local level is very limited. Large numbers of people with learning difficulties are still living in NHS institutional services, although the aim was for these to be closed. The recent Cornwall and Orchard House abuse scandals highlight that the accountability and quality of such provision is still suspect.
- While one of the concerns that government sought to address in undertaking community care reforms in the 1990s was to end 'perverse incentives' for people to be placed in residential care, disproportionately high referral of adult service users to residential services continues. It is estimated that 500,000 people are currently living in such provision and this not only includes large numbers of older people, but also disabled people of working age and young disabled people. Service users and their organisations argue that many of these people could be

supported to live in their own homes consistent with the original goals of the community care reforms.

- At the same time service users have been able to impact on policy (Thompson, 1991). A key expression of this is the introduction of direct payments schemes with new legislation in 1997 (Glendinning and others, 2000). The number of people receiving direct payments has gradually increased. The range of people has also been expanded to include a wider range of service users and children and young people. But the overall numbers in receipt of direct payments is still small in relation to numbers of social care service users overall (approximately 42,000)
- Direct payments were pioneered by the disabled people's movement. They represented a radical change in values and philosophy to underpin people's support. The aim was to put individuals in charge of the support they received by giving them control over the cash it cost; for them to decide on what support they wanted; for them to have support (from disabled people's organisations) to initiate and run such schemes and for the support to be sufficient to make it possible for them to have 'independent living'; that is to say for people to live their lives on as equal terms as possible to non-disabled people/nonservice users (Barnes, 1993).
- While this has been the policy framework for direct payments, there have been major problems and barriers undermining it. There has been strong resistance from some local authorities, who have wanted to continue to control their own services; budgetary limits have meant that often direct payments have not been sufficient to ensure independent living and there has frequently not been equity between service users; the process of assessment has continued to be dominated by traditional professional values, direct payments appear often to have been understood officially in consumerist terms (as if people were just buying services), rather than as a means of empowerment, requiring infrastructural support; and contracts have increasingly been placed away from valued disabled people's organisations to commercial

organisations which have undercut them and offered an inferior service. Problems have also been experienced by service users where local authorities themselves seek to be the service provider 'in house' for direct payments. The cumulative effect has been to subvert direct payments as a truly different approach to personal and social support.

- Recently the government has made clear its commitment to individualized approaches to support more generally as a central plank in social care policy. Such 'individualised support schemes' or 'personalised budgets' are based on bringing together different funding streams to provide support for service users (Duffy, 2004, 2006). These schemes have not originated with service users. While the aim is to mainstream such schemes, so far their development has been based on a relatively few pilot projects with a limited evidence base for their effectiveness. Service users express concerns that their long term helpfulness may be undermined and qualified by cuts in service and service users' organizations and unevidenced assumptions that such schemes will reduce costs.
- Service users and their organisations have also developed their own thinking about issues affecting them, for example, their identity and how they are perceived, new ways of understanding their situation and new (particularly non medicalised) user-led approaches to support and assistance. These include both collective and individualized support and services. Service users have in addition sought to gain greater involvement in four key areas, all of which have significant implications for social work roles and tasks and which in some cases have already begun to influence them. These are in:
    - Developing their own accounts and histories – offering their versions of their experience and views.
    - Education and training – developing user involvement in social work education and training, user trainers, training for user trainers and user led training.
    - Research and evaluation – getting involved in research, developing a more inclusive knowledge base for social

care, developing their own new research approaches and becoming researchers.

- Quality definition and measurement – developing user involvement in quality standards and user-defined outcome measures.

### *Broader Developments*

Broader developments have also had a major influence on the policy context of social care and social work. Key to this is the introduction of rights based legislation. This includes the introduction of the Disability Discrimination Act, the subsequent extension of its provisions to include a wider range of service users and situations; the passing of the Human Rights Act and in 2006 the establishment of the Disability Equality Duty, requiring public agencies and services not only to counter discrimination, but also to strive towards and promote, equality for disabled people (broadly defined). As well as embodying the original commitment of the disabled people's movement to a human and civil rights rather than welfare approach to people's needs, these developments have also fostered a wider understanding of and support for a rights based approach to health and social care policy and practice among service users.

### *Mental Health Legislation*

While disability legislation and proposals for change (including the current Independent Living Bill) have focused on rights and entitlements, the policy context for mental health has been significantly different. Since the community care reforms, there has been a growing media and political preoccupation with the perceived 'dangerousness' of mental health service users and the 'threat' they pose to 'public safety'. While there is no evidence to support highly publicized accounts of an increase in homicides by mental health service users as a result of the reforms, this has become a key driver in mental health policy and public perceptions.

Most significantly over the last nine years it has resulted in ongoing government attempts to introduce new mental health legislation increasing restrictions to be placed on mental health service users' rights, including the extension of compulsory treatment beyond hospitals and the detention of people labelled as having 'dangerous personality disorder', prior to conviction for any crime. This has led to widespread and concerted campaigning against such legislation (which has strengthened a rights based approach to conceptualizing mental health issues) and fears that attention has been diverted from continuing core problems and deficiencies of mental health services and policy.

There has been continuing questioning in policy of the specific contribution that social work and a social work background has to offer in health and social care. The first expression of this was embodied in the Community Care reforms, when the official assumption was that other professionals (for example, nurses, occupational therapists, etc.) would be just as well qualified to act as care managers as social workers. More recently the intention has been to end the approved social worker (ASW) role and put a mental health social worker role in its place which might be undertaken by other health and social care professionals.

## A Policy Context for Children and Family Social Work

Service users and indeed members of the public more generally, seem to understand social work with families and children as ultimately being concerned with keeping children with or removing them from their families. Whatever, the origins of this perception, whatever the part played by the mass media in perpetuating it, this does seem to be a view which is much more broadly internalized. In a study of another area of social work, this negative stereotype of social work as child remover seems to be a deeply held concern and fear about social work held by many people, worrying them about accessing other forms of social work support. (Beresford and others, 2007).

A process of child care and child protection policy and practice development in children and family social work based on a cycle of tragedies and follow-up enquiries has been widely recognized. This approach has tended to focus on reorganization and training as solutions to problems, although these have not been shown convincingly to be effective.

Service users highlight what they see as the arbitrary use of social work's controlling powers to remove children from parents with mental health problems and with learning difficulties, rather than ensuring the provision of appropriate ongoing support –

especially at times of particular difficulty. The removal of children related to problems of homelessness and poverty has also been identified by service users as a problem associated with social work with families and children. Inadequate funding, problems in recruiting and retaining good quality staff, insufficient management resources, over bureaucratisation and overloaded agencies are all seen to contribute to the inability of such social work to ensure adequate and reliable support for families and children to prevent problems worsening, to identify difficulties early and to ensure effective decision-making. Problems of communication and coordination with other agencies in work with children and families, as well as with adults is also recognized as a problem, which service users are aware of because of the difficulties they experience in securing suitable and integrated support where their needs cross over different agencies and policy sectors.

Over the last 25-30 years there have been radical shifts in child care and child protection policy and practice. Many of these have become high profile issues which have become part of broader, political, media and public debates. They include:

- A shift from residential provision to foster care and adoption;
- Shifts towards and away from 'same race' fostering and adoption;
- Shifts in understanding from 'relativism' in relation to culture and ethnicity, to the need to adopt effective anti-discriminatory, anti-racist policy and practice;
- Shifts in philosophy relating to removing children from families of origin and seeking to keep them with their families;
- A shift from long term retention of cases to fear of 'drift' in care;
- Shifts in approaches to fostering and adoption relating to the sexuality of potential parents and the nature of their households;
- Shifts in approaches to adoption in relation to the age of potential adopters.

Such policies and practices have changed over the years, in some cases due to shifts in social work thinking and because of child protection tragedies, rather than as a result of strongly knowledge based policy development. One thing which has remained a constant in stated policy and practice over recent years, however, has been a view of the primacy of the child in considerations and decisions relating to child care and child protection.

This originated with the 1989 Act, but a constant tension since has been the degree to which this has actually been achieved and achievable in practice. Both the Victoria Climbie tragedy and the more recent Child B case in Westminster, were defining cases where this did not happen, although it is argued that this is for different reasons (Broad, 2007). The 1989 Children Act, which provided the original underpinning for current social work with families and children, like the community care reforms introduced at the same time, placed an emphasis on the participation of children (and their families). It also placed more emphasis, than the reforms relating to adult service users on rights and entitlements as well as needs.

However, participation in relation to children and young people raises additional issues to those raised with adult involvement. Service users argue that these do not particularly follow from the ability or otherwise of children to come to realistic and sensible decisions; to make choices and to contribute their views about themselves, their circumstances and services relating to them.

Children do not have the rights of full citizenship in societies like England and the UK. In some cases they may lack the capacity to pursue their own interests independently. There is a strong tradition of adults speaking on behalf of children and interpreting what they say. As both adult and children service users have observed, there is often a particularly large gulf between political and service rhetoric about children's participation and the actual influence that they can exert to affect decisions and the direction of policy and nature of practice. In formal political processes (from which they are essentially excluded) this influence is necessarily very limited.

Much work has now been done to develop appropriate ways for children and young people (from a very early age) to get involved (including different groups of children like disabled children and those with experience of being looked after in care. Yet there is still a strong sense at the level of policy, provision and general-decision making that children have very little influence over social work and social care. At an individual level, both the Victoria Climbie and Child B cases highlighted basic problems (both with experienced and qualified social workers and overloaded and less experienced social workers) of the voice of the child not being given central consideration and the child not necessarily being spoken with or listened to. Social work with children and families includes at least five (potentially overlapping) groups of children and young people. These are:

- Disabled children and young people and their parents;
- Disabled parents and their children;
- Looked after children and their families (who may be fostered, adopted, or in state care);
- Children in the family where child care/support or child protection needs have been identified;
- Children and young people within or at risk of coming within the juvenile justice and related social control/penal systems.

The wide range of issues and circumstances included under these five headings reflect the diversity and complexity of social work with children and families.

In recent years social work and social services have identified another group which they see as coming within their orbit, relating to the second group identified above, who have been categorized as 'young carers'. A new area of policy, practice and discussion has developed in relation to this externally constructed identity. This has become a very contentious development. Many disabled people and disabled people's organizations challenge the thinking underpinning this concept and policy approach, arguing that while it often serves to blame and stigmatise disabled parents, the actual issue is the lack of adequate and appropriate support they are able to access as disabled people and parents (Mason, 2007).

## Social Work Roles and Tasks

There are some general points that need to be made before looking separately at social work roles and tasks with adults and with families and children.

### *Lacking Public Understanding*

All the signs are that the roles and tasks of social work have not been and are still not well known to the public or to service users. Studies of public and service user under standings from the 1980s and 2000s both provide evidence to this effect. Thus social work may be something that 'the public' has strong often negative attitudes about, but equally it doesn't have a clear understanding of what social work actually is and what it does. The fact that service users may not know what the nature and scope of social work practice resulted in one current text recommending that social workers needed to be much clearer to service users about what they do (Beresford, Adshead and Croft, 2007).

Lack of public familiarity with and understanding of social work seems most likely to relate to the fact that it is generally not a universalist service. Its association with deprivation, disadvantage and people who are often devalued in society mean that people are more likely to see it as for others rather than themselves. Equally, a key characteristic of social work is the enormous range of activities it includes, as well as the wide variety of approaches and ways of working with people which it encompasses. While this may be one of its strengths, it makes understanding social work more difficult. Social work is also essentially a human rather than technological service. It isn't linked with high technology, complex equipment and 'scientific discovery'. The truth is that much of it is about people talking to or communicating with each other. This is perhaps what can make it seem so unremarkable and mundane, but which is actually what makes it so complex and difficult to tie down and comprehend. We can expect that all these characteristics will also play a part in making it more difficult to understand.

From what service users say it seems that social work is an easy job to do badly, but a very difficult one to do well. In discussions, they highlight the benefits they have got from good social workers as well as the problems when social work supports is not good (Branfield and others 2005). It will be helpful to look more carefully at the roles and tasks of social work and how they are defined in turn.

### *Social Work Roles*

Two main roles for social work tend to be identified most often and service users certainly talk in these terms too. These are social work's

- Support role.
- Control role.

The first of these roles is largely uncontentious and relates to the goals and values that social work most often associates itself with, including advancing self-determination, autonomy and social justice. In more mundane terms, this means helping people live their lives to the full, negotiate with the wider world, deal with changes and difficulties they are experiencing and work out what they want to do. The control role has always been part of social work. It is not only traditionally associated with social work playing a part in ensuring that people conform to prevailing values and behaviours. It also extends to social work having powers to restrict people's rights and freedom of action. This is most associated with the child protection and mental health aspects of social work practice (with the approved social worker having powers to section or impose 'compulsory treatment' and child protection workers to remove children from their families).

Social workers can also intervene where they judge people incapable of managing their own affairs and in the institutionalization of people seen as no longer able to manage in their own homes.

The control role of social work is particularly linked with interventions to restrict the rights of some people, in order to safeguard the rights of others (for example, restricting parents' rights to safeguard children's rights, or restricting mental health service users' rights on the basis of safeguarding those close to them and other members of 'the public'. A third role however is also associated with social work; this is a role to bring about change in the individual. Thus the International Federation of Social Workers' (IFSW) definition of social work includes:

Professional social work is focused on problem solving and change. As such, social workers are change agents in society and in the lives of the individuals, families and communities they serve. While social work may see this role and goal as unproblematic, for many service users the intervention of state social work to change them can seem very much the opposite. Bearing in mind that such intervention for change is significantly based on psychiatrically based interpretations of behaviour and emotions, its appropriateness as well as its effectiveness are concerns for service users. Thus while social work's commitment to broader social change is something that service users value, seeing itself as an agent of *individual* change is a very different issue and one which needs to be given more consideration in reviewing social work roles and tasks than so far seems to have been the case.

Service users draw a distinction between social work and social workers. At least two of the core roles discussed above are cause for concern for many service users. What makes social work more acceptable to them is the extent to which good practitioners mediate underlying problems in its ideology and organization (Branfield and others, 2005). This places a big responsibility and creates large challenges for such practitioners.

### *Poverty and Exclusion*

Social work has long been associated with poverty and working with a clientele with particular problems of deprivation, although as has been said, some commentators have felt that social work has not always paid enough attention to this (Jones, 2002). New Labour governments from 1997 highlighted the related concepts of social exclusion and social inclusion and made them central in UK social policy, setting up a Social Exclusion Unit, initially chaired by the Prime Minister. Over this period, increasingly, government has seen a primary task of social work and a measure of its success the degree to which it reduces social exclusion (Barry and Hallett, 1998). Government definitions of social inclusion have emphasized the importance of people being in paid employment as a key criterion. This has also been reflected in the significance attached by government in its overall social policy, benefits and fiscal policies, to people being in paid work rather than relying on benefits.

Thus a key implicit role for social work is to support such an interpretation of social inclusion by encouraging the integration of social care service users into employment (Levitas, 1996,1998) Certainly key groups of social care services users, particularly disabled people and mental health service users, have been officially identified as having low employment rates and government policies have sought to integrate them into employment.

There has also been a growing interest on the part of government on getting single parents back into paid employment (although with regard to two parent families, the concern has been that children should be with their parents, rather than both parents be out working). Service users frequently experience these pressures to take paid employment as a problematic, crudely conceived and implemented policy, which takes little account of:

- The lack of flexibility of the labour market and its insensitivity to their needs;
- Broader discriminations in employment;
- The poverty traps that reintegration into employment may still face them with;
- Their continuing needs for support when in employment;
- The limited capacity of some service users to be in (full-time) employment, even if they are capable of making a contribution to their communities;
- Alternative ways in which service users can contribute and develop their skills, for example, through education and training, getting involved in their communities and services and as full-time parents;
- High costs and shortcomings of child care provision.
- Continuing problems with benefits policy and practice in the way of people undertaking unpaid activities which can develop their sense of self-worth and self-esteem, confidence and occupational skills, which may later help them to join the labour market.

### *Social Work Tasks*

If we take social work tasks to mean what social workers do and with what practice is concerned, then the range of work approaches and activities is truly enormous. Social work approaches include:

- Individual direct work with service users.
- Indirect work with family and friends.
- Work with loved ones and others identified in roles as 'informal carers'.
- Group work.
- Community-based and community development work.

Actual tasks are wide ranging including:

- Offering information, advice and advocacy;
- Helping people negotiate with other state agencies, particularly over benefits/financial support, housing and other services;
- Providing counselling and other psycho-therapeutic support.
- Providing practical guidance and help.
- Referring service users to other relevant agencies and service providers.
- Accessing financial support to service users.

### *What Service Users Seem to Value from Social Work Practice*

Strong consistent messages emerge both from formal research and what service users say about what they find helpful and value in social work practice. Issues they highlight include social work and the social worker's;

- Social approach.
- Relationship.
- Personal qualities.

***Social approach:*** While some service users make clear that social work is not always strongly consistent with the social approach that defines it as *social* work, nonetheless the recognize it as having an underpinning philosophy which aims to see the person in their broader context and respond accordingly. They see this as helpful. This distinguishes it from other health related professions which tend to be based more on medicalised individual models which focus narrowly on the individual, rather than their circumstances and the issues and barriers they face (Beresford and others, 2005; Branfield and others 2005).

***Relationship:*** Service users highlight the relationship with the social worker as key to the positives they associate with social work practice. It is this (ongoing) relationship which is the starting point for building trust and supporting people's self-empowerment. Service users refer to the strengths of the informality, flexibility and warmth of this relationship.

***Personal qualities:*** When asked what they want from social workers, service users consistently refer to a range of valued personal qualities. How much these qualities are inherent in practitioners and how much they are learned remains unclear. They are certainly important for service users. They include, warmth, respect, being non-judgemental, listening, treating people with equality, being trustworthy, openness and honesty, reliability and communicating well.

Service users also value the shared understanding that they believe comes from direct experience of using social work and social care services.

They argue for this to be seen as a positive in the recruitment and training of new social workers. They also highlight continuing barriers standing in the way of service users becoming social workers on equal terms with non-service users and call for these to be removed (Snow, 2002). A picture emerges of the kind of social work practice service users want and what they want from it. This includes practice which:

- Is participatory in process and purpose.
- Focused on supporting independent living and participation rather than dependence.
- Offers continuity.
- Is flexible and person-centred.
- Is holistic and social model based.
- Connects the personal with the social and political, offering personal/emotional and practical support.
- Addresses rights, risks and their complex interrelations.
- Is based on inclusive understanding of knowledge which includes the experiential knowledge of service users and

the practice knowledge of face to face workers. Service users value social workers who:

- Enable them to work out their own agendas with them.
- Give them time to sort things out.
- Who are available and accessible.
- Provide continuity of support.
- Are reliable and deliver.
- Are responsive.
- Have a good level of knowledge and expertise.
- Value the expertise of the service user.

This picture emerges from a wide range of service users and the whole spectrum of social work interventions, including work with adults, mental health service users, young people, families and children, in criminal justice, residential, day services and field work. There is remarkable consistency in data.

## Social Work Roles and Tasks with Adults

Approaches to social work roles and tasks with adults and with children and families, have if anything become increasingly differentiated over recent years.

### *Government Thinking on Social Work with Adults*

There has been little detailed discussion of social work roles and tasks in recent government discussions of adult social care. Significantly, the green paper on social care: and the subsequent joint health and social care White Paper, Our Health, Our Care, Our Say, made little reference to social work. What they do suggest is that they see the future roles and tasks of social work in terms of the social worker as 'navigator'. What this seems to mean is that the social worker will be someone who helps people negotiate the health, welfare and social care systems, agencies and practitioners they may encounter or need to turn to.

While it does not spell out clearly or fully the kind of social work it envisages for the future, what this suggests is some version of care management set out in different terms. It points to a model of social worker as organizer, manager and referral point. However, these are not the aspects of social work practice which service users have highlighted that they value. They place an emphasis on the benefits of the relationship and the range of support activities offered by good practitioners. The role of the social worker as assessor and referrer are in fact the aspects of social work practice which adult service users seem to find most problematic. For many of them, these are also the only professional social work roles they actually experience.

### *Roles and Tasks in Relation to New Approaches to Support*

This is of particular significance currently when the government has made it clear that it sees individualized budgets and individualized approaches to support (sometimes now being called 'self-directed support') as central to the future of social care support and service provision. Direct payments, developed by disabled people and the disabled people's movement, pioneered such individualized approaches to support, putting the individual service user in control of the money for their support and those providing such support, for example, through employing personal assistants (PAs) (Vasey, 2000). In this arrangement, the service user defines the support they want and decides who provides it. This has led to service users identifying a wide range of imaginative forms of support that they want, outside the box of traditional social care provision. Research has repeatedly highlighted that service users prefer direct payments; that they make it more possible for them to live independently and improve their health and general wellbeing, enabling them to be more active citizens and to contribute in various ways, including through being in employment.However, service users have identified a wide range of problems in the way in which such direct payments have in practice been implemented. These include:

- Lack of parity, according to when people access them and where they live;
- The exclusion as yet of health services and funding from such arrangements;
- The longstanding lack of enthusiasm of some local authorities for such arrangements;
- The increasing use of private and other non-disabled people contractors providing such support, leading to a lowering of its quality;

- The setting of rates for direct payments being determined by comparisons below the cost of residential care, rather than enabling independent living;
- The failure to ensure infrastructural support for direct payments to make possible their uptake by the widest range of service users;
- The failure to offer or fund legal advice should things go wrong between a personal assistant (PAs) and their employer;
- The undermining and closure of local user controlled organisations because of inadequate and insecure funding.
- The shortcomings of traditional professional social work based assessment processes in relation to such schemes (Gibbs, 2004; CSCI, 2005; Branfield and others, 2005; Beresford and others, 2005, NCIL, 2006; Morris, 2007).

We will return to this last concern shortly. While disabled people and other service users have increasingly been highlighting the problems with existing direct payments schemes, other approaches to individualized support have also recently been developing.

These are most associated with the In Control project and the Department of Health Care Services Improvement Partnership (CSIP). Neither of them have been rooted with service users or grown from their experience. Both have sought to extend the range of income streams included to pay for support and involve the service user knowing what their budget is in advance through the resource allocation system.

They originated in work with people with learning difficulties and in some cases appear to come closer to older 'indirect payment' schemes, where money is held on behalf of service users, rather than directly accessed by them themselves. They have so far placed a significant reliance on the unpaid involvement of family and loved ones, rather than infrastructural support (Turner, 2006). As has been said, the government has responded enthusiastically to these schemes, seeing them as the major plank in future arrangements for adult social care, although the research evidence for them is so far limited and the scale of pilot projects is still small.

Some disabled people are concerned these schemes will be used to replace direct payments, rather than sort out the shortcomings now associated with them; that they do not have the ownership of service users and are being advocated as being capable of offering improved support for less money. This has created considerable concern, given that service users are currently reporting cuts in services, as well as in their own user controlled organisations.

This brings us back to the issue of professional assessment. In December 2006, a two day 'Self-Directed Support Academy for people who use services and family carers, organized by CSIP, brought together service users with experience of using direct payments and other self-directed support schemes. The latter tend to be seen as different from direct payments by their advocates and were also compared adversely with direct payments by service users at this event, although direct payments can be used as part of an individual budget.

They compared positive experiences of S-DS, with what they called 'bureaucratic' and 'over-policed' arrangements for direct payments. They particularly singled out the problems of professional assessment processes in direct payments, compared with S-DS pilots which did not rely on these. It is the specific issue of assessment that we will be focusing on here. But it is also possible to see how problems and confusions over different approaches to individualized support (direct payments and S-DS) are being created by comparisons being made between small scale specially funded pilot projects and mainstream local authority policy. Problems with professional assessment. The problems that service users highlight with existing systems of professional social work referral can be summed up as relating to:

- It being based on 'professional' rather than service user definitions of issues and problems;
- That these are still not necessarily informed by 'social' or 'barriers' based models;
- Instead they continue to be based on deficit models of service users, only offering support where 'inability' is identified, rather than seeing support as a means of enabling ability and supporting preventative approaches;

- While they are meant to be 'professionally-led', they are still significantly budget-driven;
- Limited effective involvement of many service users in their assessment (some not even being aware if they have been assessed).
- Time taken to respond to assessment and requests for information from social workers thus undermining the opportunity for service users to be in control of how their personal assistance needs are met, particularly in relation to direct payments. (NCIL, 2006).

Given the future role seen for social work as navigator, professional assessment can be expected to become an even more central part (if not the main part) of the role with adult service users. Yet many service users see it currently being interpreted and operated in regressive and disempowering ways. Service users and their organisations, however, have over time developed ideas and models for enabling much more effective user involvement in the assessment process, both through the development of advocacy, information and support roles to enable service users to input their views more effectively and through more participatory tools and processes (Leader, 1995).

## Social Work Roles and Tasks with Children and Families

The policy response of government to the tragic death of Victoria Climbie was the White Paper, *Every Child Matters,* which was framed in broad terms of the rights and needs of all children and made the case for a national data system for children. Yet statutory social work has never provided a universalist service for children and families. The Victoria Climbie tragedy was related to specific failings in social work and other services (notably not communicating directly with Victoria herself) and the recent history of child care practice has increasingly been dominated by a 'very narrow model of child protection work' (Blewett and others, 2006) This has not been valued by service users (ATD Fourth World, 2006; CSCI, 2006) or indeed other stockholders.

This shift away from community-based to child protection work which emphasizes the controlling powers of social work has not been the only development narrowing the roles and tasks of social workers with families and children. As with adult work, they have been under increasing pressure to manage and commission work rather than undertake ongoing direct work with families and children. Thus the very strengths that service users value from good practitioners, to capacity to be non-judgemental, to listen, to be honest and reliable and crucially to offer a key supportive relationship are weakened rather than maximized (Morgan, 2006). This has been compounded as problems of recruitment and retention have increased.

While child protection work is associated with the use of social work's powers to restrict people's rights, it is the arbitrary and inappropriate use of such powers, without adequate information or warning which service users have long expressed most concern about. The existence of such powers does not in itself inherently exclude the possibility of service users being involved and having a say in what happens to them. But they do report concerns that this does not always happen and that safeguards are inadequate. Some service users who have developed relationships of trust with social workers even feel able to confide problems to them. Others, lacking such confidence in the practitioner will keep such problems to themselves for fear of what they see as arbitrary and punitive interventions. They also talk of the problem of social workers failing to keep them informed, perhaps because of the challenge such openness poses for some practitioners. High levels of staff turnover, promotion out of practice and constant re-organizations, also create problems in the way of maintaining ongoing relationships with service users, which in turn inhibits the development of trust in sensitive situations where it is especially important.

Two groups of parents have particular concerns. These are parents with learning difficulties and those who use mental health services (Boxall and others, 2002). Both groups may need ongoing support as parents, or support at particular times of difficulty, or over particularly difficult issues. Their concern is that rather than receive such support, they are required to change or their particular difficulties are seen as reason for removal of children.

It is not only the shortcomings of social work practice that service users refer to. They also highlight the inadequacies of placements and other follow-up action initiated by practitioners.

Here they refer to poor outcomes in terms of the inferior quality of residential placements (a continuing concern); the frequent breakdown of fostering placements in some cases; the continuing stigma associated with being in state care and the poor personal performance (for example, in relation to education, contact with the criminal justice system, etc.) still repeatedly ascribed to young people with experience of being looked after by the state. As service users say, while many policies have changed over recent years, often through 360 degrees, the problems experienced by service users continue. Policy proposals continue to be imposed from the top down and opportunities for choice are restricted as standardized prescriptions continue to be adopted – even if change significantly over time. Thus the possibility of children and families having real choice in what happens to them is limited by particular prevailing philosophies, which are often experienced as monolithic and rigid in practice. The limited say that social work practitioners have in shaping the broader landscape of social care in the context of work with children and families needs perhaps to be seen as having a key part to play in perpetuating this problem.

### *Social Work Roles and Tasks: A Neglected Exemplar*

While social work roles and tasks with both adults and children and families can be seen to be arbitrarily constrained by managerial structures, increasing bureacratisation and funding priorities, resulting in the standardizing of social work responses and referral to a limited range of support services, there is one area of social work, where a different picture seems to emerge.

This is the field of specialist palliative care social work, an area of social work that seems to have been neglected in both public and professional discussions of social work. Yet it is highly valued by service users; seems to remain truest to both traditional social work values and more recent ones of empowerment, participation and partnership. Not only do service users report it providing a wide range of supportive roles and tasks, combining practical and psychological forms of help and support and addressing personal and social issues,, but they also indicate that the response of practitioners is very much geared to the individual service user, offering whatever combination and form of help that the particular person may value and find most helpful.

There seems to be some irony in the fact that a branch of social work which has remained so true to social work values and principles, where there is much desired continuity of practice and practitioners, has been significantly marginalized by social work and in social work discussions (Beresford and others, 2007).

## Towards 2020: The Challenge for Social Work from Service Users

Service users have much to say about both the strengths and weaknesses of existing social work practice. They show a sensitivity to the rights and needs of practitioners as well as of service users. Taken together their accounts and the material they have produced offers a distinct set of discourses to set next to conventional professional and academic social work discussions. Not only are service users able to critique existing arrangements and make sense of the interrelations of social work practice roles and tasks with broader policy and social work structures and organisation. They have also developed their own theories and philosophies for social work to be based upon.

Thus their critiques of existing practice and services and government proposals offer a basis for how things could be different and better. But they also point directly to the kind of social work that they want to see. Key components of such social work practice are that it is:

- Social model based.
- Inclusive.
- Participative.
- Rights based.

Here we set out some of the key elements making up service users' vision for an inclusive, participatory, inclusive and rights based approach to social work. While it is not a complete list, it does include the main ones that service users, their organisations and discussions have highlighted and returned to frequently over recent years.

Service users want social work which is based on a barriers model/social model approach, committed to working with service users, addressing their personal and social circumstances and challenging the barriers which they face in society and supporting them to deal with these barriers and their effects as well as finding ways of minimising them.

A touchstone for social work practice for service users is the degree to which it safeguards and secures their human and civil rights. This needs to be recognised in both the process and aims of social work. The views of service users suggest that the control roles social work now has need to be subjected to fundamental review and reconsideration.

Theorising about social 'care' and support for adults has been strongly influenced by the discussions and developments of service users and their movements, beginning with the disabled people's movement and its development of the social model approach to disability and the idea of 'independent living'.

These have impacted upon policy, practice, research and theory. Social work theory about child care and child protection similarly needs to be more strongly influenced by the input and perspectives of service users (both families and children). Opportunities need to be provided to develop such discussions and for them to be included in dominant social work theorising.

The production of formal 'social work discourse' has generally been dominated by policy makers, managers and academics. Service users highlight the benefits of a more inclusive discourse which enables the fuller and more equal involvement of both service user and current face to face practitioner perspectives (Beresford and Croft, 2004).

Service users generally find technicist managerialist based models of social work unhelpful. They want a 'hands-on' approach from social workers rather than one where the social worker is essentially a referrer to other agencies, professionals and services.

They see a distinct value and contribution in social work practice which addresses both their personal, psychological needs and the broader issues and problems that face them. They see these two aspects of their lives as closely bound and inseparable. Social work needs to include both 'casework'/counselling skills and input and broader understanding of and work with service users' wider worlds. Service users value the wide range of social work approaches, including individual, family, group and community work approaches. They also want to see social work which will intervene on their behalf, offer reliable information, support and advocacy and is familiar with their rights and needs. What seems to be needed is social work practice which draws on the wide repertoire social work has to offer to respond to the particular preferences and needs of each individual.

Service users highlight the central importance of the relationship they have with social workers as a key value of social work. The organisation of social work is undermining and curtailing such relationships. Service users argue for promotion in social work to place much greater weight on enabling people to remain in practice, rather than moving out of it.

Service users want the social work role of assessment to be seen in terms of supporting self-assessment. They want assessment to be based on social and barriers based models, rather than deficit models of social care support as they frequently are now. This would support preventive approaches to social care which can make independent living possible. New related roles need to be explored and developed, for example, to support service users to have an effective say in assessment. Following the model developed by Derbyshire Centre for Inclusive Living, these could be based on developing advocacy and information roles undertaken by service users, linked with formal recognised qualifications.

Service users highlight the importance of 'person centred support' as the starting point for social work and social care. By this they mean support that is geared to meet the rights and needs of service users rather than service or budget driven support which fits service users into traditional services.

Social work and the structures associated with it have developed a negative approach to risk taking. This restricts the life chances of service users unhelpfully and prevents them gaining the opportunities that are part of making the journey to independent living. Social work needs to be supportive of positive risk taking for service users. It also needs to be more effective in safeguarding service users (both adults and children) from the risks that they currently encounter in the social care system, including serious risks of neglect, abuse, denial of rights, bullying, racism, etc.

Service users want to see social workers, as a routine part of their professional and post-qualification education and training, to be offered an effective grounding to understand access issues broadly defined, for example, in relation to the physical, communication and cultural access requirements of service users.

The government is placing an increasing emphasis on 'individual budgets' and 'self-directed support schemes'. Building on direct payments developed by disabled people, these are intended to bring together different funding streams to support service users' independent living. Strong independent evidence will be needed to ensure that they are able to achieve this and that the 'support planner', 'service broker' and 'navigator' roles associated with them work to deliver self-determination, rather than retaining control.

Much more work also needs to be done to ensure that direct payments schemes are more widely available and are less constrained by traditional assessment approaches, inadequate funding and the lack of infrastructural support as envisaged by disabled people's organisations to enable the widest range of service users access and retain them. Service user controlled organisation should be ensured equal opportunities to provide such services.

Service users emphasise that they have a particular contribution to make to each other in offering the positive support and advocacy roles associated with social work through the direct experience that they share. This raises at least three key issues, that:

1. professional social work practitioners are encouraged and supported to be based in service user controlled organisations, as well as in other settings.
2. service users are supported and encouraged to develop their own support, advocacy and advice giving roles alongside those of professional social work, rather than these being displaced by it, or it necessarily being offered instead. The specific contribution of peer support and support based on shared direct experience needs to be recognised.
3. social work education and training fully involves service users and their organisations. To achieve this means ensuring:
    - strategic support and capacity building for service users and their organisations to be involved;

- some funding resources for such involvement are provided directly to service user controlled organisations;
- that the current patchiness of implementation of user involvement in social work education is addressed and raised standards are achieved generally;
- diverse involvement of service users, including the wide range of social work service users (including those where social work's control as well as support roles are applied) and addressing difference in relation to gender, sexuality, ethnicity, culture, class, disability and age.
- Equal access of service users to professional social work education and training (this will require changes in GSCC approaches to registration of disabled people, as highlighted by the Disability Rights Commission).
- To support the development of an effective network of local user controlled organisations as recommended in Improving the Life Chances of Disabled People report and working in close and equal relationship with them. This is a key requirement is social work is to be user centred and involve service users meaningfully.
- To support the development and provision of more user-led services and support, based in user controlled organisations. Evidence highlights that such services are particularly valued by service users, but at present they compete on unequal terms with other sectors of service providers (for example, commercial and conventional voluntary/charitable organisations) to provide them.
- To explore the development of appropriate organisational and management structures for social work to maximise the contribution and effectiveness of social work practice. Such structures will need to be accessible in the broadest sense to ensure the diverse and full involvement of service users.

- To maintain and advance a strategic approach to service user involvement of service users and their user controlled organisations in social work and social care structures and organisations. This will seek to ensure that they are fully accessible and enable effective involvement on equal terms. Such structures include, for example:
- Social work and social care organisation like SCIE, GSCC, Skills for Care, CSCI, etc.
- Editorial boards and refereeing systems for peer review journals, professional journals, books and other publications;
- The management and partnerships for qualifying and post qualification and other social work education and training.

# 6

# Democratic Field of Youth in India

## The 1988 National Youth Policy

In 1998, the Government of India adopted a national youth policy. This policy defines youth as 15 to 35 years. Among the central themes of the national youth policy included youth empowerment, youth coordinating inter-sectoral mechanisms, and information, research networks, and privileges and responsibilities of youth. Eight sectors are being responsible for youth work in India : education, training and employment, health, environment, recreation and sports, participation and citizenship, and science and technology. The national youth policy also focuses attention on the disadvantaged sub-groups of youth. The Standing Committee on Youth of the Indian National Parliament follows up those matters by specific and appropriate legislation.

As of the year 2000, the youth of India (aged 15-24) representing 19% of the total population constitute a vital human resource. The Government of India had formulated a national youth policy in 1988 and has been implementing it since then, with several revisions and updates.

The national youth policy lays down the following objectives :

- To instill in youth a deep awareness of and respect for the principles and values enshrined in the Indian constitution ;
- To promote among youth the awareness of Indian historical and cultural heritage and imbue them with a sense of pride and national identity ;

- To help develop in youth the qualities of discipline, self-reliance, justice and fair play ;
- To provide youth with maximum access to education which apart from developing their all-round personality, would equip them with professional and vocational training for employment and self-employment opportunities ;
- To make youth aware of international issues and involve them in promoting world peace.

### *The 2003 National Youth Policy*

The National Youth Policy 2003 reiterates the commitment of the entire nation to the composite and all-round development of the young sons and daughters of India and seeks to establish an All-India perspective to fulfil their legitimate aspirations. It purports to enable Indian youth to be of a strong body and mind to successfully accomplish the challenging tasks of national reconstruction and social changes that lie ahead.

The National Youth Policy 2003 is designed to galvanize the youth to rise up to the new challenges, keeping in view the global scenario, and aims at motivating them to be active and committed participants in the exciting task of National Development. The Policy is based on recognition of the contribution that the youth can, and should, make to the growth and well-being of the community and end eavors to ensure effective co-ordination between the policies, programs and delivery systems of the various Ministries, Departments and other Agencies.

The thrust of the Policy centres on "Youth Empowerment" in different spheres of national life.

This Policy will cover all the youth in the country in the age group of 13 to 35 years.

It is acknowledged that since all the persons within this age group are unlikely to be one homogenous group, but rather a conglomeration of sub-groups with differing social roles and requirements, the age group may, therefore, be divided into two broad sub-groups viz. 13-19 years and 20-35 years. The youth belonging to the age group 13-19, which is a major part of the adolescent age group, will be regarded as a separate constituency.

### *Youth Empowerment*

The Policy recognizes that in order for the youth to effectively participate in decision-making processes, it is essential that they are better equipped with requisite knowledge, skills, and capabilities.

Towards this end, the Policy envisions the following :

- Attainment of higher educational levels and expertise by the youth, in line with their abilities and aptitudes, and access to employment opportunities accordingly ;
- Adequate nutrition for the full development of physical and mental potential and the creation of an environment which promotes good health, and ensures protection from disease and unwholesome habits ;
- Development of youth leadership and its involvement in programs and activities pertaining to Equality of opportunity and respect for Human and Fundamental Rights without distinction of race, caste, creed, sex, language, religion or geographic location and access to facilities relating to Sports, Cultural, Recreational, and Adventure activities.

### *Gender Justice*

The Policy recognizes the prevailing gender bias to be the main factor responsible for the poor status of health and economic well being of women in our society and that any discrimination on grounds of sex violates the basic rights of the individual concerned and it, therefore, advocates elimination of gender discrimination in every sphere.

### *Education*

The Policy acknowledges that the objective of providing appropriate education, which enables the youth to develop into good citizens of the country, should also suitably influence relevant actions of the Government and public behaviour.

It is recognized that the need of the educational system to instill, in the youth, an abiding sense of patriotism and values oriented towards the unity and integrity of the country, equally calls for the elimination of violence in all forms, adherence to good moral and ethical values and respect and reverence for India's composite culture and national heritage.

This Policy emphasizes that the learning process should minimize the stress, which the system may exert on students, especially in the early years. The thrust of the educational system, particularly in the early years, ought to be on learning, rather than on merely qualifying in examinations and memory-based tests. The Policy lays emphasis on outdoor learning as an integral part of the educational process and on Physical Education, Sports Games, and Adventure activities.

Academic institutions should be equipped with adequate sports and recreational facilities. Education, above the secondary level, should have a high degree of socialization as to enable the youth to acquire those requisite skills, which would augment avenues of employment for them. Technical institutions need to be strengthened and their number increased keeping an eye on the country's emergence as a major force in information technology.

There needs to be greater uniformity in the educational system and standardsin various parts of the country. Closer links should be developed between the educational system and prospective employers, on an institutional basis, and career counselling should be a part of the educational system, from the secondary level onwards. Programs need to be undertaken for proper dissemination of information, amongst young men and women, in respect of career options.

Programs should be undertaken to upgrade the existing skills of young artisans of traditional handicrafts and other products and for those who may wish to take up the same as a vocation. Education system should also have a rural orientation to address the varied needs of agriculture and other areas of rural economy. Educational curriculum in schools should include information on health issues including reproductive health, HIV-AIDS, and on population issues.

Youth clubs and Mahila Mandals should be encouraged to involve their members in programs like "Sarva Shiksha Abhiyan" and Total Literacy Campaign for generalization of primary education and spread of literacy, and to organize activities to promote book reading habits among the youth.

## *Training and Employment*

This Policy recognizes that the question of employment is, at present, of very serious concern for the Indian youth and that several social issues arise out of widespread unemployment and under-employment of the youth.

This Policy further acknowledges that the incidence of unemployment is more pronounced in the rural areas and in urban slums and calls for appropriate strategies and commensurate efforts to deal with it.

The current trends suggest that the growth rate of the labour force has been higher than the growth rate of population and that the growth rate of employment has not been in proportion to GDP growth.

The critical issues in this area can be described as mismatch between skills requirement and employment opportunities ; low technology levels, low wages and low productivity ; occupational shifts in employment, under-employment owing to seasonal factors, excess labour supply in relation to demand ; migration of the labour force from the rural to urban areas and limited participation of women in the work force, especially in the organized sector.

The incidence of unemployment has been accentuated with advances in technology and communications. To tackle this issue, opportunities for self-employment need to be created. Schemes to provide "seed money" to assist viable enterprises initiated by the youth need to be drawn up. Network of youth skill training centres need to be established to build up the capacities of the young people for income generation activities.

Adequate funding for both pre-job and on-the-job training for youth by government as well as other stockholders should be ensured. For proper vocational guidance and career counselling, schools and colleges should pay adequate attention to this aspect as part of their co-curricular activities.

Government, in conjunction with youth organizations, will develop training programs for young people in the rural areas, based on their needs. Special schemes would also be developed for young women, youth with disabilities and for young people returning from the urban to the rural areas, alongside flexibility in training systems and collaboration between training institutions and potential employers.

Cooperative schemes involving Self Help Groups of young people in the production and marketing of goods and services would be encouraged and strengthened with government support. Banks and Cooperatives would be advised to make identifiable allocations of soft credit to young people and their Self Help Groups and micro-credit adopted as a strategy to enable young women and men, in the rural areas, to undertake fruitful economic ventures.

### *Health*

The policy recognizes that a holistic approach towards health, mental, and physical needs to be adopted after careful assessment of the health needs of the youth.

As per the youth population projections (based on the 1991 Census), about 21.4% of the total population in 1996 was estimated to be in the age group of 10-19 years ; of these, about 78.4% lived in the rural and the remaining (21.6%) in the urban areas. The mean age of marriage in the rural areas was 21.56 years for males and 16.67 years for females. In the urban areas, the mean age for marriage was 24.32 years for males and 19.92 years for females. In other words, most women in India are married during the age of adolescence.

The Policy lays emphasis on the importance of hygiene and sanitation in promoting a healthy society. All efforts should be made to inculcate in the youtha sense of hygiene and sanitation right from early education. The youth on their part should be encouraged to organize mass awareness campaigns in their neighbourhood to promote better hygiene and sanitation. Their services should also be utilized in creating better sanitation facilities for the community, both in rural areas and urban slums.

This Policy strongly recommends introduction of health education in the curricula of regular/formal education in higher classes of schools and colleges, in non-formal education centres and in every other organized interaction with the youth. The policy advocates that every youth of India should clearly understand what, why and how of good health within his or her socioeconomic parameters. A policy of minimum physical exercise for all should be propagated.

### *Science and Technology*

As adaptation of scientific and technological principles and developments, to maximize the use of local resources, is central to empowerment in the quality of life. The Policy recognizes the importance of emerging, modern technologies, particularly in the field of information technology and electronic media, in enabling the youth to achieve their life objectives in all sectors of their interest.

The Policy also recognizes that young scientists and technologists should be extended adequate facilities for research, and that the contribution of the private sector in this field should be encouraged.

The National Youth Policy, therefore, provides for :

- Review of policies in respect of the school curriculum and the non-formal education sector so that Science may be popularized amongst all sections of the youth ;
- Support to providing exposure of the youth to the scientific temper and way of life ;
- Development of mechanisms within the system to identify and train gifted youth, as early as possible, in the fields of science and technology ;
- The best and the most positive use of information and communications technology, as well as all forms of media, including the electronic media, for youth development as well as for promoting and protecting the richness of India's culture ;
- Promoting a multi-sectoral approach involving, inter-alia, the private sector and NGOs, to orient the youth towards scientific and technological studies and research ;
- Ensuring co-ordination between the various Government Ministries/Departments and Scientific Organizations/ Institutions dealing with youth development programs ;
- Upgrading science curricula in institutions of learning to inculcate the scientific approach amongst all sections of the younger generation ;

- Linking the projects of the young scientists to the problems of the people and ensuring better interaction between labs and the industry ;
- Documentation of the large repository of physical and knowledge based resources within the country to prevent their piracy by vested interests.

*Civics and Citizenship*

Human behaviour is significantly shaped by norms and values, which are a basis for attitudinal growth. The dominant features in the Indian Society, which impingeon the cultural and other values of young people, include areas such as family life, education, work and occupational activities, gender, class and ethnic relations, religion, mass communication, artistic and creative expression, sports, recreation, politics and the economic environment.

Anti-social behaviouris a manifestation of the absence of well-accepted values, attitudes and norms in the individual and in society which can reflect itself in crime, violent action, breakdown of parental authority in family life, corruption in public life, obscenity in the media, in discipline in schools and in sporting activities and low productivity at the work place.

The Policy, therefore, envisages the following strategies :

- Embodying instruction in the values like respect for teachers and parents, religious tolerance, and compassion towards the poor and the needy. The concept of family as the basic and most important asset of Indian Society will be strengthened.
- To motivate the youth to resist fragmentation of society on the basis of caste, religion, language and ethnicity and for promotion of democratic values enshrined in the constitution of the country.
- To mobilize the youth to create local pressure groups within the community to fight corruption at all levels and to ensure that the benefits of development reach those for whom they are intended and are not controlled by middlemen and the powerful.
- Laying emphasis on the economic and social security of the youth belonging to underprivileged sections of our

society and those who are mentally and physically challenged.

- In the Present set-up of our so-called democracy where muscle power and money are ruling the nation there is an urgent need for the youth to unite and take charge of political affairs of the country in order to impose the faith of a common man in democracy.

In India youngsters are not given any importance, this can be proven by a fact that most of the heads of youth organizations are persons aged above 40 or sometimes even 60 plus. I wonder sometimes, how a person above 40 years can be termed as a 'Youth'. India needs a movement to eradicate the evils of Corruption, Red-Tapism, Mafia raj etc. The educated class of youth should be promoted as the representatives of the largest democracy in the world; they have the vision, compassion, dedication to do something meaningful, all they need is support.

Youth can be the saviours of democracy which will otherwise be concentrated and exploited at the hands of the rich and mighty. The problem here arises in the present mental set-up of youngsters who only want to study and indulge themselves in a 9-5 job, earning a handsome amount of salary from their foreign employers. They should understand that if they stand united there is nobody who can stand against them, they are the power house of energy and should motivate the citizens to exercise their right and give them a chance to make a change in our country.

Ours is a young country and the power of youth should be utilized positively in order to make India even more powerful. They should provide some rest to our ageing politicians who have given so much to our country like caste divisions, reservations, unemployment, corruption, poverty etc. Our current democratic leaders have presented an entirely new definition of the word "Democracy" which means government elected by the people from the power of money and to earn the money.

On one hand politicians oppose castecism and on another they introduce reservations, what kind of hypocrisy and double standards are these? I think they have ruined the future of millions of youngsters to safeguard their own vote-banks. The young generation should promote a single sacred religion of 'Indian' and urge people to vote for the candidate based on his character and work rather than on his caste or religion. The young leaders should promote relaxations in fees for poor segment and should oppose reservations based on caste or religion.

They should chalk out an overall development plan for the country and promote rural industrialization, privatization of ailing government sectors, employment opportunities, eradicate illiteracy, corruption etc. The youth has the power to present a new face of India in the global market and the talent to make India a developed country. All these factors are the only options left to instill faith of common man in democracy. We must understand that a nation can only progress on young and innovative minds. It's the duty of every Indian family to motivate and promote their children to come forward and reconstruct our nation for the sake of the world's largest democracy comprising of 100 crores of citizens. The future of India lies with the generation X of today.

## Services for Student Youth

### *Youth Services*

The Youth Services Bureau of the Ministry of Education and Social Welfare have been implementing systematically programmes catering to the need and development of the student and non-student youth. The National Youth Board was reconstituted during the year. The Board which has undertaken a critical review of the programmes for the welfare of student and non-student youth will advise the government on the formulation of a National Youth Policy.

### *National Service Scheme*

During the year 1978-79, the National Service Scheme was continued in colleges and universities with the same objective with emphasis on bringing the students closer to the community and to enable them to contribute towards national development. The response to NSS programme continues to be encouraging and it is now in operation in all the States and universities. The coverage is likely to reach the figure of 4 lakh students at the end of current year. A Review Group was set up to review the Scheme The Review Group was of the view that the performance under the Scheme was good and it was desirable to strengthen the programme and expand it further. The Review Group while reiterating the objectives of the NSS viz inculcating a sense of social consciousness and dignity of labour amongst the students and developing their personality, also emphasised that this Scheme should provide them an opportunity to discharge their social obligation towards the community.

The NSS students did commendable work in the wake of floods in different parts of the country. Their contribution to flood relief in Delhi, Bihar, Orissa, West Bengal and Uttar Pradesh was acclaimed by the press and public alike. During the year under report, NSS personnel-teachers, students as well as the supervisory staff-gave high priority to the involvement of students in National Adult Education Programme. In this effort the NSS personnel are working closely with those responsible for organisation of various activities under National Adult Education Programme.

### *National Service Volunteer Scheme*

The National Service Volunteer Scheme which was started in 1977-78 continued in its second year with about 450 volunteers who have been deployed with 130 Nehru Yuvak Kendras and over 30 volunteer agencies. The volunteers are working mainly in the field of adult education with these agencies. While the voluntary agencies have the discretion in deploying them in any activity of adult education, a uniform pattern of work has been evolved for the volunteers deployed with the Nehru Yuvak Kendras. Each volunteer is expected to set up 15 to 20 Chetna Sanghs. A Chetna Sangh is a method of organising youth between the age-group of 15 to 35 for activities like adult education, sports and recreation, cultural activities, adventure programmes etc. It is intended to be an instrument for organised action for development. Each Chetna Sangh has an organiser who is given an honorarium of Rs. 50 per month. The work of the organisers is supervised by the National Service Volunteer who is paid a stipend of Rs. 175 per month. The volunteers, before taking the work in the field, are given one month's intensive training.

### *Planning Forums*

Initiated by the Planning Commission in 1955 and transferred to the Ministry of Education in 1968, the Scheme of Planning Forums aims at developing the consciousness regarding planned development of the country among the educated youth and through them among the general public. The Planning Forums numbering about 1000, organise various programmes like seminars, debates, discussions, plan information centres about planning process and development. It has been decided that from 1979-80, the implementation of the Scheme be taken over by the University Grants Commission.

### *National Integration Samitis*

The object of the Scheme is to familiarise the students and teachers with the diverse perspectives of our composite culture and civilisation and to undertake activities which would eradicate communalism in all its forms and to take such other steps as would directly promote the cause of National Integration. About 130 Samitis had been functioning in universities and affiliated colleges. The implementation of this Scheme has been taken over by the University Grants Commission from 1978-79.

### *Nehru Yuvak Kendras*

The scheme of Nehru Yuvak Kendra was continued in 1978-79 with the same objective of organising Non-student Youth in constructive activities. Out of 255 sanctioned Kendras, over 185 Kendras have become operational and are functioning in all the states. The scheme continues to be fully financed by the Central Government.

In the current year, a one-week seminar in the context of National Adult Education Programme for the Youth Coordinators for the Southern States at Hyderabad; and a one-week Refresher Training Course at Udaipur were organised. A one month Orientation Training Programme is proposed to be organised in March 1979 at Udaipur.

The Scheme of Nehru Yuvak Kendras was reviewed by a Review Group which had representatives from State Governments, Voluntary Organisations, Planning Commission and Youth Coordinators. The Group was of the view, that on the basis of 5 years' experience of the implementation of the scheme, there has been ample evidence to show that Nehru Yuvak Kendras are characterised by vitality and inventiveness and the autonomy of the Kendras should be continued to be maintained. The Group however felt that there is need for greater conceptual clarity for evolving a system. It also felt that more emphasis for the involvement of women and youth belonging to the weaker sections of the, society in the activities of the Nehru Yuvak Kendras should be given. All the activities of the Nehru Yuvak Kendras-Adult education, vocational training, social service, sports and physical activities, cultural programmes etc. should be taken up in an integrated manner to create awareness amongst the youth and to develop leadership amongst this section of the youth. The Government has accepted the recommendations of the Review Group. It has been decided that during the current plan period the scheme would continue to be a Central Scheme. However, after the expiry of this plan period, the scheme may be transferred to the State Governments.

### *Financial Assistance to Voluntary Organisations Working in the Field of Youth*

This scheme has been evolved to provide a frame-work for Voluntary Organisations to involve youth for developmental activities specially in the rural areas. It is designed to promote involvement of youth on a full time basis for undertaking programmes of rural development, educational developmental activities in urban slums, promotion of plastic, graphic and folk arts, and mass media. This scheme aims at larger involvement of voluntary agencies in the implementation of youth programmes viz. to impart training in skills to non-student youth with a view to improving their functional capacities for full time employment, self-employment or subsidiary employment. It is also designed for training of young persons who can act as catalysts to bring out social chance Registered Societies, public trusts and non-profit companies are eligible for assistance under the scheme. This scheme was revised in 1978 incorporating essential features of the scheme of establishment of work centres which has been discontinued from 1978-79. The scheme of Youth Leadership Training Programmes has also been merged with this scheme. About 30 organisations have been extended assistance totalling about Rs. 11 lakhs up to the end of December 1978, under the scheme.

### *Commonwealth Youth Programme*

India continued to participate in this programme and made the annual contribution to the Commonwealth Youth Programme of Rs. 5.00 lakhs-50% in foreign exchange and 50 percent in Indian currency. The Youth Development Centre, with an Indian Director, continued to organise basic training for the youth of Asia-South Pacific region.

### *Scouting and Guiding*

Central continued to participate in this programme and made the shape of organisational and administrative grants and grant-in-aid for training camps, rallies, jumborees etc. conducted by the Bharat Scouts and Guides and All India Boy Scouts Association. Scouting and Guiding, which is an international movement, is aimed at developing the character of boys and girls to make them food citizens by inculcating in them a spirit of loyalty, patriotism and thoughtfulness for others. Scouting and Guiding also promotes balanced physical and mental development of boys and girls. Social service and community welfare work is an important aspect of this movement.

### *Programmes for Promotion of National Integration*

A Review Group was appointed to study the various aspects for promotion of National Integration. On the basis of the deliberations of this Group the Scheme for Programmes for Promotion of National Integration has been formulated.

The Scheme of Programmes for Promotion of National Integration has two basic aims : (i) to facilitate visit of youth living and working in the border states to states with marked cultural difference and an exchange visit by youth of those states to the border states in order to promote greater understanding of historical and cultural heritage of the country, of the problems being faced by the people of different regions and of the environment, social customs etc. in different parts of the country, (ii) the scheme also provides for financial assistance to voluntary agencies which are engaged in creation of public opinion, against forces promoting disintegration, and organisation of social groups for action to serve the objective of national integration through camps, seminars, research and publication, cultural activities, exchange programmes etc. Under this scheme, teachers, students and non-student youth who are members of voluntary agencies, members of peasants and workers organisations, recognised educational institutions, registered voluntary organisations, Nehru Yuvak Kendras and

State Governments/Union Territory Administrations are eligible for provision of financial assistance. Up to the end of December 1978, assistance totalling about Rs. 1 lakh was sanctioned to 10 organisations under this programme.

### *Scheme for Promotion of Adventure*

The scheme of Promotion of Adventure aims at encouraging the spirit of adventure, risk-taking, cooperative team work, capacity of ready and vital response to challenging situations and endurance amongst the youth of the country. In this process it is expected that youth would become familiar with the rich heritage of flora and fauna of the country and develop well-balanced personality and character. This Scheme was reviewed by a Review Group appointed by the Ministry and has been revised in the current year. Under this Scheme financial assistance is given for undertaking programmes such as mountaineering, trekking hiking, exploration for collection of data, study of flora and fauna in the mountain, forest desert and sea with emphasis on conservation, canoeing, coastal sailing, raft expeditions, swimming, skiing, cycling, motorcycling, ice skating etc. Assistance is provided for training in the above activities as well as for establishment and development of institutions, camp sites and base camps to facilitate adventure activities. Under this scheme individuals, mountaineering institutes, educational institutions, registered voluntary organisations, Nehru Yuvak Kendras and State Governments/Union Territory Administrations are eligible to get assistance. In addition, financial assistance is given regularly to the Himalayan Mountaineering Institute, Darjeeling. Up to the end of December 1978, assistance totalling Rs. 9.00 lakhs was sanctioned to about 75 institutions/groups under this scheme.

### *Different Colours of Education System in India*

Upanayana is a word that has very deep attachment with India education which is known as formal admission ceremony. This ceremony is treated as the re-birth of the child and was known as "Dvijya".

Upanayana is a word that has very deep attachment with India education which is known as formal admission ceremony. This ceremony is treated as the re-birth of the child and was known as 'Dvijya'. In ancient time 'Parisads' word was for higher learning where primary mode of learning was Sanskrit. But now primary mode of language is differ from state to sate. Sravana, Nidhyasana and Manana are the three modes of education in India.

Shrutis is a type of education in which knowledge and skill are passed orally where as Manana in which pupils had to think themselves about what they have heard and made their own inferences and assimilate about the lesson taught by their teacher and Nidhyasana means complete information about the truth and its uses in the life.

At that time women also got equal right in the education sector. Vikramshila, Nalanda and Taxila were the most important universities of India in the ancient times.

Among these three Taxila University was famous for medical studies, Nalanda was a university with high numbers of colleges with residential campus. Students not only form India but also from different countries especially from South Asia came here for higher education. Vikramshila is famous for religious teachings. Now the time has changed and education system in India follows an implantation of British rulers what they had left in 1958.

As compared to previous education system now the education system in India has divided into many categories like pre-primary, primary, middle, secondary, higher secondary, undergraduate, post graduate and finally research degree courses.

Now India has long list of different types of universities, colleges and educational institutes that have excellence reputation worldwide. IITs and IIMs are among the top institutes of technology and MBA colleges of India. Not in regular courses India has also have remarkable records for distance education in india where it offers quality distance education to its students for various sections.

It is a given that the knowledge industry will thrive only on mass higher education. It is a given that the knowledge industry will thrive only on mass higher education. We can't break into the big league without a highly skilled gen-next. Are we then headed in the right direction? Indian higher education is stranded between selective notions of socialism and free enterprise. In the glory days of socialism, we promoted higher education at the cost of universal primary education. Now in the midst of reforms, we can't shake off our reservations against private investment in higher education. The result is that we neither have China's impressive early gains nor America's high quality.

With 342 universities and over 5,000 recognised colleges, India's education system is among the largest in the world. The same numbers look ridiculous when seen against the backdrop of our immense challenges. All these institutions cater to only 4.2 percent of the country's youth. As India churns out 2 million graduates every year, another 28 million young people are added to its population.

Out of its 2 million graduates, only 5 percent are of international quality, another 20 percent are barely employable with training and the remaining 75 percent are seriously sub-standard. Indians may be poor but at 50 percent, their share of household expenditure on education (as percentage of total national expenditure) is very high compared to 3.5 percent in Netherlands, 5.1 percent in France and 24.1 percent in United states, according to UN figures.

Private funding for higher education allows more government funds to go into primary and secondary education. The students expect and get higher quality when they pay for education. Higher expectations fuel competition, which improves quality and lowers costs. The government can be the main facilitator and regulator of quality. It can address the issue of low-cost education for the weaker sections by giving targeted subsidies and loans directly to the needy.

Technology has already revolutionized the concept of distance learning. Imagine virtual universities without classrooms, campuses or fixed faculty-student ratios. Teaching material in public domain rules out bad teaching and on-line exams handle dramatic numbers with ease. The NIIT provides specialized teaching services to 5 lakh students in 30 countries including the United States. Another Indian company, Aptech, has taught 4 million students in 50 countries in less than two decades. The time has come, perhaps, to replicate our own success stories besides learning from others.

## Student Assistance Programs are Vital for Youth

### *Youth Development also Means Providing Youth Counselling Services*

In a Student Assistance Program a counsellor often sees high-risk youth who have problems, sometimes incidental and sometimes long standing. These can include problems with alcohol or other drugs, emotional problems, behavioural problems, relationship, academic, or family problems (including physical or sexual abuse) often due to parental addiction.

### *An Early Intervention Program*

The Student Assistance Program was started as an early intervention program specifically for Children of Alcoholics (COAs) in the 70s as a response to the overwhelming problems that COAs faced at home. These problems posed serious issues at school including emotional neglect, or physical or mental abuse. Often the only adult that could be trusted in the life of a young COA was the youth counsellor in the school.

In the 80s, the program expanded to focus upon all youth who abuse alcohol and other drugs. In the 90s the programs again expanded to focus upon all youth who are at-risk for a number of life problems: alcohol/drug abuse, delinquency, relationship and family issues, and academic underachievement and school drop-out. Finally, the SAP has once again evolved to integrate the risk and protective factor model of prevention into the counsellor's role.

A Student Assistance Program can be extremely effective. As a result of referral to a youth counsellor schools have found reductions in use of alcohol and drugs by youth, decreases in family problems, reductions in personal problems, reductions in maladaptive behaviours, and reductions in academic problems.

### *Advantages of SAPs*

SAPs have distinct advantages over community-based youth counselling programs. Because they are school-based they are more easily accessible for youth than community-based services, and are more likely to be used by youth. They also have a lower "no-show" or premature drop-out rate. Experience also shows that while many youth may be referred from the school, the number of self-referrals of youth is greater. SAPs also provide free services to youth, without regard to the ability to pay.

SAPs provide both crisis management services, educational services, and individual and group counselling. For situations which are more critical, such as suicidal ideation or active addiction, the programs refer to a number of other community-based providers better equipped to handle problems of that level of severity.

School-based Youth Counselling Programs can be very effective, and have been recommended as a core component in the overall system to fight drug abuse ("Background Research", Centre for Prevention Research and Development, Institute of Government and Public Affairs, University of Illinois, July 2005.) Clearly, the provision of services such as these are a key element in both the control and eradication of illicit drug use, and the overall stabilization and development of youth with serious problems.

### *An Ounce of Prevention is Worth a Pound of Cure*

It has been reported that for every one dollar invested in prevention or treatment, society sees a return of seven to twenty-three dollars in savings ("Benefit Cost Analysis of Residential and Outpatient Addiction Treatment in the State of Washington", French, M.T., Salome, H.J., Krupski, A., McKay, J.R., Donovan, D.M., McLellan, A.T. Durrell, J., Evaluation Review, 24(6), 2000.) Certainly, an ounce of prevention is worth a pound of cure. The SAP is a critical service for youth-in-need, and there is no better way to enhance education while improving lives than by providing assistance and support to our youth.

## Role of Youth in Development

### *Children and Youth in Sustainable Development*

Youth comprise nearly 30 percent of the world's population. The involvement of today's youth in environment and development decision-making and in the implementation of programmes is critical to the long-term success of Agenda 21.

### *Programme Areas*

Advancing the role of youth and actively involving them in the protection of the environment and the promotion of economic and social development Basis for action It is imperative that youth from all parts of the world participate actively in all relevant levels of decision-making processes because it affects their lives today and has implications for their futures. In addition to their intellectual contribution and their ability to mobilize support, they bring unique perspectives that need to be taken into account.

Numerous actions and recommendations within the international community have been proposed to ensure that youth are provided a secure and healthy future, including an environment of quality, improved standards of living and access to education and employment. These issues need to be addressed in development planning.

***Objectives***

Each country should, in consultation with its youth communities, establish a process to promote dialogue between the youth community and Government at all levels and to establish mechanisms that permit youth access to information and provide them with the opportunity to present their perspectives on government decisions, including the implementation of Agenda 21. Each country, by the year 2000, should ensure that more than 50 percent of its youth, gender balanced, are enrolled in or have access to appropriate secondary education or equivalent educational or vocational training programmes by increasing participation and access rates on an annual basis.

Each country should undertake initiatives aimed at reducing current levels of youth unemployment, particularly where they are disproportionately high in comparison to the overall unemployment rate.

Each country and the United Nations should support the promotion and creation of mechanisms to involve youth representation in all United Nations processes in order to influence those processes.

Each country should combat human rights abuses against young people, particularly young women and girls, and should consider providing all youth with legal protection, skills, opportunities and the support necessary for them to fulfil their personal, economic and social aspirations and potentials.

### *Activities*

Governments, according to their strategies, should take measures to:

(a) Establish procedures allowing for consultation and possible participation of youth of both genders, by 1993, in decision-making processes with regard to the environment, involving youth at the local, national and regional levels;

(b) Promote dialogue with youth organizations regarding the drafting and evaluation of environment plans and programmes or questions on development;

(c) Consider for incorporation into relevant policies the recommendations of international, regional and local youth conferences and other forums that offer youth perspectives on social and economic development and resource management;

(d) Ensure access for all youth to all types of education, wherever appropriate, providing alternative learning structures, ensure that education reflects the economic and social needs of youth and incorporates the concepts of environmental awareness and sustainable development throughout the curricula; and expand vocational training, implementing innovative methods aimed at increasing practical skills, such as environmental scouting;

(e) In cooperation with relevant ministries and organizations, including representatives of youth, develop and implement strategies for creating alternative employment opportunities and provide required training to young men and women;

(f) Establish task forces that include youth and youth non-governmental organizations to develop educational and awareness programmes specifically targeted to the youth population on critical issues pertaining to youth. These task forces should use formal and non-formal educational methods to reach a maximum audience. National and local media, non-governmental organizations, businesses and other organizations should assist in these task forces;

(g) Give support to programmes, projects, networks, national organizations and youth non-governmental organizations to examine the integration of programmes in relation to their project requirements, encouraging the involvement of youth in project identification, design, implementation and follow-up;

(h) Include youth representatives in their delegations to international meetings, in accordance with the relevant General Assembly resolutions adopted in 1968, 1977, 1985 and 1989.

The United Nations and international organizations with youth programmes should take measures to:

(a) Review their youth programmes and consider how coordination between them can be enhanced;

(b) Improve the dissemination of relevant information to governments, youth organizations and other non-governmental organizations on current youth positions and activities, and monitor and evaluate the application of Agenda 21;

(c) Promote the United Nations Trust Fund for the International Youth Year and collaborate with youth representatives in the administration of it, focusing particularly on the needs of youth from developing countries.

## Children in Sustainable Development

### *Basis for Action*

Children not only will inherit the responsibility of looking after the Earth, but in many developing countries they comprise nearly half the population. Furthermore, children in both developing and industrialized countries are highly vulnerable to the effects of environmental degradation. They are also highly aware supporters of environmental thinking. The specific interests of children need to be taken fully into account in the participatory process on environment and development in order to safeguard the future sustainability of any actions taken to improve the environment.

### *Objectives*

Governments, according to their policies, should take measuresto:

(a) Ensure the survival, protection and development of children, in accordance with the goals endorsed by the 1990 World Summit for Children;

(b) Ensure that the interests of children are taken fully into account in the participatory process for sustainable development and environmental improvement.

### *Activities*

Governments should take active steps to:

(a) Implement programmes for children designed to reach the child-related goals of the 1990s in the areas of environment and development, especially health, nutrition, education, literacy and poverty alleviation;

(b) Ratify the Convention on the Rights of the Child (General Assembly resolution 44/25 of 20 November 1989, annex), at the earliest moment and implement it by addressing the basic needs of youth and children;

(c) Promote primary environmental care activities that address the basic needs of communities, improve the environment for children at the household and community level and encourage the participation and empowerment of local populations, including women, youth, children and indigenous people, towards the objective of integrated community management of resources, especially in developing countries;

(d) Expand educational opportunities for children and youth, including education for environmental and developmental responsibility, with overriding attention to the education of the girl child;

(e) Mobilize communities through schools and local health centres so that children and their parents become effective focal points for sensitization of communities to environmental issues;

(f) Establish procedures to incorporate children's concerns into all relevant policies and strategies for environment and development at the local, regional and national levels, including those concerning allocation of and entitlement to natural resources, housing and recreation needs, and control of pollution and toxicity in both rural and urban areas.

## Community Programme for Youth Development

Adolescence is the pivotal period between childhood and adulthood. It is the time when youth need to acquire the attitudes, competencies, values, and social skills that will carry them forward to successful adulthood. It is also the time when they need to avoid choices and behaviours that will limit their future potential. Parents and families play a crucial role in helping young people navigate this phase. In the past, schools, neighborhoods, and communities extended and enhanced positive development and supported young people. Indeed, an enduring image of American life is the participation of neighbours and community members watching out for children, taking responsibility for their safety and well-being, and helping to steer them in the right direction.

In recent decades, a number of social forces have changed both the landscape of family and community life and the expectations for young people. A combination of factors have weakened the informal community support once available to young people: high rates of family mobility; greater anonymity in neighborhoods, where more parents are at work and out of the home and neighbourhood for long periods, and in schools, which have become larger and much more heterogeneous; extensive media exposure to themes of violence and heavy use and abuse of drugs and alcohol; and, in some cases, the deterioration and disorganization of neighbourhoods and schools as a result of crime, drugs, and poverty. At the same time, today's world has become increasingly complex, technical, and multicultural, placing new and challenging demands on young people in terms of education, training, and the social and emotional skills needed in a highly competitive environment. Finally, the length of adolescence has extended to the mid-to late twenties, and the pathways to adulthood have become less clear and more numerous.

Concerns about youth are at the centre of many policy debates. The future well-being of the country depends on raising a generation of skilled, competent, and responsible adults. Yet at least 25 percent of adolescents in the United States are at serious risk of not achieving "productive adulthood" and face such risks as substance abuse, adolescent pregnancy, school failure, and involvement with the juvenile justice system. Depending on their circumstances and choices, they may carry those risks into their adult lives. Public investments in programs to counter such trends have grown significantly over the past decade or so. For the most part, these efforts have targeted specific problems and threats to young people. Substantial public health investments have also been made to prevent such problems as teen smoking, sexually transmitted diseases, unintended pregnancy, and alcohol and other drug use. Major funding has been allocated to the prevention and control of juvenile delinquency and youth crime. These efforts have led to some successes. On one hand, adolescent well-being and behaviour have shown substantial improvement in some areas since the late 1980s.

Serious violent juvenile crime has declined, teen pregnancy has decreased, and more young people are graduating from high school and participating in volunteer and community service. On the other hand, cigarette smoking, HIV infection, school violence, and obesity have increased during this period, particularly among youth in high-risk urban neighbourhoods and very poor rural communities. In addition, many youth are entering the labour market with inadequate knowledge skills, such as the ability to communicate effectively, resolve conflicts, and prepare for and succeed in a job interview.

Continued efforts to prevent and control these and other problems are clearly needed. An exclusive focus on problems, however, narrows the vision that society should have for all of its young people. Many who study adolescent development and work with young people have increasingly come to believe that being problem-free is not fully pre pared. Beyond eliminating problems, one needs skills, knowledge, and a variety of other personal and social assets to function well during adolescence and adulthood. Thus a broader, more holistic view of helping youth to realize their full potential is gaining wider credence in the world of policy and practice. This approach is not viewed as replacing the focus on preventing problems, but rather creating a larger framework that promotes positive outcomes for all young people. Public and private organizations are now engaged in a wide array of activities that fall within this framework.

Such programs include mentoring, school-based community service programs and other volunteer activities, school-to-work transition programs, parenting skills, arts and recreation activities, among others. All are part of a new direction in public policy that places children and adolescents once again at the centre of neighbourhood and community life, where they can engage with caring adults inside and outside their families, develop a sense of security and personal identity, and learn rules of behaviour, expectations, values, morals, and skills needed to move into healthy and productive adulthood.

Recent increases in funding from federal agencies, foundations, state and local governments, and the private sector have given impetus to these efforts and, at the same time, focused attention on the need to assess program effects and provide objective, reliable information to guide future investment.

There is great diversity among the organizations that offer these programs, as well as the programs' emphases, curricula, and populations served. Organizations offering youth programs range from large national youth-serving agencies, such as 4-H, Boys and Girls Clubs, Girls, Inc., Boy Scouts, and Girl Scouts, to more local youth sports organizations, community centres, schools, libraries, faith-based institutions, museums, arts centres, service clubs, and numerous other grassroots organizations.

Programs may target youth broadly or focus on a subset of them, defined by characteristics such as neighbourhood, ethnic group, or special need. The focus of these programs may be general or specific (e.g., centred on sports, religion, or academic success). This report focuses broadly on community-based programs for youth and examines what is known about their design, implementation, and evaluation. These are programs located in the communities in which the youth live. In the context of this report, communities may include neighbourhoods, block groups, towns, and cities, as well as non-geographically defined communities based on family connections and shared interests or values.

### *The Committee Charge*

The Committee on Community-Level Programs for Youth was es-tablished by the Board on Children, Youth, and Families and the Committee on Adolescent Health and Development (formerly the Forum on Adolescence).

The specific charge to the committee was:

- Review and synthesize available data on community interventions and programs to promote positive outcomes for adolescent development;
- Assess the strengths and limitations of data sources and indicators commonly used to characterize youth health, development, and well-being;
- Assess the strengths and limitations of methodologies and approaches used to evaluate these activities; and
- Identify gaps and central questions for the design of a unified conceptual framework and research agenda to promote the healthy development of youth.

To the extent feasible, the committee was asked to identify those programs with sufficiently strong evidence to suggest that they could serve as models for communities that are enhancing their youth programs.

Support for the committee's work came from private foundations and federal agencies. All those supporting this study share a common desire to understand more about how community programs for youth can be designed to promote the positive development of youth. Foundations seek guidance about wise investments in adolescent programming; policy makers seek guidance regarding effective prevention and youth development approaches; and program practitioners and managers seek assistance as they work to design and evaluate their programs.

The committee examined programs that target young people ages 10 to 18. While we made the decision to focus our review and analysis on programs promoting a "youth development" perspective, we rejected the often polarized view of youth programming as either "prevention/problem-centred" or "youth development" centred. Our view is that both approaches are valuable and necessary and that, in practice, the distinction between the two is often blurred. The committee turned to multiple types and sources of information for this report—theory, practical experience, and qualitative and quantitative research and data—in order to gain as broad a perspective as possible on positive youth development. Based on its analysis of this information, the committee generated a set of conclusions and recommendations organized around two primary themes: (a) policy and practice; and (b) research, evaluation, and data collection.

In beginning its work, the committee agreed on a set of four core concepts that serve as a foundation for this report:

- Some youth are doing very well;
- Some youth are taking dangerous risks and doing poorly;
- All young people need a variety of experiences to develop to their full potential;
- Some young people have unmet needs and are particularly at risk of participating in problem behaviours (e.g., dropping out of school, participating in violent behaviour). These include young people who often, but by no means always, live in high-risk neighbourhoods, are poor, experience repeated racial and ethnic discrimination, and have a substantial amount of unsupervised time during nonschool hours. Other youth who are in special need of more programs include youth with disabilities of all kinds, youth from troubled family situations, and youth with special needs for places to find emotional support.

Although the committee stresses the importance of providing support for all youth regardless of economic status, we were also particularly interested in understanding community programs for young people who have the greatest need coupled with the fewest resources. We found very little research to talk specifically about the kinds of programs that would be particularly appropriate for these disadvantaged and under served youth, including youth who are gay and lesbian, youth who are bullied at school, and youth who have experienced sexual and other forms of harassment.

# 7

# Volunteer Management

## Planning Volunteer Projects

### *Why do you want to Involve Volunteers*

Before starting to plan a volunteer programme, it is useful to take some time to consider *if* and *why* your organisation should involve volunteers.

Volunteers:

- widen the scope and flexibility of your organisation's work
- increase diversity
- allow greater participation by the local community
- complement paid work and bring 'added value' to your work
- have a chance to learn new skills and take on challenges.

Why is planning your volunteer involvement important?

- Volunteers are a huge resource for your organisation, giving time, skills, experience and energy, but they are not free of cost. They need proper management so that the experience is equally useful for you and for them.
- If you want to make the most of your volunteers, it is always worth making a real investment in volunteer training, support and personal development.
- If you use targeted recruitment, you can match volunteers' skills and experience exactly so that you have the right volunteers with the right skills for exactly the tasks that need to be done.

- Funders recognise and appreciate investment in volunteer involvement.

Most funding applications are stronger if they include some volunteering. They are more likely to be successful if you can show clearly that you understand that volunteers need and deserve proper supervision, training and expenses.

What kind of structure do you need?

Creating a structure for volunteering could include:

- designing volunteer policies
- implementing standard procedures
- giving regular individual or group supervision
- supporting volunteers' training and personal development needs
- clarifying boundaries and roles
- designing a whole project focused on volunteer development
- recruiting or designating a member of staff as a volunteer co-ordinator
- carrying out safety and risk assessments which cover the way volunteers and clients work together.

Won't formalising volunteering put off some of our community volunteers?

Many smaller organisations are worried about 'formalising' their volunteering, and worry that it will put off some community members who 'just want to help'. However, planning the structure of your volunteer involvement doesn't need to include formal agreements or a formal management style for volunteers. The important thing is that the organisation itself reviews and plans its volunteer involvement to make sure that volunteers are used in the most effective and developmental way – an advantage for you, for them and for your clients

## Involving other Staff

Volunteers are often a large percentage of the team, so increasing their role or numbers will impact on the whole organisation. It is very important to involve all existing staff, management committee members and volunteers themselves in planning their involvement. If everyone in the organisation understands why volunteers are there and everyone takes some responsibility for welcoming and supporting them as a vital part of the organisation, volunteers will feel more involved and, as a result, will want to stay longer.

The benefits of Investing in your Volunteers;

- You will recruit more volunteers more easily.
- They will be able to contribute more to your organisation.
- They will stay longer because they feel valued and are enjoying developing their skills and self-confidence.
- Your organisation will develop a good reputation in the wider community when volunteers talk about you to others (you never know who they might know at home) such as potential fund-raising.

## Budgeting

### *Essential Issues*

- How much training will volunteers need? Where will it come from? How much will that cost?
- What sort of support will volunteers need? How much supervision should they have? Are there any specificrisks involved? Will volunteers face particular pressures?
- Do you want to offer personal development to volunteers as part of the project?
- Will volunteers have any specific access needs such as child care or physical disability?
- What project resources/materials will they need?
- What input will your organisation need to make?

### *Overhead Costs*

If the funder allows it, you could claim up to 10% of the total you are applying for as general management costs. Check their guidelines carefully.

### *Social Events*

As any payments apart from volunteer-related training and

exact expenses would jeopardise volunteers' benefits and your employer status, occasional social events for volunteers are usually very much appreciated as well as being motivating.

### *Running Costs*

Remember to include some running costs for the general organisation, if there is room in the budget, for stationery, rent, heating, lighting, management time etc. This should not usually be more than 10% of the total application budget.

### *Evaluation Costs*

Any funder will need a report on the project, and it can be very useful for further fund-raising. An external evaluator can charge more but you evaluate internally you may want to charge for extra staff hours, or for the costs of an event that would involve your volunteers and service users in the evaluation. You should also include the costs of printing several copies of the report so you can send them to other potential future funders and share what you have learnt with other organisations.

### *Police Checks*

If your organisation is working with vulnerable people as clients or as volunteers, you may need to have police checks done on some staff and volunteers. It may be worth registering your own organisation for this if you have over 10 volunteers and staff who need checks. There are likely to be changes, as the system is under review.

### *Interpreting and Translation*

You may want to translate your volunteer policy or recruitment materials, or provide interpreters for training. Capital items and other project resources and materials You may need a desk, computer and so on for the volunteer manager, or for an increased number of volunteers so that you can use their time constructively. There may also be items needed for the specific project, such as books, maps, noticeboards etc.

### *Volunteer Expenses*

These will normally include exact travel costs and lunch expenses, and sometimes care costs. But in order to budget, you will have to estimate these according to where you think your volunteers will come from and what groups you will recruit from? For example, will most be very local and only have bus fares? Will some be women travelling after dark who need taxis? Will they be working all day and need lunch expenses? Remember, volunteers will not be working 365 days a year. The examples below are based on the assumption that they will do around two days a week each for 45 weeks of the year.

### *Volunteers Budget Checklist*

- Staff (recruitment ads, salary, travel, training)
- Administration/office overheads
- Volunteer training
- Volunteer expenses (travel, lunch, care costs)
- Police checks
- Internal supervision
- External supervision
- Project materials (translation, leaflet production, volunteer packs)
- Social events
- Capital items (computer, overhead projector, books, personal alarms)
- Evaluation.

## Fund-Raising

It is significant that fewer than 5% of refugee-led community organizations (RCOs) have a dedicated volunteer project or volunteer co-ordinator, compared to around 70% of mainstream organisations.

### *Probable Reasons for This*

- Refugee-led community organisations do not consider making applications specifically for this.
- When they make funding applications for volunteer programmes they focus on the service delivery and not on investing in support for their volunteers.

It is therefore important to consider making funding applications for your volunteer involvement, as a separate item from your core services. It is also important not to underestimate how much volunteer investment will cost. Many applications are rejected by funders because they leave out costs that are important to the success of the project. 'It is important to be realistic. You should apply for an amount that allows you to run the project professionally and creatively… Submitting an unrealistically low budget will not increase your chance of funding.'

## Grants Officer, CO-volunteering Projects Funder

### *There are 4 Ways to Fundraise for Volunteer Costs*

1. Make applications for small grants (around £1,000–£10,000) just for volunteer expenses and training.
2. Include volunteer costs as part of your organisation's general overhead costs in all funding applications.
3. Include proportional volunteer costs in project applications if the project involves volunteers.
4. Fundraise for a whole volunteer project including paid staff to manage volunteers.
    - What Service do you want to Provide?
    - Could the service benefit from volunteer involvement? Or is it specifically volunteer-focused (such as a befriending project, or a project providing personal and career development for ex-service-users)?
    - What roles would volunteers have?
    - What support and training would they need to deliver these roles successfully?

What is the need for the service?

- Have there been client requests? Is there a gap in local services? Is an existing service you provide over-stretched? Would you like to improve or extend a successful service?
- How can you *prove* that there is the need? Can you provide statistics of casework or research?

Would the service benefit from volunteer involvement? Would it:

- increase number of workers at little extra cost?
- increase client trust?

- increase the organisation's range of skills, diversity of knowledge and representation it provides?
- develop the potential for users to become volunteers later?
- Or should the whole project be specifically volunteer-focused?
- Are volunteers going to be the main deliverers of the service (such as befriending)
- Should the focus therefore be on their support and training rather than on a paid worker?
- Should the paid worker therefore be a volunteer co-ordinator?
- What support and training will volunteers need to deliver these roles successfully?

### *Top Tips for Making an Application*

- Plan in the context of your organisation's existing work.
- Create a draft 'ideal' project plan and costs.
- Research appropriate funders.
- Understand your funders' priorities, and speak to them in person if you can.
- Explain exactly why the project is needed and how it will work.
- Don't give more or less information than is asked for.
- Prepare in good time and ask someone outside your organisation review the application.
- Be realistic about expected outcomes. Consider when to modify the size and range of work (such as target area, groups targeted, users or volunteer numbers, staff hours). Re-estimate your budget after any modifications.

## Volunteer Co-Ordinator Posts

### *Staff Recruitment*

Most funders will require you to follow a clear equal opportunities-based recruitment process. You should therefore include a realistic amount in the budget for staff recruitment via the local or national press as well as through your other networks.

### *Salaries*

The average salary is probably about Rs.1,44,000-Rs. 2,44,000 volunteer co-ordinator/manager posts in India, depending on how administrative or managerial the post is. It might be helpful to check salaries in similar posts in other organizations.

### *Job Description*

Remember that any dedicated volunteer co-ordinator post will probably include recruitment, policy and practice development and supervision, reporting to funders and planning the work.

This level of responsibility should be reflected in the salary and position of the post in your organisation, so it should be comparable to a project co-ordinator or middle-management post.

### *Job Title*

Usually 'Volunteer Manager', 'Volunteering Project Coordinator', or project-related, for example, 'Befriending Project Coordinator'.

## Responsibilities to Consider for a Volunteer Manager Role

### *Project/Service Development*

- Expand services by recruiting more volunteers
- Diversify the volunteer team, such as by recruiting more ex-service users/young people/host community/asylum seekers as volunteers
- Review, design or develop volunteer roles
- Create a project plan and realistic exit strategy
- Fundraise for the continuation of the project
- Develop or improve volunteer policies and procedures.

### *Project Co-ordination*

- Provide project service cover
- Match volunteers appropriately to clients, manage and assign their workloads and monitor and supervise their work
- Keep volunteer and service statistics for evaluation.

### *Supervision and Training*

- Provide day-to-day/regular/monthly/weekly one-to-one and/or team supervision of volunteers
- Develop and deliver internal/external training for volunteers
- Assess individual development needs of volunteers and design training programmes to support their personal and professional development.

### *General Duties*

- Provide monthly/weekly/annual written reports to the management committee/steering group/funder/director
- Network with other relevant projects in the borough/ region/nationally
- Develop written resources/a library/information for the project
- Administer the volunteers' expenses
- Manage the project budget in co-ordination with the finance worker/director.

### *Further Information*

Talk to organisations of a similar size and type to your own who already have a volunteer coordinator in place – the funder you are applying to may be able to put you in touch with them.

## Designing Volunteer Roles

### *Why have Specific Roles?*

Many organisations recruit general volunteers and then decide what work they will be doing. But if you do it the other way round – define specific roles, and then recruit people for these roles – a lot of things will be easier.

1. You can look at the services that you offer and work out exactly where volunteers would be most useful.
2. It is much easier to select the right volunteers if you have a role description which describes what skills you need and how much time they have to give.
3. People are more likely to stay if they have chosen a role

they think involves work that they're good at or is a way of gaining skills and experience and is also fun.

4. It's much easier to plan what training and supervision you need to offer if you know exactly what volunteers will be doing.
5. If the volunteer, other staff, and service users know what the volunteer is meant to be doing, you are less likely to have problems with boundaries, volunteers doing the wrong thing, or volunteers being asked to take on too much work.
6. Clear roles give volunteers status and a sense of responsibility so they will be more reliable.

You will need to look at the kind of work volunteers do in your organization and work out which roles they might possibly take on.

### *Key Roles*

- Assistant advice workers (e.g. benefits, housing, education)
- Advocates (e.g. interpreting and rights support)
- Befrienders/mentors (e.g. elders, new arrivals, unaccompanied young asylum seekers)
- Support group leaders (e.g. parenting group)
- Trainers/speakers (e.g. health promotion)
- Community champions (e.g. representation at local meetings)
- Events organisers (e.g. social events, celebrations)
- Fundraisers (e.g. applying for small grants for events).

### *Support Roles*

- Administration roles (e.g. reception, database, office work)
- Computer maintenance
- Newsletter/website editor
- Translator (e.g. leaflets, posters)
- PR (e.g. distributing leaflets, posters).

### *Writing a Role Description*

You will Need a Description for each Role which States:

- what tasks you want the volunteer to do

- what kind of skills they need to have
- what hours you need them to work
- how long you need them to stay
- who will be supervising them
- what training they will get.

Be realistic. Your description shouldn't describe the perfect volunteer; it should just list the skills, time and commitment you realistically need for each role.

When you are Designing Roles Remember:

- You can't expect volunteers to have the same skills as paid staff. Part of the reason most people volunteer is to gain experience.
- Very few volunteers can, or want, to work full time. It is easier to find three people to work one or two days a week than one person full time.
- Volunteers can and will leave. If a role is really important break it down into several smaller roles so that you don't have to rely on just one person. If you can't do this then you may have to look for funding to make it a paid role.
- Volunteers won't stay if they don't enjoy what they're doing or don't find it rewarding. It 's better to give really boring or unpleasant jobs to paid staff.
- If you replace paid staff with volunteers, you could end up with lots of legal problems – at worst your organisation could be taken to tribunal and sued.
- You can always change and adapt roles to suit different people or different services.

***Recruitment***

Once you have designed specific volunteer roles, you will find recruiting volunteers much easier. You will know how many people and what skills you need from these groups.

You Might want to Recruit:

- Current or Ex-Service Users: they will know your organisation well and may want to give something back.
- Other People From Your Community: they may want to

help their own community. They will know your culture and will have appropriate language skills.

- People With Similar Experiences to Your Service Users: refugees from other communities may not know your language and culture but may have been through similar experiences to your service users.
- People with Special Skills: for example, if you wanted someone with legal skills, you might think about recruiting trainee lawyers who have the skills but need experience.
- Host Community: people in the host community may have specific knowledge of the locality or have knowledge of services that would be useful for your organisation.

Look at your role description and decide who would be most appropriate for it. You will also need to think about which groups are most likely to benefit from volunteering for you. Then you can decide where to target your recruitment for best results. But do remember, if you only target one group, fewer people are likely to come forward.

## Recruitment Methods

### Word of Mouth

The most common way for people to hear that an organisation needs volunteers is when someone tells them. Make sure that all your current volunteers, staff and service users know that you are looking for volunteers so they can tell anyone they know, who they think might be interested. Lots of organisations rely on word of mouth to recruit people. This is all right but it will mean that you only recruit from your own community, so you may find it hard to involve the host community or get people with specialist skills.

### Advertising

Advertising for volunteers is just like selling a product. You need to tell people why you need them and what they will get out of helping you.

A volunteer recruitment advert should:

- attract people by presenting the need for volunteers
- describe how they can help

- dispel some of the reasons that might put them off helping
- sell the position to them by describing how they will benefit from volunteering for you.

Once you have written your advert you can:

- make posters or leaflets and distribute them wherever you think potential volunteers might see them (such as libraries, other RCOs, schools, colleges etc.)
- put it in your newsletter, local paper etc
- make leaflets and hand them out at any events that your organisation is attending.

### *Volunteer Centres*

Most boroughs have a volunteer centre which has a database of different volunteer opportunities in their area. If people are not sure where they want to volunteer, they will often go to a volunteer centre and look through the vacancies on the database. It is usually free to register your vacancies with them and once you've registered you will also be able to access any other services that they offer, such as training and support for volunteer management.

However, most volunteer centres only provide the contacts; they do not actively recruit or manage volunteers for you, so you will still need to interview and, if necessary police check people they send.

### *Recruiting Service Users*

It is good to involve your service users as volunteers; they are the people who know your service best. However there can be problems if someone is using a service as well as volunteering in it.

- You need to be clear when someone is helping out, and when someone is *being* helped, otherwise people will get confused. You could decide that people may not volunteer and use your services on the same day, or, if you have several different services, you could decide that people can only help a service that they are not currently using.
- Volunteers have access to information about other service users. You need to have a clear confidentiality policy and make sure volunteers follow it.

- Service users who are volunteering should not receive a better service than other people as this can create conflict. Most funders will expect you to show that everyone receives an equal service.

## Selection

### *Why Select?*

Not all volunteers are suitable for all roles but if you make sure that someone is right for the role before they start, it will save a lot of time and effort. If you have decided the volunteer is right for your organisation and the volunteer feels that your organisation is right for them, the relationship is much more likely to be successful. 'I only volunteered for a couple of months for my community because they only wanted volunteers for administration, but if I could have used some of my skills from my previous youth work in Bosnia, I might have stayed much longer…'

### *Selection Procedures*

Volunteer interviews need to be very different from paid staff interviews. The volunteer has to decide whether they want to help you just as much as you have to assess whether they have skills you can use. You will not need formal selection procedures like those for paid staff. The best way to decide whether someone is right for your organisation is to invite them in for an interview. Some organisations ask volunteers to fill out application forms, but if you are interviewing them, this should provide all the information you need, so you don't really need them to fill out a form as well.

The interview is a chance for you to decide whether the volunteer is suitable; it is also a chance for the volunteer to find out a bit more about your organisation and decide whether they want to work with you.

You will find out much more about them if there's a relaxed atmosphere where you and the volunteer feel comfortable and relaxed. You will need to find a space where you won't be interrupted and make sure that everyone knows that you are in an interview and shouldn't be disturbed.

### *Role Descriptions*

It's much easier to select volunteers if you have a description for each role that says:

- what you want the volunteer to do
- what kind of skills they need to have
- what hours you need them to work
- how long you need them to stay.

The description shouldn't describe your perfect volunteer. It should list the minimum skills, time and commitment you realistically need to get the work done.

The role description will be your basic selection guide and you will need to check in the interview that the volunteer meets all the needs you have listed.

Do remember that if someone is good but is missing one of the skills you need, you might be able to offer training or split the role into two and look for another volunteer with the missing skill.

If you are having problems finding anyone suitable, it could be because you are expecting the volunteer to do too much. Try dividing up the role. You will probably find that it is easier to find five volunteers to work one day a week than one volunteer to work full time.

### *Interviews*

As well as checking that volunteers meet all the needs that you have identified in the role description, you will also need to check the following issues.

- Why do they want to volunteer for you? If they have a particular reason (such as training, getting a reference, meeting new people) and your organisation can't provide that, then they are not likely to stay with you for long.
- Are they happy with the level of support your organisation can offer? If they will be expected to work on their own and be in charge of their own work, you will need to find out if they can cope with this.
- Are there any resources that they would need in order to volunteer (such as child care expenses, special equipment)?

### *At the End of the Interview*

- Make sure that you offer them a chance to ask you any questions they might have and give them information about your organisation to take away.
- Agree about what will happen next and when you expect to be in touch again.
- If you definitely don't think they are suitable, tell them immediately, but firmly and kindly, and try to refer them on for more support (perhaps to a job club or support group) or to another voluntary organisation, or to your local volunteer centre so they can volunteer for someone else who might need their skills.

### *Training*

Your volunteers will need to be trained to be able to carry out their roles. The type of training you need to give will depend on what your volunteers are doing. You need to think about the following issues. What will they need to know?

- How your organisation works.
- What policies and procedures they have to follow.
- Health and safety information.
- The specific issues and needs of the community you serve and the context of your work in the UK.
- How to do their job. Remember, the culture and style of service delivery differ between cultures and countries, and extra orientation will be important so your volunteers understand both the client group and the host community context. Will they need training before they start volunteering?
- For some roles (such as giving advice or emotional support) it wouldn't be safe for the volunteer to start until they'd been trained. These roles will need formal training. You may want to train groups of new volunteers together or consider the possibility of sending volunteers on external training courses.
- With other roles (office work, practical tasks) the volunteer can learn the necessary skills by working with a staff member or another volunteer, who can show them what

to do. For these roles you will still need to think about ongoing training. You might want to run training sessions for your whole volunteer team on important topics or make sure that all staff training is open to volunteers.

### *Who Will do the Training?*

- You could run your own training sessions. If you want to learn how, a number of organisations run courses on delivering training.
- Check with your local CVS. In some areas there is a lot of free training available for volunteers via local statutory or voluntary organisations. However, these will be general courses so they may not be culturally appropriate or suitable for people who are not confident with their English.
- You could pay an external trainer to deliver custom-made courses for groups of volunteers, specialised to your needs.
- Remember to budget for venue hire costs, refreshment costs and creche costs for your training sessions.

Funders are usually very happy to see applications that include volunteer training costs – it proves you want to support them and help them to work professionally and safely.

### *Volunteer Management Training*

Many local volunteer centres run training courses on basic volunteer management that are free to local organisations. They can also advise you on where you can find more in-depth courses. You may also want to train other staff and your management committee on working with volunteers. Volunteer projects are usually far more successful and sustainable if the whole organisation understands and values volunteer involvement.

### *Supervision and Retention*

Support and supervision are very important for volunteers. If someone is giving you their time for free and feels bored, are stressed, or feel they are not respected and that their work is not important, they will leave. You have to supervise volunteers to make sure they are doing the work you need them to do, and to support them to make sure that they are happy.

### *Induction*

The first few days that a volunteer is with you are really important. They will be deciding whether your organisation is right for them. If they feel nervous or confused, they may not come back. It is a good idea to plan an induction for them, to make sure that they feel comfortable, and know what is expected of them.

### *Ongoing Supervision*

Even if your volunteers are very skilled and independent, you will need to supervise their work to make sure they are doing what you want them to do and are happy with their work. It is important that each volunteer has a person who is monitoring their work, who they can go to with any problems. This could be someone who is responsible for all the volunteers in the organisation, or it could be the person who is responsible for the part of your organisation they work in. Through support and supervision you can let volunteers know what they are doing well, discuss any problems with their work, and check whether they are happy. There are several different methods.

### *Formal*

Regular one-to-one meetings (usually monthly). Formal supervision is best when the volunteer has a complicated or difficult role. It is useful when a volunteer wants to gain work experience because you can check how they are progressing and help them plan how they could develop their work.

### *Informal*

Regular contact with the volunteer – making sure you spend five minutes chatting with them every time they come in. This works best when the volunteer is based in your office and you have regular contact with them. It only works if you make sure you spend time regularly with each volunteer.

### *Group*

Volunteers regularly meet up as a group to discuss their work. This type of supervision works best if you have lots of volunteers performing similar roles. It is good because it means that volunteers support each other but you still have to make sure you have informal contact so as to be aware of individual problems.

### External

If your volunteers will be dealing with difficult emotional issues for clients (such as domestic violence, counselling), it may be appropriate to involve an external supervisor for their casework.

Whatever method you use, you need to make sure you:

- thank them for their time and praise any work you feel they've done particularly well
- discuss current work, future plans, any problems they may have, or any that you have with their work
- ask what aspects of their role they enjoy and which bits they don't like, and see how you could develop the role
- check if there's anything you could do to make their role easier or if there's any training they feel they need
- ensure they feel part of the organisation, not just service providers. Ask them if they have any ideas for the whole organisation and tell them whether and how this can be acted on.

### *Dealing with Problems*

It is much easier to deal with problems if you have clear roles so that each volunteer knows exactly what they are meant to do and when they are meant to come in. It is also a good idea to have a 'volunteer agreement' saying what you expect from your volunteers. You will need to ask them to:

- stick to your organisation's rules and procedures
- come in when they have said they are going to, or let you know in advance if they won't be able to make it
- attend training and supervision sessions.

If someone is not carrying out their role properly or is not sticking to the agreement, you will need to discuss it with them as part of their supervision. It is a good idea to have a disciplinary procedure so everybody knows how problems will be sorted out.

### *Sample Disciplinary Procedure*

- If there is a problem with your work we will discuss it with you and try to find a solution.
- If a problem recurs over and over again, we may need to ask you to leave.

- If you are violent, abusive, break the law or do something that might harm someone, then we will have to ask you to leave straight away.

*Getting them to Stay*

People have lots of different reasons for volunteering. You will keep your volunteers for longer if you find out why they are volunteering and you make sure that you are supporting them and meeting their needs.

For example, if a volunteer wants to meet new people, don't make them work in a room on their own. If a volunteer wants to learn new skills, don't give them just very basic work to do.

Through support and supervision you need to find out what each volunteer's aims are and see if there is any way you can help to achieve them. If a volunteer wants something that you definitely can't provide, it may be better for them to go to an organisation which can.

Volunteers are more likely to stay if they know they are appreciated and that your organisation values their work. You can do this by:

- reimbursing expenses
- including them in staff meetings and decision making
- featuring them in newsletters and annual reports
- holding events where volunteers can socialise and have fun
- having ongoing training
- giving them references for work or education
- developing their roles to help them gain the skills they want
- saying thank you.

*Safety*

*What's your Legal Responsibility?*

As an organisation you have a legal obligation called a 'Duty of Care' towards staff, volunteers and clients. This means you have to do everything you can to make sure that no one is hurt or harmed. If someone is harmed and it is your organisation's fault, your organisation or management committee can be sued. The court would investigate whether you had reasonable safety procedures in place. If they felt you didn't, they could order your organisation to pay compensation. If the organisation didn't have enough money then the trustees/management committee may be expected to pay.

## Four Steps to Make Sure your Organisation is Safe

### *Do a Risk Assessment*

Look at what your organisation does and write a list of things that could go wrong, these are your 'risks' or 'hazards'. Once you have your list look at each item and see if there are any policies, procedures, rules or training that could stop the hazards occuring.

*Example:* A lunch club for elderly people Hazard: People getting food poisoning Solution:

- All volunteers preparing food must have training in food hygiene.
- Notices on the wall in your community language about food care.

### *Have Safety Policies and Procedures*

The solutions you find will include ideas for policies and procedures. These don't have to be very complicated, in fact the simpler you make things, the easier it will be to apply. Once your policies and procedures are in place you will have to decide how to let people know about them, otherwise there's no point in having them.

### *Make Sure Everyone is Trained*

Giving volunteers training to do their role is important. Remember that training doesn't have to expensive or formal. It could be a current volunteer or member of staff showing someone how to perform a task, or one person from your organisation going on a course and sharing what they have learnt.

Some roles do not need much training but some are very high risk (such as giving health advice). You need to make it clear that only volunteers who have received proper training should carry out these roles.

### *Make Sure your Insurance Covers Volunteers*

Employers Liability or Public Liability Insurance can cover volunteers, but you need to make sure your insurance company knows that you have volunteers and that they are included in your policy. This doesn't usually cost any extra money. If you haven't told them, they could refuse to pay out for an incident involving a volunteer.

### *Working Safely with Vulnerable People*

'11% of people experience sexual abuse as a child. 82% of these are abused by someone from their own community.' NSPCC prevalence survey 2000.

If your organisation works with vulnerable people, you will need to be particularly careful that you have training, policies and procedures in place to make sure they are not harmed. Your risk assessment will need to take into account any extra hazards resulting from working with children or elderly people.

You are legally allowed to run a police check on any staff or volunteers who will be working with:

- people under 18
- people with learning or physical disabilities
- people with a physical or mental illness including addiction to drink or drugs
- elderly people who are frail.

Many organisations are worried about applying for police checks but if a vulnerable person was abused and you hadn't done the check, you would be failing in your duty of care. Don't decide that police checking isn't right for you because you are a community organisation. There is a lot of support, information and advice available to help you make the right decision for your organisation.

### *Writing a Volunteer Policy*

If you are involving volunteers, you will find it useful to have a volunteer policy. This policy should say how your organisation manages volunteers, and should refer to other policies like health and safety, confidentiality and equal opportunities that affect volunteers.

### *Your Volunteer Policy*

- makes it clear to everyone (including potential funders) how and why you involve volunteers.
- means all your volunteers are treated equally.
- gives you a simple plan of how you manage volunteers.

Involve volunteers, staff and management committee members in developing the policy. It's more likely to be useful if everyone can contribute ideas.

Most importantly, try to keep the policy simple and readable, and only create policies that you will actually put into practice in your work. Policies do not have to be long, but they must be accessible – you may want to have copies in your mother tongue as well as in English. A cupboard full of policy files is not useful if the people in the organisation who should be using it cannot read them and no one knows what is in them! What Should be in it?

Why do you Involve Volunteers?

- Try to think beyond 'We can't afford to pay' to 'We can involve the whole community', 'It gives us a chance to involve service users' etc.
- Consider which are volunteer roles rather than paid roles and why?

### *Recruitment and Selection*

- Where will you advertise for volunteers?
- How will you select volunteers? Will you have an application form or will you interview people?
- Do you ask for references or carry out police checks?
- What are your policies?

### *Induction and Training*

- Is there a Volunteer Agreement which tells volunteers what you expect from them?
- Do you have a list of items that will be included in volunteers' induction?
- What initial training do you give?

## Glossary

*Accountability.* Holding someone, some group or some entity responsible for its actions and failures, outputs and results.

*Audit committee.* A subcommittee of a board of directors/ trustees that includes a high proportion of independent directors and those competent in accounting and auditing. It receives and acts upon the financial recommendations of outside auditors.

*Benefactor.* Person who uses their money to set up a trust or foundation during their lifetime or through their testamentary will.

*Beneficiaries.* Persons for whose benefit property (including money) is held, or for whom services are offered, by trustees or NGOs.

*Bequest.* A charitable gift by a donor. Often it comes with the entitlement to have your name associated with the gift.

*Board of directors or trustees.* The group of directors (or trustees) that has dayto-day operational control and oversight over an NGO or international organization (IO). Different names are used in each jurisdiction or legal tradition.

*Breach of trust.* Acting in a way inconsistent with your fiduciary duties to act in the best interests of the NGO above your own gain.

*Case law.* Law and principles made when judges or arbitrators decide cases and disputes and write up their decisions. It is non-statutory law, meaning it is not created by the legislature or sovereign.

*Certificate of incorporation or charter.* Formal document that establishes a corporate entity and frequently defines its scope and powers. It is usually fi led with a government official, department or court responsible for registering such entities.

*Character assassination.* Extreme acts against a person's reputation or business integrity often as part of a protest campaign.

*Charity.* An entity set up for the purpose of providing educational, scientific, religious, artistic, or philanthropic relief to members of the general public. Many jurisdictions have long-standing specialized laws for the establishment and regulation of charities. Does not normally include private clubs and mutual societies for the benefit of its members.

*Chief operating/executive officer or managing officer (CEO).* Person who is the highest executive officer responsible for running the daily operations of an NGO. Often called a coordinator in more collective NGOs.

*Cites.* The Convention on the International Trade in Endangered Species of Wild Fauna and Flora, which entered into force in 1975, attempts to regulate the global trade in animals, plants and their products. Some NGOs have been able to play a useful role in monitoring countries' adherence to their treaty promises under this regime.

*Civil action or suit.* A legal case brought by one private citizen or company.

*relief or damages.* Not initiated by the state or police prosecutors.

*Class action.* A civil suit brought collectively by a group of people who are affected by the same activities or negligence (e.g., consumers of a faulty drug or victims of an environmental accident).

*Code of conduct.* Voluntary guidelines and principles for how NGOs may conduct themselves and their affairs. Not established by the state through force of law.

*Commingling of funds.* Improper mixing of personal finances with those of an NGO.

*Compact (social contract).* Term referring to various legal and administrative arrangements between a government and a private or NGO social service provider, such as in the health or education fields.

*Conflict of interest.* Improper mixing of personal and fiduciary business interests, where a director or officer would gain personally from a business decision taken by the NGO. Such situations are best avoided by the conflicted director excusing herself from the board meeting, leaving the matter to be decided by the other impartial directors.

*Constitution.* Formal legal document as to how a state, international organization or NGO is organized and run.

*Constitutive documents.* Formal legal documents, such as charters or memoranda of incorporation, which are used to set up (constitute) the existence of an NGO or other legal entity.

***Control system.*** Any system established to ensure financial and legal commitments are made by the right persons upon proper authorization and crosscheck.

***Convention or treaty.*** International agreement between two or more states and/or international organizations. NGOs are usually not allowed to be formal parties in their own right to treaties.

***Criminal laws.*** Body of law and principles that refer to illegal acts that are prohibited by the state on force of fi ne or imprisonment.

***Crosschecking.*** Prudent financial or business management procedures to safeguard against fraudulent or negligent business decisions. Usually involves another more senior officer or body overseeing the work of the more junior operative.

***Direct action.*** Any activity or demonstration that involves one-on-one confrontation, as opposed to more indirect means, such as boycotts, negotiations and lobbying to change policy.

***Direct mailings.*** Approaching the general public for a contribution to an NGO through a bulk mailing campaign of brochures usually accompanied with pledge forms.

***Dissolution of an NGO (winding-up of an NGO and its operations).*** Various procedures required in each jurisdiction to end the operations of an NGO and pay out its creditors in an orderly way.

***ECOSOC.*** The Economic and Social Council of the United Nations is assigned to coordinate the economic, social, and related work of various parts of the UN. It receives advice from numerous NGOs, as well as academics and representatives from the business sector.

***European Convention on Human Rights.*** The European Union's version of the Universal Declaration of Human Rights. It copies very closely the wording of many of the UN's sections. It also established a European Court of Human Rights, which has heard many cases upholding the rights of controversial NGOs to establish and register themselves in countries such as Greece and Turkey.

***Executive fi at.*** An order from a government official whose decision is necessary to authorize actions or procedures, such as the registration of NGOs. Often marked by a high degree of unpredictable discretion that is frequently unchecked by another independent body or court.

***Fiduciary duty.*** Duty of trust owed by a director, trustee, or officer to act in the best interests of the NGO, rather than for personal advancement.

***Foundation.*** Usually a large-scale charitable or public purpose organization that may be established under a variety of laws. Some foundations are also incorporated as non-profits (e.g., World Economic Forum in Switzerland). A favoured form for grant-giving trusts or societies for the support of the arts.

***Founder.*** Person, company or group that establishes or originates an NGO.

***Four-eyes principle.*** So-called because at least two people will check a financial transaction before it is implemented. Based on the old military "two-keys" principle that the agreement of two officers is required before a weapon can be launched.

***Franklin dam campaign.*** In 1982 environmentalists interfered with planned hydro construction works on state forest land in Tasmania, Australia to stop the destruction of a UN common heritage wilderness area. Their televised actions and arrests popularized the struggle and bought time for federal government intervention and ultimately successful court challenges to halt the works.

***Freedom of information laws.*** Term to refer to various laws and disclosure practices in progressive jurisdictions that allow the general public to access nonsensitive government documents and archives. Certain non-public NGO reports and filings might be disclosed to the public or media if such laws apply to the government departments that collect these reports.

***Freedom to associate.*** A bedrock principle for NGOs and their members to peacefully congregate to pursue their agenda. Often also enshrined in democratic constitutions or bills of rights.

***Fund-raising ratio.*** Amount of money raised against the costs of raising it.

***General assembly.*** Most common term used to refer to the periodic meetings of all the members of an NGO. Universally must be held at a minimum on an annual basis, but can be more frequent depending on the terms of the constitutive documents or the business needs of the NGO.

***Gifts-in-kind.*** Instead of giving money, personal property such as clothes, food or services may be contributed by donors.

***Governance.*** Manner in which power is exercised by someone, some group or some entity in management.

***Governing body.*** Term referring to the highest management group of an NGO. Often synonymous with the board or even the general assembly.

***Group guarantee.*** The repayment of a microfinance loan is guaranteed by the other members of the borrowing village group, not just by the debtor herself. Group support is thought to encourage higher peer pressure to honour a loan.

***Guantanamo detainee case.*** In the case of Hamdan the US Supreme Court decided in June 2006 to invalidate military commissions which had been set up in violation of the Geneva Conventions at the US-run prison at Guantanamo Bay for detainees from the campaigns against terror.

Notable for a powerful judicial check on the executive branch's interpretation of their powers to act in times of a national emergency and for upholding international humanitarian and treaty principles in the face of domestic derogations or exceptions.

***Improper personal profit.*** Any personal financial or business gain at the expense of the best interests of the NGO.

***Indirect action.*** Myriad of NGO activities that do not involve one-on-one confrontation or physical acts, most of which are legal.

***Institutional memory.*** The tacit knowledge and know-how possessed by staff who work for an NGO or IO. It is rarely written down or passed on to new personnel. Frequently it is lost to an entity when the long-serving staff leave, unless the entity introduces knowledge capture and management programs.

***Internal governance.*** Procedures set up inside an NGO to ensure it is operated in an efficient and ethical manner.

***Legal identity or personality.*** Capable of having legal rights and duties separate from the individual members. At law persons can be natural (real human beings or individuals) or artificial (companies or other formal entities, including registered NGOs).

***Libel.*** Term referring to various criminal and civil laws that protect persons and companies (sometimes even their products) from unfair or untrue public accusations.

***Limited term charitable licensing.*** Instead of having a perpetual license to operate indefinitely, a charity must periodically convince the registration authorities that it is operating responsibly and in the public interest before it can receive a renewed license. This reform is being considered in light of criticism that some large charities have become complacent and non-responsive to the reasonable demands of government and the general public.

***Management board or advisory board.*** Often a board of outside advisers who are experts in their field and are selected to give independent guidance and comments to managers on the operations and programs of an NGO.

***Matching gift program.*** Some companies will match the amount of money their employees give to a charity or qualified NGO through these programs.

***Memorandum of Understanding.*** A written arrangement to collaborate on some project or activity often in the form of an exchange of letters between parties such as IOs, government departments and NGOs. It is not intended to have the force of being legally binding, although the parties will usually honour their promises to each other. It is widely used because it is more convenient to prepare and may not require the formal approval of higher authorities with legal and financial commitment powers.

***Mission.*** The strategic direction or purpose of an NGO. Can be multiple but not too diffuse.

***Montreal Protocol.*** One of the most successful treaties of all time, the Montreal Protocol on Substances That Deplete the Ozone Layer has enjoyed widespread adoption and implementation by countries since it was first opened for signature in 1987. Also has a multilateral fund that helps developing countries pay for their obligations under the treaty to phase out the use of ozone-depleting substances. Especially noteworthy for its fast negotiation after the scientific problem was understood.

***Moral turpitude.*** Serious violation of normal moral standards, most usually involving the commission of a crime or a heinous personal act.

***Narmada Dam campaign.*** In the 1980s local people formed a movement to protest their displacement for the construction of a major dam project on the Narmada river in India. The World Bank withdrew financial support after an independent review of the implementation of the project.

***Not-for-profit company.*** A corporation set up under a special section of the company laws for an identified non-commercial reason, such as educational, charitable, social or humanitarian purposes. While NPOs may have the traditional management structure of a company, i.e., CEOs, officers and boards of directors, they do not have shareholders who receive profits or distributions of its assets.

***Open letter.*** A protest or complaint letter addressed to the target of a campaign (e.g., CEO of an offending company) that is publicly displayed by the writer usually in a paid advertisement of a newspaper. Now more frequently posted on the Internet, which is cheaper but less visible.

***Outside oversight.*** External checking by an independent body of an NGO's operations and governance.

Overhead or administrative expenses. Back office expenses that must be met to deliver aid or service in the field to the Beneficiaries in need. Frequently criticized if too high or misspent on lavish rent and perks for HQ executives.

***Parody or hate site.*** Web site with the purpose of making fun or criticizing its target, which might be a government, company or individual.

***Partnership.*** Relationship among people carrying on a common business for shared profit, but who are not members of an incorporated company.

***Philanthrocapitalism.*** Newly-coined phrase that refers to the new breed of wealthy capitalists or celebrities who are socially active in their preferred charities or causes.

***Public benefit.*** An important concept for NGOs in order to obtain tax privileges and exemptions because their activities are beneficial to the general public good of society rather than being for a money-making endeavour or for members' personal enjoyment.

***Public liability insurance.*** New form of insurance that covers an NGO for its damage or negligence to members of the general public. It may have to be offered by a government agency; commercial insurance companies may not find it a lucrative enough market to enter.

***Sarbanes-Oxley Act or SOX.*** More formally the Public Company Accounting Reform and Investor Protection Act of 2002. After the Enron scandal, US legislators Sarbanes and Oxley sponsored this wide-sweeping reform of corporate governance of publicly traded companies in the United States. Certain provisions are also relevant for large NGOs and foundations. Similar legislative reforms have taken place around the world; these are frequently known as SOX reforms.

***Self-dealing.*** Improper mixing of personal business interests with those of the NGO, where a director or officer causes an NGO to enter into a financial or business arrangement for the benefit of the director or officer. Self-regulation. Instead of being controlled by the government, an NGO or a sector of civil society undertakes to police its own activities.

***Sharp practice.*** While not strictly illegal, this activity may cross the bounds of what is normally considered ethical or a good business practice for an NGO.

***Special-favour deals.*** A business deal where an advantage is offered to an insider or a person connected with the managers of the NGO. Most often these are unfair and improper to the disadvantage of the NGO.

***Stakeholder.*** Any person or group with an interest in an NGO or IO or their operations and programs. Does not have to be a member or volunteer and is often someone who is being helped by the NGO's programs.

***Statute or statutory law.*** Laws formally written down by legislatures or parliaments in enactments, as opposed to judge-created case law.

***Subsidiarity.*** Useful concept developed by the EU to mean taking important decisions at the lowest and most efficient level so as to encourage more direct involvement of the persons usually affected. Also sometimes known as "new localism."

***Tax exemptions and privileges (tax breaks).*** Generic terms to refer to the myriad of tax relief provisions offered by governments for both the NGO and persons who donate money to registered NGOs that qualify for such privileges.

***Transparency.*** Allowing outsiders to see the inside workings and decision-making processes of an NGO or its management body. Also known as "information flows."

***Trust.*** Has many legal definitions; for our purposes mainly refers to a form of NGO set up by a wealthy individual (benefactor) either during their lifetime or through a testamentary will for a non-commercial purpose, frequently for the benefit of others or a philanthropic activity.

***Trustee.*** One who holds property or money on trust for others, or provides services for the benefit of others; the managers of a trust.

***Unincorporated association.*** A group that has not taken formal legal action to organize itself into a separate legal entity; such a group is unincorporated, not a corporate body of associated people. Many NGOs begin in this form but find they must evolve into a more formal entity as they grow.

***Universal Declaration of Human Rights.*** The United Nations General Assembly's first bill of rights dating from 1948. While it is not strictly legally binding on states, it has long been recognized as declaratory of customary international human rights law.

***Venality.*** Being susceptible to corruption or bribery or using one's position of trust for an improper personal benefit or dishonest gain.

***Watchdogs.*** Usually independent NGOs that oversee (with or without permission) the operations of other NGOs or IOs that are active in areas of particular interest, such as the environment or indigenous peoples.

***Whist leblower.*** Usually an inside person who discloses wrongdoing or sharp business practices in an NGO, IO or company. Many progressive jurisdictions protect them from retaliation that could affect their employment prospects.

# 8

# Promoting Women in Social Work

Women, especially those in the low-income strata, traditionally have contributed to productive activities such as agriculture (mostly small-scale), agro-processing crafts and home industries, trade and commerce, but there has been a tendency to underestimate their economic roles and to undercount their participation due to inadequate data, prevailing definitions of economic activity and current sampling and interviewing procedures employed in obtaining national statistics. More attention has been focused, especially in national plans and programs, on their reproductive and child-nurturing roles.

In general, women have benefitted increasingly from programs in the social sector, as evidenced by the large increases in school enrolment of the female population at all levels of education and a rise in life expectancy. However, severe health, nutritional and educational problems still remain to be resolved, especially in the case of women in rural areas and low-income women in the urban centres.

While modernization has opened up economic opportunities in some areas, on the other hand it has led to a decline in traditional sources of income for many women, e.g., those engaged in the production of handmade and homemade items. In the agricultural sector the introduction of mechanization and new technologies generally has displaced small producers and disrupted traditional systems of production and complementarity between the roles of the two sexes in the smallholder family.

Low productivity in the campesino economy on the whole, the displacement of small producers, lack of income-generating opportunities and of social services in rural areas have caused both men and women to emigrate to the cities. These migratory flows have deeply affected women's roles in two ways. In the urban centres there has been a rapid entry of migrant women into the work force, with females being concentrated in low-level or unskilled jobs and services. Women are involved in the urban informal sector, largely in retail trade and in small scale enterprises. In the rural areas, wherever male outmigration has been strong, women who remain had to increase their workload and to assume full responsibility of carrying out both agricultural and household duties.

It is also within this context that one observes within the region a large number of female-headed households, particularly in the low-income strata. Various studies emphasize the disadvantaged position of female heads of households: They are most likely to be living below the poverty line, they score lower than low-income men on educational attainment and are more apt to be unemployed or employed in low-skilled or service occupations.

Moreover, the economic crisis of the 1980s in Latin America and the hitherto unprecedented levels of unemployment and underemployment which adversely affected particularly the poorest segments of the population, have had serious repercussions for women in particular.

On the one hand, this situation led to relatively fewer income-generating opportunities available on an overall basis. On the other hand, cutbacks in social services have seriously affected women's level of health, nutrition and education, important determinants for their productivity and effective participation in the economy and society as a whole. The interaction of these factors creates a vicious circle in which low-income women in particular are caught. The mounting economic responsibilities of these women thus make combatting their poverty a crucial development goal.

The Bank recognizes that if women are to be effective agents of human capital development, particular attention should be paid to enhancing their contribution and taking into account their needs, multiple roles and changing economic and family situations. This means that more recognition must be give to their current and potential contribution as producers, as decision-makers and as income-generators. Recognizing the pressing situation of poor women within the region, the Bank will pay attention to supporting activities that address their needs in both rural and urban areas. Many Latin American countries are making significant efforts, as evidenced by the establishment of Women's Desks Bureaux and both national and regional planning units to promote the integration of women into the national development process. The fields of action proposed within this policy are thus formulated with a view of assisting national efforts and leading to a more effective participation of women in development.

## *Objectives*

Within its general objectives of promoting social and economic development, the Bank through its lending and technical cooperation programs will assist member countries in their efforts to bring about the fuller integration of women into all stages of the development process and improvement in their socioeconomic situation. The Bank will support initiatives aimed at:

- Recognizing and enhancing women's actual and potential role in productive and social activities and their contribution to the national development process;
- Facilitating women's access to productive resources, services and to social and economic benefits derived from Bank operations;
- Reducing social, legal and economic constraints that depress women's ability to effectively participate in and benefit from productive and other development-oriented programs.

Improving the effectiveness of institutions responsible for fostering the social and economic participation of women in the development process.

## Fields of Activity

Employment Opportunities. One of the objectives of the Bank's operations has been to increase job opportunities and to raise the level of incomes of project participants. With a view to the fact that women increasingly bear economic responsibilities but tend to be concentrated in low-productive and low-paid jobs, the Bank will support efforts that aim at generating employment, upgrading women's productivity and promoting their access to productive employment or other income-earning activities. In line with the criteria established within the Urban and Rural Development Policies (OP-751 and OP-752), the Bank will cooperate in increasing and improving both the financing and management of small enterprises, endeavoring to mobilize the efforts of women entrepreneurs.

Bearing in mind that the issue of generating employment for women is not only related to their need for training and skills acquisition programs, but also to the demands on women associated with family and household responsibilities, the Bank will support existing programs or the establishment of appropriate ones and other incentives aimed at reducing or eliminating obstacles to women's participation in income-earning activities. These may include the financing of child day-care centres or other project-related arrangements to assist women in their child care responsibilities, and the support of special employment programs which offer flexible schedules and/or take into account women's daily and seasonal burden of domestic and productive tasks.

Education, Training and Extension. To ensure that women benefit fully from investments in project-related training programs, the Bank will give special consideration to training programs in any sector which promotes and/or facilitates the participation of women, the upgrading of their skills and the development of their productive potential. Programs in both rural and urban areas should take into account the specific factors that affect the availability and effectiveness of educational and training programs to women working in the agricultural sector or in urban-based enterprises: location of training centres, convenience of the hours of courses and the relevance of curricula and teaching materials, use of appropriate methods to transfer technology. Within this context, the Bank will support:

a) the development and establishment of extension programs, programs at technical and vocational centres, formal and non-formal educational programs and literacy campaigns appropriately designed to facilitate women's access as well as active promotion and outreach efforts to disseminate information on these courses;

b) the setting up of training courses for technical personnel to sensitize them to women's specific educational needs and problems and to increase their capacity to implement appropriate plans and projects;

c) fforts to increase the number of female extension agents;

d) efforts to identify and remove limitations to women's participation in project-related training programs; and

e) training programs connected with the maintenance and administration of project-related facilities.

***Credit.*** One of the principal constraints facing low-income groups, in particular women, is the lack of adequate financing. Access to credit is one of the keys to an improved standard of living and higher productivity for small farmers and entrepreneurs in both rural and urban areas.

Women's participation in formal credit programs particularly has been constrained by legal barriers, cumbersome application procedures, relatively high opportunity and transaction costs, sociocultural constraints or by their lack of secure title to property and other forms of collateral, even if they play a major role in production and marketing in the agricultural sector.

In urban areas, women experience similar difficulties in their efforts to establish or expand their own enterprises and sources of self-employment, so that they are often forced to turn to informal, high-cost sources of credit.

The Bank will therefore pay special attention in its credit programs to the support of programs or other mechanisms which facilitate women's access to credit and thus raise their productivity, either individually or through groups organized into productive units. These measures can include:

a) the appropriate training of employees of formal credit institutions;

b) the support of financial extension services specifically geared to reach out to potential female borrowers;

c) the strengthening of intermediary credit institutions and associations such as formal or informal savings cooperatives where women are predominantly involved; the use of active outreach and promotion efforts to inform women of the availability of credit programs; and

d) measures that would remove or ameliorate legal or other inhibitions to equitable treatment for women in obtaining credit.

***Research and Studies on the Participation of Women.*** As the information and statistical data available on the involvement of women in economic and social development and other related topics is still limited, the Bank will support and encourage the collection and publication of sex-disaggregated data and qualitative information on the participation of women, especially research on women's actual and potential participation in productive activities, decision-making structures and social activities; and on mechanisms to enhance their contribution.

Knowledge of these roles and of the factors that enhance or limit women's ability to carry out these roles can contribute to the improvement of project design so that women can actively participate in and reap more benefits from the development process.

The Bank will also assist in:

a) carrying out research to reappraise concepts, approaches and practices associated with gathering statistics in order to improve data-gathering on the role of women;

b) studying solutions for dealing with the obstacles restraining women's participation and ways of promoting income and employment for low-income women; and

c) studying means to adapt and transfer appropriate technology to women.

As far as possible, any studies undertaken will be coordinated with and complement the actions of national institutions and other international organizations.

In order to enhance the implementation of this policy, the following section provides specific pointers on operational instruments and mechanisms for Bank action in the programming, analysis, administration and evaluation of loans in key sectors.

### *The Programming Process*

As part of the programming process, when the Bank is developing a strategy and identifying operations in a particular country, attention should be given to gaining an informed understanding of women's roles in the economy and society as a whole.

Although due to a general lack of base line and disaggregated data, only approximations may be obtained in some cases, an assessment—however, general—of women's real contribution to the economy and identification of any key issues affecting their participation at an early stage is a prerequisite for: a) ensuring the efficiency, effectiveness and the success of operations where women's participation would be a significant contributing factor to the achievement of project goals; and b) more effectively involving women in specific programs and projects, thus enhancing their advancement.

## Women, Participation and Development: A Case Study from West Bengal

The importance of Women's Organisations for bringing women within reach of the development process is a recognised policy for women's development in India.

However, nature and functional role of such organisations were not always clearly defined. In recent years, it was increasingly being felt that such grassroot organisations with certain definite objectives and roles can serve as key instruments for mobilising women to develop their economic activity in an organised manner-by ensuring access to needed development inputs and to strengthen women's voice in development decisions and in the political process.

In other words, such grassroot organisations are expected to serve as participatory and mobilising mechanisms rather than mere delivery agencies in the planning and development process. Introduction of an economic component in grassroot women's organisations is gradually emerging as a critical need not only to alleviate poverty but also to reduce exploitation of the most vulnerable groups of women workers and to stabilise the participatory and mobilising mechanisms.

However, the need for such organisations of rural women was thought of in the fifties as a part of the community development programmes and various organisations did come into existence in India. But they ran into difficulties because no economic component was envisaged and as a result the organisations became the monopoly of affluent section of the rural women.

Government was also not clear about the functions and roles of these organisations which depended largely on government support and assistance. As a results most of them collapsed when government assistance was withdrawn. There were exceptions in a few states because of the presence of some women with clear vision in the state administration who did not see these organizations as mere delivery agencies.

When the Committee for the Status of Women in India in its report severely criticised the government's approach and pointed out the disturbing decline in the status of rural women and suggested economic activity as an important component for such organisations, the Committee's views were endorsed by the Committee on Panchayati Raj and Working Groups on Employment of Women, Adult Education for Women and Development of village Level Organisations of Rural Women.

The mid-seventies was also the period of increasing realisation of growing rural inequality which affected the implementation of progressive legislations for Abolition of Bonded Labour, Land Reforms measures, Minimum Wages Act etc. The Committee appointed by the Ministry of Education for review of adult education programme for adult women, while trying to explain the failure of the programme to reach illiterate adult women who constitute three fourth of all adult illiterates in India recommended that such women could only be reached through forming organisations for both learning and earning activities.

These recommendations were however articulating the need for a new strategy and approach but did not spell out the possible obstacles adequately. It was not realised that in the context of existing politico-economic class relations and inequalities in the rural areas the female section of the rural poor could not be fully mobilised through usual forms of workers' organizations. In West Bengal for instance, the government was holding rural camps under 'Operation Barga' for successful implementation of land reforms by promoting Organisation of poor farmers and agricultural workers. It was found that participation of women or women's organisations was marginal in such camps and the Land Reforms Commissioner resorted to holding a special camp to look into specific problems of rural poor women at Jhilimil, Bankura in 1980. Studies on peasant movements and organisations reveal that while women are militantly involved in struggles of the poor peasantry they are seldom represented in the organisations or the leadership. It is only in this context that some voluntary organisations developed separate organizations of poor women workers.

Both Government and Voluntary Organisational, however had to face several issues. Of theses two critical ones were the needed methodology for development of such organisation and required stabilising mechanisms for these organisations which are mainly formed by landless and asset less illiterate poor women depending mainly on wage labour.

The solutions to these issues are likely to emerge through a learning process and from various instances of success and failure in the context of set goals and objectives. In the context of these two critical issues-the need for intermediaries between grassroot level organisations and developmental agencies has been identified as a temporary solution and preliminary methodology. But this solution or methodology has not yet passed the severe test of time, and competing involvements and pressures.

## Lessons from Current Development Programmes

The ongoing developmental efforts through IRDPP, ITDP, DWCRA, ANP, NREP etc. plan the creation of durable productive assets and income generating activities for the rural poor and mention women as the most vulnerable section of the target group. Most of these developmental thrusts aim at building on existing local skills and occupations and utilizing local raw materials and marketing outlets. To fortify these approaches basic instruments designed so far are cheap credit, some amount of braining in production skills and subsidized distribution of technological equipment/livestock/seeds etc. The objective of all these programmes is to make these poor households economically viable through increased opportunities for 'self-employment'. Field evaluations have, however, increasingly revealed that;

(a) 'self-employment for individuals or households' at this level of poverty is an impossibility because of their own limitations and structure of the rural market economy, and

(b) small assets without training in economic management of such assets only intensifies the vulnerability of those households.

The structural constraints are provided by inequalities and limited purchasing power of the majority of the rural population, dominant influence of urban products which depress the demand for locally produced goods, difficulties in getting raw materials etc. The local power elites normally the employers (often the money-lenders) are reluctant to see them acquire economic viability-as that would prevent the formers' ability to exploit their labour and need.

All these problems affect women from such households even more adversely. In addition, they have to face some special constraints emanating from their familial responsibilities and their depressed status in the local community-which men do not share. All these problems are intensified when these households take to seasonal migrations for survival.

Strategies for improving poor rural women's access to development must, therefore, face several challenging obstacles: (i) identifying an economic activity which will be viable and within reach of the women's skills, understanding, resources and marketability; (ii) transforming the dependency of wage workers to the self-reliance of entrepreneurs and managers; (iii) finding a mechanism that can help to combat their special vulnerabilities/ constraints, and to provide them basic services.

Grassroot level organisations of rural women had been introduced to meet the last challenge as early as the Second Plan (Mahila Mandal, Mahila Samitis, Mahila Samajams, Mader Sangams). At that time, however, employment generation had not been seen as a priority for women, and only training taken up through these bodies was in household activities (nutrition, childcare, sewing and embroidery etc.). As a result, the organisations could not draw the rural poor women and remained confined to women of the rural elite. These became inactive the moment government support was withdrawn.

The new perspective-of economic independence for women, coupled with the strategies for eradication of poverty gives a new dimension to the formation and development of these grassroot organisations. For the first time these are being viewed as possible instruments for employment generation and viable economic development as well as channels for sociopolitical development of the most oppressed and deprived section of the rural populations. IRDP/ITDP assistance for acquiring livestock, for sericulture and household industry though given to male heads of households generally increase the work burden of women particularly with livestock and sericulture. But women have no control over the disposal of The structural constraints are provided by inequalities and limited purchasing power of the majority of the rural population, dominant influence of urban products which depress the demand for locally produced goods, difficulties in getting raw materials etc. The local power elites normally the employers (often the money-lenders) are reluctant to see them acquire economic viability-as that would prevent the formers' ability to exploit their labour and need.

All these problems affect women from such households even more adversely. In addition, they have to face some special constraints emanating from their familial responsibilities and their depressed status in the local community-which men do not share. All these problems are intensified when these households take to seasonal migrations for survival.

Strategies for improving poor rural women's access to development must, therefore, face several challenging obstacles: (i) identifying an economic activity which will be viable and within reach of the women's skills, understanding, resources and marketability; (ii) transforming the dependency of wage workers to the self-reliance of entrepreneurs and managers; (iii) finding a mechanism that can help to combat their special vulnerabilities/ constraints, and to provide them basic services.

Grassroot level organisations of rural women had been introduced to meet the last challenge as early as the Second Plan

(Mahila Mandal, Mahila Samitis, Mahila Samajams, Mader Sangams). At that time, however, employment generation had not been seen as a priority for women, and only training taken up through these bodies was in household activities (nutrition, childcare, sewing and embroidery etc.). As a result, the organisations could not draw the rural poor women and remained confined to women of the rural elite. These became inactive the moment government support was withdrawn.

The new perspective-of economic independence for women, coupled with the strategies for eradication of poverty gives a new dimension to the formation and development of these grassroot organisations. For the first time these are being viewed as possible instruments for employment generation and viable economic development as well as channels for sociopolitical development of the most oppressed and deprived section of the rural populations.

IRDP/ITDP assistance for acquiring livestock, for sericulture and household industry though given to male heads of households generally increase the work burden of women particularly with livestock and sericulture. But women have no control over the disposal of assets, or the use of credit. These low capital, labour intensive activities, to achieve viability, need some scale of investment and production. A household dependent on daily earnings of its members cannot wait for future income-from multiplication/maturity/sale of its products. At the household level such scale can only be achieved by land-owning affluent farmers, not assetless households. Collective activity-through grassroot organisations offers the added advantage of channelising vital social services-which the poor rural women (and their children) cannot normally avail of. Story of Gramin Mahila Sramik Unnayan Samitis (GMSUS) in Bankura District of West Bengal.

### *The Area and the Women*

Bankura is one of the most economically and industrially backward districts of West Bengal and within Bankura, Ranibandh block occupies the south-western corner touching the borders of

Purulia and Medinipur districts. The entire block is hilly and forested and forms a part of the drought-prone region. Agriculture is dependent on rain and a single crop of paddy is taken from the undulating land if there is timely rain. Backyard cultivation of maize is undertaken by almost all households who have some land. On the high lands babui grass is cultivated in some areas mainly for rope making. The forest-which was once a source of food, fuel, fodder and occasionally of livelihood-still provides for fuel and some income from minor forest products.

However collection of Kandu and Sal leaves, Mahua flower, Neem, Mahua, Zamun, Amlaki, Haritaki, Kusum and Sal fruits, and various kinds of medicinal herbs and barks still constitute a supplementary source of livelihood for the women. Kheria and Sabar. Other communities living in the area are Oriya Brahmins, a conglomerate of lower castes of Bengal who have embraced Baisnabism, other backward communities like Mahato, Deswali Majhi, Kora (Mudi), scheduled castes like Sunris, Kaira, Chamar, Dom etc. and a host of occupational and service castes like Kumbhakar, Karmakar, Teli, Napit, Dhobi etc. Of all the communities, the Oriya Brahmins, Sunris and some Baisnabs are prosperous (obviously at the cost of Bhumij and Santal), and others largely belong to the group falling below the poverty line.

After being dispossessed of their land and after forest resources depleted or went under the control of others, the tribal groups took to seasonal migration for agricultural work in the adjacent district of Burdwan and Hoogly for the sake of survival. In view of multiple cropping in these areas intensity of seasonal migration increased and in these treks women were in majority.

The social costs of such intermittent nomadism were-high infant mortality, physical decline of women resulting in low life expectancy, denial of all schooling training and healthcare opportunity to the children who went with their mothers, increasing incidence of alcoholism and domestic violence, frequent destruction of family life and stability, sexual assault by employers/labour contractors, growing number of young unmarried women with little prospect of marriage, frequent collapse of homesteads from bad weather during families' absences, perpetual state of indebtedness etc. Various other evil effects are also visible at the community level and in the socioeconomic milieu of the area. Involvement of the Centre for Women's Development Studies at Bankura. Some of these facts surfaced during a 'Re-orientation Camp for Migrant Women Agricultural Labourers' organised by the Government of West Bengal at Jhilimili in May 1980-in which representatives from Centre for Women's Development Studies (CWDS), New Delhi participated. Apart from Government officials, the camp was also attended to by the Minister for Land Reforms. The Minister, after the camp, requested the CWDS representatives to assist the Government of West Bengal in amelioration of the conditions of these women.

Policy branch of the International Labour Organisation to implement a project on "Employment Opportunities for Rural Women through Organisations" in a few States of India, and CWDS decided to plant itself in the Ranibandh Block of Bankura district. The Ministry of Labour, Government of India, also wanted CWDS to undertake a survey on vocational training needs of rural women in Bankura.

The Minister's request paved the way for various needed supports, the ILO assistance provided the financial support needed for mobilisation and implementation and the Labour Ministry's work gave a chance to survey two clusters of villages in the Ranibandh Block for basic socioeconomic data. (The survey not only confirmed the various statements made by the women in the Rural Camp but also added new dimensions. Women everywhere identified seasonal migration as an evil necessity and stable employment in their own area as their most critical need. They felt that other needs-healthy education, social security etc. will follow after stable employment locally has been ensured).

### *The Samitis*

They were about 30 in number-coming from several villages in and around Jhilimili. CWDS field workers contacted these women through the local Panchayat Sabhapati and the Pradhans.

They moved from one village to another and held meetings and discussions. Some of the women who participated in the Re-orientation Camp often accompanied the CWDS field-team and narrated their experience of the Camp to other women. The discussions used to emphasize on their problems first and then used to move on to the possible solutions for the same. The crucial point on which the women stressed repeatedly was generation of employment opportunity locally and they realised that in the context of existing politico-economic class relations and inequalities in the rural areas they cannot achieve anything without being united into an Organisation of their own (and the CWDS was constantly supporting this ideology).

Thus the first Gramin Mahila Sramik Unnayan Samiti (GMSUS) was born at Jhilimili in the beginning of 1981. Although it started with less than 100 members originally by end of 1982 the membership crossed 200 who came from a cluster of eight settlements around Jhilimili. About 20 kilometers away from Jhilimili and near the Block headquarter the second GMSUS was formed at Bhurkura in the middle of 1981-drawing its more than 100 members from four settlements.

Each GMSUS (hereafter mentioned as 'Samiti') was registered as a Samiti and has a memorandum of association. Once a year, it elects an Executive Committee through democratic means. The Executive Committee elects a President, a Secretary and a Treasurer from among the executive committee members. In order to ensure a permanent relationship with the CWDS (and to provide a locus standi for CWDS field staff) each Samiti has nominated the Director, CWDS as its permanent Joint Secretary. Initially the Samiti members on account of being mostly illiterate were highly apprehensive of accountability conditions attached to any funds they might receive from Government. They, therefore thought that by keeping the Director CWDS as permanent Joint Secretary of the Samiti they would be able to tide over various difficulties. At the initial stage the Director, CWDS could play the role of spokesperson on behalf of the Samitis in dealing with Government and other agencies.

The three Samitis, locationally form the apexes of an imaginary isolateral triangle within the Ranibandh Block. Members consist of unmarried adult women, married women with or without children, widows, divorced/separated/deserted. All of them are agricultural workers and most of them had the bitter experience of seasonal migration. Most of them are also illiterate. The deserted/divorced/widows, the married women without children and the unmarried girls were found to be more active and enthusiastic. The traditional tribal ethos of Collective activity (for instance in fuel collection, minor forest produce collection, festivals etc.) helped in providing the base of collective approach.

All the three Samities immediately after their formation were in desperate search for suitable activity which would generate local employment for their members. The CWDS is a research and professional institution specialising in women's developmental problem and it had no fund to contribute for actual development activities (Its project staff and other field expenses are supported by the ILO's Rural Employment Policies branch with the approval of government of India). Naturally, the samitis had to depend on State/Central Governments and/or other developmental agencies for funding such activities. At that moment, Government of West Bengal and the local Panchayat Sabhapati came to their help. The GMSUS (Jhilimili) undertook the agency of Kandu leaf and Sal seed collection from local LAMP (Large Size Multipurpose Cooperative Society) and provided employment to some of its members for about three months.

The GMSUS (Bhurkura) managed to procure an absolutely rocky patch of wasteland by persuading its owners to donate the same to the Samiti and decided to develop the same for cultivation of Asan/Arjun plants with the aim of rearing Tassar cocoons. (This was once a traditional occupation in the area-although not exactly with the women-but had been abandoned with the recession of forest and establishment of government control over all forest areas). The Government of West Bengal provided a grant of one lakh rupees to this samiti to undertake the activity. The other two samitis were not able to mobilise such local sources and were getting frustrated in their search for some income/employment generating activities.

Towards the end of 1981, the CWDS project staff came across a simple machine with the help of which plates and cups could be manufactured our of sal leaves. After discussion with the GMSUS (Chhandapathar) and GMSUS (Jhilimili) steps were taken to procure a few machines (the financial assistance at that time came from Government of West Bengal and subsequently from the Department of Science and Technology, Government of India). These are simple foot operated machines with a pair of dies-which are heated by blow lamps. Stitched Sal leaves with a thin layer of Polythene in between are placed between the two heated dies and pressed by the pedal. The plates and cups of specific sizes are obtained. These plates and cups can be used in lieu of paper plates. Some of the Samiti members from the two Samitis were trained on these machines and limited employment could be generated through training and production of Sal plates on machines and collection of Sal leaves from forest as raw material.

Meanwhile, the district as a whole was passing through a period of severe drought which continued upto mid 1983. There was immediate need for some activities and actions to help out the poor women. The frantic efforts of the CWDS and the Samiti members to augment financial resources from government and other developmental agencies, and mobilise local resources, were getting frustrated at various levels and for various reasons. The GMSUS (Jhilimiii) and GMSUS (Chhendapathar) took the step of getting themselves affiliated to the West Bengal Tribal Development Cooperative Corporation (WBTDCC) in the hope of augmenting cash credit to continue the activity of machanised manufacture of Sal plates. One of the samitis even participated in a WBTDCC organised workshop at Calcutta to plead for their right to carry on trade in minor forest produce independent of the LAMPS with which their relationship was somewhat strained by that time due to differential treatment meted cut to them by the LAMPS in regard to Sal seed and Kandu leaf agency.

Fortunately, it was possible to bring these woman face to face with two Ministers and a few Government officials through a Rural Camp orgenised by CWDS in October 1982 at Jhilimili. A few of them had also met the Chief Minister of the State while inviting him to the Rural Camp. Everytime the women stressed on their rights and state of present condition. They expressed that they are basically workers and therefore their right to work should be ensured and employment opportunities should be created. These dialogues were helpful in many ways subsequently.

For the whole of 1982 and the first half of 1983, the GMSUS (Jhilimili) and GMSUS (Chhendapathar) were primarily experimenting with machanised manufacture of Sal plates.

The GMSUS (Bhurkura) was primarily pro-occupied with motherly care of Asan/Arjun plates. The CWDS project staff were trying to find out other sources of activities-such as – possibilities of rope making out of Babui grass, animal husbandry programmes, expansion of Tassar cultivation in Bhurkura and in the other areas, cultivation of cash crops which are less dependent on rain, trade in those minor forest produce in which the LAMPS is not involved, etc. The absence of appropriate technology, adverse climatic conditions, delay in mobilising local resource and above all, inadequate financial resources were posing as major obstacles to any such effort. The CWDS also by this time conducted a market survey on possibilities of sale of Sal plates in the industrial belt of West Bengal and in the city of Calcutta, and established contacts with the various marketing agencies like WBTDCC Ltd. Bengal Home Industries, BENFEB and a few private traders. All these efforts generated some hope both among the Samiti members and CWDS project staff.

The October 1982 Rural Camp where two Cabinet Ministers and a host of officials of the State Government, Panchayat office bearers, special invitees, ILO representatives and CWDS field team were present and listened to the Samiti representatives one by one for three days provided the occasion of a thorough reappraisal of the whole approach. The Ministers and Government officials-on return took steps to clear some of the pending proposals of the Samitis for employment generating activities in March-April 1983. It is then that the Samitis could diversify their activities-by way of setting up poultry and goatery units, expanding Tassar plantation areas in Bhurkura, adding Sal plate machines in Jhilimili and Chhendapathar etc.

The success of Tassar plantation in Bhurkura has been noticed by other two Samitis and they were in constant search of wasted land in their respective areas. Both the Samitis ultimately found some land and persuaded the owners to donate the same to the Samitis. The Jhilimili Samiti went ahead with plantation of Asan/ Arjun on a two acre plot without waiting for government assistance. It also obtained a cash credit from the West Bengal Tribal Development Cooperative Corporation Ltd. (WBTDCC) for Sal plate manufacturing activity.

Jhilimili Samiti also started a small piggery unit on experimental basis. All these activities provided employment to some members but not to all. The Samitis, therefore, decided to share amongst all whatever employment opportunity could be created. They owned all the assets collectively and took all actions-also collectively.

Till March 1984 (i) the Bhurkura Samiti had added four acres of Tassar Plantation to its earlier seven acres, set up two goatery units of 22 animals each and a poultry unit of more than 100 birds, (ii) the Chhendapathar Samiti had procured six Sal plate machines, set up two goatery units of 33 animals each, a poultry unit of more than 150 birds and had obtained a seven acre plot for Tassar plantation, a two acre plot for fodder cultivation and two small plots for setting up two more goatery units under the Government of West Bengal nutrition programme for which this Samiti was chosen(iii) the Jhilimili Samiti had procured ten Sal plate machines, set up four goatery units, a poultry and a piggery unit, and had obtained two plots of wasteland-on one of which plantation of Asan/Arjun was completed.

Apart from emphasis on employment generation, the Samiti members realised that they needed some amount of education to discharge certain activities (e.g. transaction with banks, government functionaries etc.). Each Samiti, therefore, started adult education units in its area.

On the request of CWDS, the West Bengal Illiteracy Eradication Association trained a few Samiti members as teachers. Several months' effort to this and prepared certain members to read and write elementary things and they were able to carry on transactions with banks, government functionaries without the help of CWDS field team.

Since all the basic activities were based on local resources and existing skill of Samiti members the only other inputs necessary were augmentation of financial resources and some training to upgrade the traditional skills of the women. To these ends-the Samitis (and the CWDS team) have been partially successful. It was possible to obtain grants from Government of West Bengal for Tassar plantation, animal husbandry, adult education, nutrition-improvement activities and for purchase of Sal plate manufacturing machines. Credit was procured by one Samiti from the WBTDCC for Sal plate manufacture. But these were not enough-and the Samitis went on submitting one scheme after another (e.g. scheme for Babui rope making, construction for worksheds) to government of West Bengal and Government of India.

The training input came in regard to Tassar plantation, mechanized manufacture of Sal plates and adult-education. The district sericulture department was persuaded to provide one month's on-the-field training to Bhurkura women in Tassar cultures Training was also given to almost all women of the Jhilimili and Chhandapathar Samiti in the manufacture of Sal plates and in service and repair of Sal plate-machine. However, several vital trainings are immediately necessary for the survival and self-reliance of the Samitis and their activities. The trainings are required in the field of animal husbandry (poultry, goatery, piggery), accounts keepings and management of the Samiti. At the moment, suitable institution/individuals are being identified by the CWDS team for bringing these training facilities to the illiterate Samiti members who have hardly ever managed any assets themselves and who have their whole life been dependent on others giving them work. The content materials of the training, therefore, need to break several barriers and take the women out from the psychology of dependence to psychology of self-reliance and independence.

*Employment Generation*

The main objective of all three Samitis has been to generate employment locally for the members. Fulfillment of this objective would depend on Samitis' ability to augment financial resources, to mobilise local resources and to stabilise the assets owned and created. Synthesis of all these efforts can lead the Samitis towards achievement of the main objective. To this end the three Samitis have not been equally successful. A review in September 1982 and again in September 1983 showed that due to Tassar plantation oriented activity, supported all through by the Government of West Bengal, the Bhurkura Samiti generated 10,000 person-days of employment every year. The other two Samitis did not have any such sustained activity. The mechanised manufacture of Sal plate used to get stopped occasionally for such reasons as breakage of machines, scarcity of kerosene, lack of storage space for leaves, slackening of market demands and finally lack of experience in planning various activities. In spite of all these difficulties the annual rate of employment generation by the Jhilimili and Chhandepathat Samiti was 5000 and 3000 person-days respectively. The estimated person-days of employment generation during October 1983 to September 1984 by the three Samitis would be 15,000 (Jhilimili) 10,000 (Chhendapathar) and 20,000 (Bhurkura).

### *Future Plan*

The future plan of activity of the Samitis depends on several issues. On the one hand, each Samiti has a series of objectives to achieve for its members and on the other hand it needs various support-financial moral, political and material-to fulfil those objectives. Both the CWDS team and the Samiti members realised from the beginning that secondary and tertiary sector activities would be unsuitable from the marketing point of view. A distant and/or an urban market would be difficult to control or capture by goods produced by women whose production skill to produce goods for competitive market would take longer time to grow.

Fortunately, the Samiti members also never demanded initiation of any such activity in which they have no preliminary skill. Half of the operation i.e. collection, selection, grading, stitching etc. of Sal leaves, in mechanised manufacture of Sal plates was already known to the women and therefore they readily accepted the activity. Both Tassar culture and animal husbandry programmes are close to the women's heart and with that in view both CWDS team and the Samitis would like to diversify in such activities for which raw materials, skills and market could be easy to obtain. The primary emphasis therefore will remain an wasteland development oriented activities e.g. Tassar cultures fodder and fuel cultivation, introduction of suitable cash crops (papaya, sun flower, pulses, medicinal herbs etc.), animal husbandry (poultry, goatory, piggery and sheep rearing and cattle and rabbit rearing on experimental basic) and babui rope making and rope products. The Samitis desire for forestry based activities may come into conflict with both political and other vested interests in the region. The uncertain climatic condition and chronic problem of drought come in the way of primary sector activities and activities relating to wasteland development. The locational disadvantages increase investment costs as almost everything is required to be brought from a minimum distances of 50 kms.

Apart from economic activities the Samitis desire to undertake certain support service and social security activities. Education, health care, child and mother care, nutrition etc. will form the core of support services. Group insurance, maternity benefits, old-age care and Dharmagolas (for paddy, Mahua etc.) will be the components of social security measures. The Samitis also need to develop its own support services for successful implementation and management of various economic activities. The normal dependence on available facilities (e.g. veterinary, sericulture etc.) has caused a great deal of damage to the Samitis and therefore acquiring some basic knowledge and internalisation of the same in the Samitis' regular function have become imperative. Another important area on which the Samitis' survival depends to some extent is the local power structure. The Samitis are currently taking several steps to establish closer relationship as well as to demonstrate their rights and a share in the development process.

# 9

# Problem Solving Theory in Social Work

## Social Work Approach to Tribal Development

### *Tribal Development Approaches for their all Round Development*

The tribal population of India constitutes around 8% of total population over 94,000 tribal villages. Tribals are mainly concentrated in Andhra Pradesh, Chhattisgarh, Odisha, Jharkhand, Gujarat, Madhya Pradesh, Rajasthan, Maharashtra, West Bengal, North-Eastern States and North-Western Himalayan States.

The small, marginal, fragmented, unirrigated and mono crop agriculture holdings and low productive livestock population do not offer adequate opportunitiesto to the tribals. Tribals in remote areas are still devoid of common infrastructure facilities of road and communication, health and education and safe drinking water, which do not allow them to absorb technological and financial facilities provided by government.

So for their All Round Development, In 1972, Tribal Development Directorate established for effective implementation of Tribal Welfare Schemes. In 1976 Tribal Development Commissionerate was established for All Round Development of Tribal. In 1984 separate Tribal Development Ministry was established to strengthen the Tribal Development Department, Directorate was merged into Commissionerate in 1992. The comprehensive Tribal Development Approach involves the following components;

- Orchard development (fruit/plantation/herbal crops & forest plants) as the core componen
- Soil conservation in the wadi
- Water resources management (conservation and use)
- Sustainable agriculture
- Human resource development (community development)
- Women development-A special emphasis is given for involvement of women in all spheres of the programme.
- The components include drudgery reduction measures, on-farm and non farm income generating activities and self help groups for inculcating thrift and credit habits.
- Community Health
- Micro-enterprises for landless people
- Processing & marketing
- Other auxillary components to dovetail with above activities.

*Objectives of Tribal Development Approach*

- To promote sustainable participatory livelihood programmes
- To take up promotional efforts such as capacity building, exposure visits, training, developing literature, sensitization programmes etc.
- To implement sustainable livelihood programmes
- To support promotional activities for micro-credit, promotion of SHGs, Income
- Generating Activities for landless, SC/ST communities and other weaker sections of the community
- To support activities related to development of tribal market
- To support other relevant activities as approved by NABARD.

*Participant Groups (PGs)*

The core activity will be a family based programme and will be undertaken by the member of tribal family. For better planning and management, the individual project participant will come together as small groups of about 10 members each. It is necessary for people to understand the relationship between their poverty and the degraded environment in which they live in. They must also be provided with an equally good, if not better, economic alternative. Social empowerment, improvement in quality of life including health and women development, in tribal predominant areas of the country through demonstration projects supported through Non Government Organisations (NGOs)/Community Based Organisations (CBOs)/GOs.

## Rural Development

Literally and from the social, economic and political perspectives the statement is valid even today. Around 65% of the State's population is living in rural areas. People in rural areas should have the same quality of life as is enjoyed by people living in sub urban and urban areas. Further there are cascading effects of poverty, unemployment, poor and inadequate infrastructure in rural areas on urban centres causing slums and consequential social and economic tensions manifesting in economic deprivation and urban poverty. Hence Rural Development which is concerned with economic growth and social justice, improvement in the living standard of the rural people by providing adequate and quality social services and minimum basic needs becomes essential. The present strategy of rural development mainly focuses on poverty alleviation, better livelihood opportunities, provision of basic amenities and infrastructure facilities through innovative programmes of wage and self-employment. The above goals will be achieved by various programme support being implemented creating partnership with communities, non-governmental organizations, community based organizations, institutions, PRIs and industrial establishments, while the Department of Rural Development will provide logistic support both on technical and administrative side for programme implementation. Other aspects that will ultimately lead to transformation of rural life are also being emphasized simultaneously.

Though the percentage of persons below poverty level in Tamil Nadu has come down significantly between 1993-94 (35.03%) and 1999-2000 (21.12%) as a result of the implementation of various

Central and State sponsored schemes, the level of poverty both in absolute numbers (130.40 lakh persons) and percentage of population below poverty line (21.12%) in Tamil Nadu is highest among the four southern States. In spite of huge investments on wage and self-employment programmes, the level of unemployment as per the NSSO 55th round (1999-2000) for Tamil Nadu compared to All India is the second highest among major States in 1987-88 and 1993-94 and third highest in 1999-2000.

The Government's policy and programmes have laid emphasis on poverty alleviation, generation of employment and income opportunities and provision of infrastructure and basic facilities to meet the needs of rural poor.

For realising these objectives, self-employment and wage employment programmes continued to pervade in one form or other.

As a measure to strengthen the grass root level democracy, the Government is constantly endeavouring to empower Panchayat Raj Institutions in terms of functions, powers and finance. Grama sabha, NGOs, Self-Help Groups and PRIs have been accorded adequate role to make participatory democracy meaningful and effective.

### *Goals, Objectives and Strategy*

The prime goal of rural development is to improve the quality of life of the rural people by alleviating poverty through the instrument of self-employment and wage employment programmes, by providing community infrastructure facilities such as drinking water, electricity, road connectivity, health facilities, rural housing and education and promoting decentralization of powers to strengthen the Panchayat raj institutions. The Chief Minister's 15 Point Programme is a visionary programme which seeks to make Tamil Nadu the best State in the country by way of creating growth opportunities in rural areas and eradicating rural poverty.

### *Centrally Sponsored Schemes*

The magnitude of poverty and disparities that existed between the various social groups necessitated planned state intervention to provide succour and relief particularly to the disadvantaged and marginalised groups such as SC/ST, women etc. Keeping this in view and having regard to the positive aspects as well as deficiencies, the earlier self employment programmes like TRYSEM, SITRA, GKY, DWCRA, IRDP and MWS were merged and a new self employment programme viz.

SGSY was launched w.e.f.1-4-1999. The SGSY is conceived as a holistic programme of micro enterprises covering all aspects of self employment and establishing effective linkages between the various components viz., organization of the rural poor into Self Help Groups (SHGs), their capacity building, planning of activity clusters, infrastructure build up, technology, credit and marketing etc.

The main objective of the programme is to bring the existing poor families above the poverty line. Among the rural poor, special emphasis will be given for the welfare of SCs/STs, women and disabled. The programme lays emphasis on organization of poor into Self Help Groups (SHGs) and their capacity building.

The SHGs may consist of 10 to 20 persons. 4 to 5 key activities will be identified in each block based on the resource endowments, occupational skills of the people and availability of markets and these activities will be implemented in clusters. 10% of the SGSY fund will be set apart for training, wherein emphasis will be given for skill development through well designed courses.

SGSY is a Credit cum Subsidy programme with the involvement of banking and financial institutions. The expenditure under SGSY is shared by the Centre and the States in the ratio of 75:25. Subsidy will be provided at 30% of the project cost subject to a maximum of Rs. 7,500 and 50% for SC/ST subject to a maximum of Rs. 10,000. For groups, the subsidy is 50% subject to a ceiling of Rs. 1.25 lakhs.

(i) To impart EDP and Vocational training for about 5 lakh rural women to start micro enterprise for economic independency.

(ii) To train 3 lakh unemployed youth to take up self employment.

(iii) To construct one Self Help Group Centre per Panchayat to conduct meeting, store and display their products and to hold training programmes for the members of SHGs.

(iv) To establish District Information Service Centre in each district to provide backward and forward linkages in marketing.

*Sampoorna Grameen Rozgar Yojana (SGRY)*

Creation of sustained employment opportunities for securing a minimum level of employment and income for the rural poor necessitated continuous need for special employment programmes. Keeping the above aim and to strengthen the need based infrastructure at the village level to boost the rural economy the erstwhile wage employment programmes JGSY and EAS were merged and a new scheme namely SGRY was launched from 15th August 2001. The main objective of the new programme is to provide additional wage employment in the rural areas as food security by creation of durable community social and economic assets and infrastructure development in rural areas. Towards this end the SGRY envisages distribution of food grains @ 5 kg per manday to the workers as part wages.

While the cash component will be shared by the Centre and States in the ratio of 75:25, the Central Government will supply the food grains free of cost to the States. The scheme will be implemented in two streams. The first stream will be implemented at the District and Panchayat Union levels. 50% of the funds and food grains available under the programme will be distributed between the District Panchayat and the Panchayat Union in the ratio of 40:60.

The second stream will be implemented at the Village Panchayat level. The entire allocation under this stream will be distributed among the Village Panchayats through the DRDAs/ District Panchayats. To augument the storage capacity of the tanks maintained by the local bodies towards increasing the availability of water for drinking, irrigation and other purposes it has been proposed to renovate one tank per panchayat under this scheme.

*Rural Housing*

The aim of the State Government is to provide a dwelling for each family giving special emphasis to rural poor and deprived. The on going rural housing programmes will be given a new thrust.

### *Indira Awaas Yojana*

With a view to meeting the housing needs of the rural poor, Indira Awaas Yojana (IAY) was launched in May 1985 as a sub-scheme of Jawahar Rozgar Yojana. It is being implemented as an independent scheme since 1 January 1996.

It aims at helping below poverty line rural households belonging to SCs/STs, free bonded labourers, widows of next of kin of defence personnel, ex-servicemen and retired members of the paramilitary forces and also non SC/ST rural poor by providing them with grant-in-aid for construction of new dwelling units and upgradation of existing unserviceable kutcha houses. 3% of funds are reserved for the benefit of disabled poor below the poverty line in rural areas.

The assistance ceiling for each house in plain area is fixed at Rs. 20,000/-and for hill/difficult areas Rs. 22,000. In order to enable fire proof RCC roofed houses to be provided, the State Government provides additionally Rs. 12,000 per house as additional cost apart from its usual matching share to the Central grant. The expenditure towards provision of RCC roofing is met under Adidravida Welfare head.

Therefore, the unit cost including sanitary latrine under this scheme is Rs. 32,000/-in normal terrain and Rs. 34,000 in difficult terrain. 80% of the IAY funds is earmarked for construction new houses and 20% is towards upgradation of unserviceable kutcha houses at the rate of Rs. 10,000/-per unit. The funds under IAY are shared between Centre and States in the ratio of 75:25. During the Tenth Plan it has been proposed to construct 1,54,090 new houses and to upgrade 78,970 unserviceable kutcha houses into pucca houses. The proposed outlay during the Tenth plan under IAY under SCP is Rs. 292.89 crores.

### *Credit cum Subsidy Scheme*

The Credit-cum-Subsidy Scheme has been conceived for rural households having an annual income upto Rs. 32,000/-. Subsidy upto Rs. 10,000/-and loan up to Rs. 40,000/-from commercial or coop. banks is provided to eligible households for construction of houses. Out of the total outlay of Rs. 9.15 crores, 25% share of the State Government will be Rs. 2.29 crores. The physical target under the scheme will be 914.

### *Innovative Stream for Rural House and Habitat Development Scheme*

This scheme intends to popularize low cost technology and usage of locally available materials in construction of buildings in rural areas. Innovative technology adopted for the rural house type design in the scheme are:

(i) Rattrap bond brick work, hollow blocks and soil stabilized cement mortar for construction of walls.

(ii) Filler slab roofing using Mangalore tiles as filler material for roofing.

(iii) Ferro cement/pre cast RCC doors, window, frame and shelter and

(iv) Brick baf with plastering for flooring.

Under this scheme free houses are constructed for the rural poor. Infrastructure facilities such as drinking water, drainage, street formation etc., are provided by dovetailing funds under other ongoing schemes in the habitations developed under this scheme. This scheme is fully funded by the Government of India.

### *Pradhan Mantri Gramodaya Yojana (PMGY) (Rural Shelter Component)*

This scheme has been introduced by the Government of India under additional Central assistance for providing shelter in the rural areas to supplement the efforts in the sphere of rural housing considering the magnitude of the task. The guidelines of Indira Awaas Yojana are applied for this scheme also. 60% of the total allocation is earmarked for SC/ST beneficiaries. During Tenth Plan it has been proposed to construct 34,475 rural shelters with an allocation of Rs. 111.14 crores. III. Member of Parliament Local Area Development Programme The Government of India introduced this scheme in 1993. Each MP (Lok Sabha and Rajya Sabha) was allotted Rs. 2 crore per annum to take up developmental works in his constituency. The District Collectors and in respect of Chennai, the Commissioner of Chennai Corporation implement the scheme. In Tamil Nadu, there are 39 Lok Sabha MPs and 18 Rajya Sabha MPs and hence Rs. 114 crores is received annually from Government of India under this scheme. A Member of Rajya Sabha may select any district of the State for exercising the choice of works under the scheme. The executive authorities concerned after studying the feasibility of the proposals of members will execute the works by following open tender system. The list of works that can be taken up under this scheme includes school buildings, village roads/approach roads, and irrigation canals, bus shelters, desilting of village ponds etc. An outlay of Rs. 570 crores has been proposed under this scheme during Tenth Plan period, which will be directly released to the District Collectors by GOI for executing the works.

### *Pradhan Manthri Gram Sadak Yojana (PMGSY)*

The Pradhan Mantri Gram Sadak Yojana (PMGSY) is a Government of India Scheme introduced in the year 2000-2001 with the objective of providing road connectivity through good all weather roads to all unconnected rural habitations having population above 1000 by 2003 and all unconnected habitations having population of 500 and above by end of Tenth Plan period (2007). Under this programme the approved works are grouped into packages costing more than Rs. 1 crore but less than Rs. 5 crores and executed through tender system. The guidelines stipulate that district master plans would be prepared. A District Rural Road Plan is prepared for each district indicating the habitations in each block with the existing status of road connectivity. The scheme will be fully funded by the Government of India and an allocation of Rs. 750 crores has been proposed for the Tenth Plan, which will be shown under the chapter Rural Roads.

### *National Project on Biogas Development*

Biogas Development programme aims to promote an ecofriendly Non-conventional Energy Source with multiple benefits. The role of biogas as a major source of renewable energy has been recognized by the Government of India by including this scheme as an item in the 20 Point Programme. Prevention of deforestation, production of enriched manure and to improve sanitation and hygiene by linking sanitary toilets with biogas plants are the objectives of this rural energy programme. This is a Centrally sponsored programme with a subsidy component of Rs. 1800/-for general category and Rs. 2300/-for scheduled category and Rs. 3500/-for hilly areas. An amount of Rs. 500/-is provided in addition for installation and maintenance of the plant to the Turnkey agent. 10,000 bio-gas plants will be constructed during the Tenth Plan. The scheme is fully funded by the Government of India and Rs. 8.05 crores is provided for the Tenth Plan which will be directly released to the District Collectors.

## Medical Social Work

Medical Social Work is a sub-discipline of social work, also known as Hospital social work. Medical social workers typically work in a hospital, skilled nursing facility or hospice, have a graduate degree in the field, and work with patients and their families in need of psychosocial help. Medical social workers assess the psychosocial functioning of patients and families and intervene as necessary. Interventions may include connecting patients and families to necessary resources and supports in the community; providing psychotherapy, supportive counselling, or grief counselling; or helping a patient to expand and strengthen their network of social supports. Medical social workers typically work on an interdisciplinary team with professionals of other disciplines (such as medicine, nursing, physical, occupational, speech and recreational therapy, etc.).

### *History*

***Britain and Ireland:*** Medical social workers in Britain and Ireland were previously known as Almoners, or Hospital Almoners. In Ireland, the origins of medical social workers go back to Dr. Ella Webb who in 1918 established a dispensary for sick children in the Adelaide Hospital in Dublin, and to Winifred Alcock who had trained as an Almoner and worked with Dr. Webb in her dispensary.

In 1945 the Institute of Almoners in Britain was formed, which in 1964 was renamed as the Institute of Medical Social Workers. The Institute of Medical Social Workers was one of the founder organisations of the British Association of Social Workers which was formed in 1970. In Britain. Medical Social Workers were transferred from the NHS into local authority Social Services Departments in 1974, and generally became known as Hosptital Social Workers.

***United States:*** The Massachusetts General Hospital was the first American hospital to have professional social workers on site in the early 1900s. The position was created by Richard Clarke Cabot to help patients to deal with areas of their life that made treatment difficult. This was important from an epidemiological point of view, as it made it easier to control and prevent outbreaks of syphillis and tuberculosis.

## The Medical Social Worker Profession

### *Role and Required Skills*

The medical social worker has a critical role in the area of discharge planning. It is the medical social worker's responsibility to ensure that the services the patient requires are in place in order to facilitate a timely discharge and prevent delays in discharge that can cost the hospital thousands of dollars per day.

For example, the medical doctor may inform the medical social worker that a patient will soon be cleared for discharge (a term that means that the patient no longer requires hospitalization) and will need home care services. It is the medical social worker's job to then arrange for the home care service to be in place so that the patient can be discharged. If the medical social worker fails to arrange for the home care service, the patient may not leave the hospital resulting in a delay in discharge. In such situations the treating physician is ultimately held responsible for the delay. Nevertheless the medical social worker often bears the brunt of the blame for the delay in discharge and his or her failure to perform often attracts the attention of management.

Other skills required of the medical social worker is an ability to work cooperatively with other health care staff as part of a multidisciplinary treatment team. They need to have good analytical and assessment skills, an ability to communicate clearly with both patients and staff, and an ability to quickly engage the patient in a therapeutic relationship. The Medical Social Worker will inevitably have to be able to process almost a never-ending flow of paperwork, whilst retaining a willingness to advocate for the patient, especially in situations where the medical social worker has identified a problem that may compromise the discharge and put the patient at risk in the community.

For example, the medical doctor reports that a frail elderly patient is medically cleared for discharge and plans to discharge the patient home with home care services. However, after assessing the patient's psychosocial needs, the medical social worker determines that the patient does not have the requisite ability to direct a home care worker and recommends that the discharge be deferred pending further assessment of this problem. In such a case, it is the medical social worker's ethical duty to inform the medical doctor that the discharge may place the patient at risk and advocate for another, more appropriate discharge even if it means that the patient's discharge has to be postponed. It is precisely in such cases that the medical social worker proves his or her worth-by placing the needs of the patient above all other considerations.

### *Challenges*

As medical social workers often have large caseloads and have to meet tight deadlines to arrange for necessary services, medical social work is a highly demanding job and as a result the turnover rate is high. In addition, medical social worker often confront highly complex cases involving patients with multiple psychosocial issues, all of which requiring intervention and leading to delays in discharge. For instance, in a major urban acute care medical centre, it is not uncommon for the medical social worker to assess patients who are simultaneously homeless, without health insurance coverage, have multiple chronic medical and psychiatric conditions, are unemployed, have just been released from incarceration, and have substance abuse problems. Any of these, separately and together, can impede timely discharge. Sometimes situations as mundane as the patient needing carfare or shoes can lead to delays in discharge, especially if these needs are not identified early. This is why a complete and timely assessment of the patient's psychosocial needs is critical.

### *School Social Worker*

School social workers are one of the three professional pupil services groups that provide counselling services to children and adolescents in schools in the United States. School social workers have worked in schools for over 100 years and are recognized in a majority of U.S. states and several foreign countries. Most school social workers hold a Master of Social Work degree and have specialized training in helping students within the context of local schools.

## *Historical Highlights*

School social work has an extensive history, dating to 1906-07, when it was established in New York, Boston, Chicago and New Haven, CT. At its inception, school social workers were known, among other things, as advocates for equity and fairness as well as home visitors. The expansion of school social work services was encouraged by a number of factors. By 1900 over two-thirds of the states had compulsory attendance laws and by 1918, each state had passed compulsory attendance laws, making school attendance obligatory, and not simply a privilege. Child labour legislation, the Progressive Movement which saw social work efforts initiated in the schools, and community settlement programs also led to its growth. A 1917 study of Truancy in Chicago supported "findings that the need for school attendance officers who understood the social ills of the community" and school social workers were best equipped for that responsibility (Allen-Meares, 1996). Mary Richmond, one of the founding mothers of social work, devoted an entire chapter to the visiting teacher in her 1922 book on *What is Social Casework?* The testing movement influenced school social work growth as well. Through the testing movement, educators were gaining knowledge about individual differences, underscoring the need for some children to attend school, children whose social conditions related to their test scores. Lastly during this time, leaders in the field like Sophonisba P. Breckinridge, expressed concerns of how school and education would relate to future success and happiness, and expressed the need to connect school and home in order to relate to the needs of children.

In the 1920s, the mental hygiene movement was concerned with treating nervous disorders and behavioural problems in difficult children. In the 1930s, like school counselling, school social work also declined. From the 1940-1960 casework in schools had become an established specialty, the profession began to emphasize collaboration and communication with teachers and others school personnel. Now the school social worker was an expert who could help schools on psychosocial issues. School social workers were affected by governmental reforms and education research. In the 1960s, pupil-personnel laws called for a greater emphasis by school social workers on the development of school policies. Like school counsellors, social workers were now called upon to address student needs while also addressing the sources of student troubles within the school. In the 1970s, school social work services were officially recognized by the U.S. passage of the Education of All Handicapped Children's Act of 1975 (P.L. 94-142), renamed the Individuals with Disabilities Education Act in 1990. In the latter part of the 1970s, inflation was rising at an alarming rate and budget cuts threatened the profession of school social work, especially as many social workers were being replaced by other school personnel claiming similar roles. The National Association of Social Work (NASW) published a newsletter to bring attention to the issue and get responses from practitioners. Through this, NASW conducted research and replicated the findings of others' studies on the roles of school social workers and models of practice, and school social work continued to expand. In the 1980s, this led to NASW giving more attention to the profession and more service to meet the needs of this social work group. NASW participation in the profession eventually led to a school social worker credential in 1992—the first time the School Social Work Credential Exam was given. From then until now, there has been a trend of integrative collaborative services. (Allen-Meares et al., 1996) In July 1994, driven by a need for more specific services for school social workers, a group of about 64 school social workers from across the country met in Edwardsville, IL. The group decided to form the School Social Work Association of America and drafted the first constitution and by laws for the organization. In June 2009 a second national organization incorporated, the American Council for School Social Work, after reviewing the direction of the profession and concluding that a stronger, enhanced national voice would benefit the profession.

## Theoretical Framework and Services

### *Traditional Model*

School social work is structured around a range of ever expanding practice models. Alderson first described these as the traditional-clinical model; the school change model whose major focus was the dysfunctional conditions of the school; the community school model which urged school social workers to employ community organization methods; and the social interaction model which de-emphasized a specific methodology and required the worker to intervene with the systems interacting with the target system. While many school social workers use an approach that draws on components from all of these, the traditional model, focusing on working with students with social and emotional difficulties and their parents, continues to predominate. In the clinical model, school social workers work primarily through casework methods supplemented by group methods with students and family members. In today's practice, a greater emphasis is placed on evidence based and promising intervention methods (Raines, 2008).

### *School-community-pupil Relations Model*

Of all the models, this one, first articulated by Lela Costin, seems to be the most comprehensive. It focuses on the school, community, and student and the interactions among the three. In this model, school social workers serves as mediators, negotiators, consultants, and advocates for students and school personnel, listening to student grievances. They also set up informal groups for students, teachers, and other school personnel. This model also encompasses the evaluation by the school social worker of characteristics of students, the school, and community conditions that may affect the availability and quality of educational opportunities for target groups (students with chemical dependency, disabilities, and so on). They are grounded in social learning theory and systems theory.

### *Education and Training*

States regulate school social work practice in different ways. Approximately 33 jurisdictions license or certify school social workers, most require a masters degree in social work (MSW), but a smaller number of states also license bachelors of social work (BSW). The National Association of Social Workers with 150,000 members also offers a Specialty Certificate in school social work but this is not required for employment in the schools.

The Council on Social Work Education (CSWE) is the national accrediting body for social work education at the BSW and MSW level. It specifies foundation social work program components, but social work specialties areas are defined by the individual accredited MSW programs. "Social work education is grounded in the liberal arts and contains a coherent, integrated professional foundation in social work practice from which an advanced practice curriculum is built at the graduate level." (CSWE, Educational Programs and Accreditation Standards. For a list of BSW and MSW programs accredited by the Council visit their web site. Other specialties in social work may include a content in policy, planning, administration, and a range of practice areas including child and family services, health, mental health, and aging.

### *School Counsellor*

A school counsellor is a counsellor and educator who works in elementary, middle, and high schools to provide academic, career, college readiness, and personal/social competencies to all students through advocacy, leadership, systemic change, and teaming and collaborating with other stakeholders as part of a comprehensive developmental school counselling program. Older, dated terms for the profession were "guidance counsellor" or "educational counsellor" but "*School Counsellor*" is preferred due to professional school counsellors' advocating for every child's academic, career, and personal/social success in every elementary, middle, and high school (ASCA, 2005). In the Americas, Africa, Asia, Europe, and the Pacific, the terms school counsellor, school guidance counsellor, and guidance teacher are also used with the traditional emphasis career development. Countries vary in how a school counselling program and school counselling program services are provided based on economics (funding for schools and school counselling programs), social capital (independent versus public schools), and School Counsellor certification and credentialing movements in Education departments, professional associations, and national and local legislation. The major accreditation body for Counsellor Education/School Counselling programs is the Council for the Accreditation of Counselling and Related Educational Programs (CACREP), which provides international program accreditation in Counsellor Education disciplines including school counselling.

Worldwide, there are large achievement, opportunity, funding, and attainment gaps for who has access to a quality elementary, middle, and high school education and can then pursue additional educational resources including college. In some countries, school counselling, frequently career education/development/counselling, is provided by educational specialists (for example, Botswana, China, Finland, Israel, Malta, Nigeria, Romania, Taiwan, Turkey, United States). In other cases, school counselling is provided by classroom teachers who either have such duties added to their typical teaching load or teach only a limited load that also includes school counselling activities (for example-India, Japan, Mexico, South Korea, Zambia). There are groups in Africa, the Americas, Asia, and Europe that have provided international counselling conferences but most have not had an exclusive school counselling focus. The IAEVG focus is primarily on career development and has some international school counselling foci in publications and conferences.

The history of school counselling varies on how countries and schools provide academic, career, college readiness, and personal/social skills and competencies to elementary, middle, and high school children and adolescents based on economic and social capital resources in a school counselling program..

### *In Botswana*

In Canada, most provinces have adapted K-12 comprehensive school counselling programs similar to those initiated by and adapted in the ASCA National Model. Various school counsellors reported in 2004 at the Canadian Counselling Association (CCA) conference in Winnipeg on issues such as budget cuts, lack of clarity about school counsellor roles, high student to school counsellor ratios, especially in elementary schools, and how using a comprehensive school cousneling model helped to clarify school counsellor roles with teachers and administrators and strengthen the profession.

In China, discussed the main influences on school counselling as being Chinese philosophers Confucius and Lao-Tsu, who provided early models of child and adult development that later influenced the work of Abraham Maslow and Carl Rogers. China also developed mental testing over 3,000 years ago, which was used for civil service examinations initially and eventually adopted by the British in the mid-1800s and later in the USA. Currently only 15% of high school students are admitted to college in China, so the entrance exams are fiercely competitive and those who do enter university graduate at a rate of 99%. Much pressure is put on children and adolescents to study and be able to attend college and this pressure is a central school counselling focus in China. An additional stressor is that there are not enough places for students to attend college, and over 1/3 of college graduates cannot find jobs, so career and employment counselling and development are central in school counselling. There is a strong stigma related to personal or emotional problems and even though most universities and many schools now have counsellors, there is a strong reluctance of many students to seek counselling for issues such as anxiety and depression. There is no national system of certifying school counsellors. Most are trained in Western-developed cognitive methods including REBT, Rogerian, Family Systems, Behaviour Modification, and Object Relations and also recommend Chinese methods such as qi gong (deep breathing), acupuncture, and music therapy. shared that Chinese school counsellors always work within a traditional Chinese world view of a community and family-based system that lessens the primacy of focus on the individual. In Hong Kong, Hui (2000) discussed work on moving toward comprehensive whole-school counselling programs and away from a remediation style model.

In Finland, specific legislation has been passed in terms of the school counselling system. The Basic Education Act of 1998 states that every student must receive school counselling services. All Finnish school counsellors must have a teaching certificate as well as master's degree in a specific subject and a specialized certificate in school counselling.

In Ireland, school counselling began in County Dublin in the 1960s and went countrywide in the 1970s. However, legislation in the early 1980s severely curtailed the movement due to budget constraints. The main organization for school counselling profession is the IGE or Institute of Guidance Counsellors, which has a code of ethics.

In Israel, a 2005 study by Erhard & Harel of 600 elementary, middle, and high school counsellors found that a third of school counsellors were delivering primarily traditional individual counselling services, about a third were delivering preventive classroom counselling curriculum lessons, and a third were delivering both individual counselling services and school counselling curriculum lessons in a more balanced or comprehensive developmental school counselling program; school counsellor roles varied due to three elements: the school counsellor's personal preferences, school level, and the principal's expectations. Erhard & Harel stated that the profession in Israel, like many other countries, is transforming from various marginal and ancillary services to a comprensive school counselling approach integral in the total school's education program.

In Japan, school counselling is a very recent phenomenon with school counsellors being introduced only in the mid-1990s and then often only part-time with a strong emphasis on assisting with behavioural issues.

In Korea, school counsellors must teach a subject besides counselling, and not all school counsellors are appointed to counselling positions, even though Korean law has required school counsellors in all middle and high schools.

In Malta, school counselling services were begun in 1968 within the Department of Education based on recommendations from a UNESCO consultant and the titles: Education Officer, School Counsellor, and Guidance Teacher and through the 1990s they included school counsellor positions in primary and trade schools in addition to secondary schools. Guidance teachers are mandated at a 1:300 teacher to student ratio.

In Nigeria, school counselling began in 1959 and it exists in some high schools but not all and little at the elementary school level. Where there are federally funded secondary schools, there are some professionally trained school counsellors but in many cases there are only teachers who function as career masters/ mistresses. School counsellors often have teaching and other responsibilities that take time away from their school counselling tasks. The Counselling Association of Nigeria (CASSON) was formed in 1976 to promote the profession, but there is not yet a code of ethics. However, a certification/licensure board has been formed. Aluede, Adomeh, & Afen-Akpaida (2004) discussed the overreliance on textbooks from the USA and the need for school counsellors in Nigeria to take a whole-school approach and lessen the focus on individual approaches and honour the traditional African world view that values the family and community's roles in decision-making as a paramount for effective decision-making in schools.

In the Philippines, the Congress of the Philippines passed the Guidance and Counselling Act of 2004, with a very specific focus Professional Practice, Ethics, National Certification, and the creation of a Regulatory Body, and specialists in school counselling are subject to this law.

### *In Romania*

In Taiwan, school counselling traditionally was done by "guidance teachers." Recent advocacy on the part of the Chinese Guidance and Counselling Association pushed for licensure for school counsellors in Taiwan's public schools. Prior to this time, the focus had been primarily on individual and group counselling with a focus on play therapy, career counselling and development, and stress related to national university examinations.

In the United States, the school counselling profession began with the vocational guidance movement at the beginning of the 20th century, now known as career development. Jesse B. Davis was the first to provide a systematic school guidance program. In 1907, he became the principal of a high school and encouraged the school English teachers to use compositions and lessons to relate career interests, develop character, and avoid behavioural problems. Many others during this time did the same. For example, in 1908, Frank Parsons, "Father of Vocational Guidance" established the Bureau of Vocational Guidance to assist young people in making the transition from school to work. From the 1920s to the 1930s, school counselling and guidance grew because of the rise of progressive education in schools. This movement emphasized personal, social, moral development. Many schools reacted to this movement as anti-educational, saying that schools should teach only the fundamentals of education. This, combined with the economic hardship of the Great Depression, led to a decline in school counselling and guidance. In the 1940s, psychologists and counsellors selected, recruited, and trained military personnel. This propelled the counselling movement in schools by providing ways to test students and meet their needs. Schools accepted these military tests openly. Also, Carl Rogers' emphasis on helping relationships during this time influenced the profession of school counselling. In the 1950s the government established the Guidance and Personnel Services Section in the Division of State and Local School Systems. In 1957, the Soviet Union launched Sputnik I. Out of concern that the Russians were winning the space race and that there were not enough scientists and mathematicians, the government passed the National Defence Education Act, spurring growth in vocational guidance through larger funding. In the 1960s, new legislation and professional developments refined the profession (Schmidt, 2003).

The 1960s was also a time of great federal funding for land grant colleges and universities in establishing Counsellor Education programs. School counselling shifted from an exclusive focus on career development to add personal and social issues paralleling the rise of social justice and civil rights movements. In the early 1970s, Dr. Norm Gysbers began shifting the profession from school counsellors as solitary professionals into having a comprehensive developmental school counselling program for all students K-12. He and his colleagues' research evidenced strong correlations between fully implemented school counselling programs and student academic success; a critical part of the evidence base for the profession based on their work in the state of Missouri.

But school counselling in the 1980s and early 1990s was absent from educational reform efforts. The profession was facing irrelevance as the standards-based educational movement gained strength with little evidence of systemic effectiveness for school counsellors. In response, consulted with elementary, middle, and high school counsellors and created the ASCA National Standards for School Counselling with three core domains (Academic, Career, Personal/Social), nine standards, and specific competencies and indicators for K-12 students. A year later, the first systemic meta-analysis of school counselling was published and gave a wake-up call to focus on outcome research in academic, career, and personal/social domains.

Also in the late 1990s, a former mathematics teacher, school counsellor, and administrator, Pat Martin, was hired by The Education Trust to focus the school counselling profession on closing the achievement gap that harmed children and adolescents of color, poor and working class children and adolescents, bilingual children and adolescents and children and adolescents with disabilities. Martin developed focus groups of K-12 students, parents, guardians, teachers, building leaders, and superintendents, and interviewed professors of School Counsellor Education. She hired a school counsellor educator from Oregon State University, Dr. Reese House, and they cocreated what emerged in 2003 as the National Centre for Transforming School Counselling (NCTSC).

The NCTSC focused on both changing School Counsellor Education at the graduate level and changing school counsellor practice in local districts to teach school counsellors how to prevent, intervene with, and close achievement and opportunity gaps. In the focus groups, they found what Hart & Jacobi had indicated---too many school counsellors were gatekeepers for the status quo instead of advocates for the academic success of every child and adolescent. Too many school counsellors used inequitable practices, supported inequitable school policies, and were unwilling to change. This professional behaviour kept many students from nondominant backgrounds (ie, students of color, poor and working class students, students with disabilities, and bilingual students) from getting the rigorous coursework and academic, career, and college readiness skills needed to successfully graduate from high school and pursue post-secondary options including college. They funded six $500,000 grants for six different Counsellor Education/ School Counselling programs, with a special focus on rural and urban settings, to transform their school counselling programs to include a focus on teaching school counsellor candidates advocacy, leadership, teaming and collaboration, equity assessment using data, and culturally competent program counselling and coordination in 1998 (Indiana State University, University of Georgia, University of West Georgia, University of California-Northridge, University of North Florida, and Lewis & Clark University) and then over 25 other Counsellor Education/School Counselling programs joined as companion institutions in the following decade. By 2008, NCTSC consultants had worked in over 100 school districts and major cities and rural areas to transform the work of school counsellors.

In 2002, the American School Counsellor Association released the ASCA National Model: A framework for school counselling programs, written by Dr. Trish Hatch and Dr. Judy Bowers, comprising key school counselling components into one model—the work of Drs. Norm Gysbers, Curly & Sharon Johnson, Robert Myrick, Carol Dahir & Cheri Campbell's ASCA National Standards, and the skill-based focus for closing gaps from the Education Trust's Pat Martin and Dr. Reese House into one document. In 2003, the Centre for School Counselling Outcome Research was developed as a clearinghouse for evidence-based practice with regular research briefs disseminated and original research projects developed and implemented with founding director Dr. Jay Carey. One of the research fellows, Dr. Tim Poynton, developed the EZ Analyse software program for all school counsellors to use as free-ware to assist in using data-based interventions and decision-making.

In 2004, the ASCA Ethical Standards for School Counsellors was revised to focus on issues of equity, closing gaps, and ensuring all K-12 students received access to a school counselling program. Also in 2004, Pat Martin moved to the College Board and hired School Counsellor Educator Dr. Vivian Lee. They developed an equity-focused entity on school counsellors' role in college counselling, the National Office for School Counsellor Advocacy (NOSCA). NOSCA has developed research scholarships for research on college counselling by K-12 school counsellors and how it is taught in School Counsellor Education programs. On January 1, 2006, the USA Congress declared the first week of February National School Counselling Week, which grew out of advocacy from ASCA members.

In 2008, The first NOSCA study was released by Dr. Jay Carey and colleagues focused on innovations in selected College Board "Inspiration Award" schools where school counsellors collaborated inside and outside their schools for high college-going rates and strong college-going cultures in schools with large numbers of students of nondominant backgrounds. In 2008, ASCA released School Counselling Competencies focused on assisting school counselling programs to effectively implement the ASCA Model. Also in 2008, in support of the ASCA Model and new vision school counselling, Dr. Rita Schellenberg introduced *standards blending* as a crosswalking approach to align school counselling with the academic achievement mission of schools as well as two data-based reporting systems, SCORE and SCOPE..

In 2009, NOSCA released a national study under the leadership of Dr. Vicki Brooks-McNamara addressing the school counsellor/ principal connection with specific recommendations for best practices in collaborative leadership in school counselling. In 2010, the Centre for Excellence in School Counselling and Leadership (CESCAL) co-sponsored the first school counselling conference devoted to the needs of lesbian, bisexual, gay, and transgendered students in San Diego, California.

The history of the school counselling profession internationally shifts as more parents, guardians, teachers, building and district leaders, and government officials support the changes in roles, expectations, and skills of current and future school counsellor candidates and as the evidence base and equity-building skills of school counsellors develop school counselling programs delivering academic, career, college, and personal/social competencies for every child and adolescent. Both the IAEVG and the Vanguard of Counsellors have been active in promoting school counselling internationally.

## School Counsellor Roles, School Counselling Program Framework, Professional Associations, and Ethics

Professional School Counsellors ideally implement a data-driven, evidence-based comprehensive school counselling program that promotes and enhances student achievement, career and college readiness, and personal and social competencies at the elementary, middle, and high school levels. A fully-implemented school counselling program ideally delivers academic, career, college readiness, and personal/social competencies to every student K-12—just as the district's mathematics program is for 100% of the students. Professional School Counsellors, in most U.S. states, usually have a Master's degree in school counselling from a Counsellor Education graduate program. In Canada, they must be licensed teachers with additional school counselling training and focus on academic, career, and personal/social issues. China requires at least three years of college experience. In Japan, school counsellors were added in the mid-1990s, but only on a very part-time basis and primarily focused on behavioural issues. In Taiwan, they are often teachers with recent legislation requiring school counselling licensure focused on individual and group counselling related to academic, career, and personal issues. In Korea, school counsellors are mandated in middle and high schools.

They are employed in elementary, middle, and high schools and in district supervisory, counsellor education faculty positions (usually with an earned Ph.D. in Counsellor Education in the USA or related graduate doctorates abroad) and post-secondary settings doing academic, career, college readiness, and personal/social counselling, consultation, and program coordination. Their work is varied, with attention focused on developmental stages of student growth, including the needs, tasks, and student interests related to those stages (Schmidt, 2003).

Professional School Counsellors meet the needs of student in three basic domains: academic development, career development, and personal/social development with an increasing emphasis on college readiness. Knowledge, understanding and skill in these domains are developed through classroom instruction, appraisal, consultation, counselling, coordination, and collaboration. For example, in appraisal, school counsellors may use a variety of personality and career assessment methods (such as the or (based on the) to help students explore career and college needs and interests.

Delivery methods include academic, career, college and personal/social planning for every student; developmental classroom lessons for all students; and individual and group counselling for some students who need more intensive assistance beyond classroom lessons or planning/advising sessions. Classroom lessons and the school counselling curriculum are designed to be preventive in nature and include academic, career, college, and personal/social skills and competencies including self-management and self-monitoring skills. The Responsive Services component of the Professional School Counsellor's role provides individual and/or small group counselling for students. For example, if a student's behaviour is interfering with his or her achievement, the Professional school counsellor will observe that student in a class, provide consultation to teachers and other personnel to develop (with the student) a plan to address the behavioural issue(s), and then work together (collaboration) to implement the plan. They also help by providing consultation services to family members such as college readiness, career development, parenting skills, study skills, child and adolescent development, and help with school-home transitions.

Additionally, professional school counsellors may lead classroom lessons on a variety of topics within the three domains such as personal/social issues relative to student needs, or establish groups to address common issues among students, such as divorce or death. The topics of character education, diversity and multiculturalism (Portman, 2009), and school safety are important areas of focus for school counsellors. Often counsellors will coordinate outside groups that wish to help with student needs such as academics, or coordinate a state program that teaches about child abuse or drugs, through on-stage drama (Schmidt, 2003).

The ASCA National Model operationalizes much of the above into four main areas of focus: Foundation (a written school counselling program mission statement, a beliefs and philosophy statement, and a focus on the ASCA standards and competencies and how they are implemented for every student; Delivery System (how lessons and individual and group counselling are delivered); Management System (use of calendars, time, building leader-school counsellor role agreements, creation of action plans); and Accountability System (use of a SC program audit, results reports, and School Counsellor Evaluations based on 13 key competencies. The model is implemented using key skills from the Education Trust's Transforming School Counselling Initiative: Advocacy, Leadership, Teaming and Collaboration, and Systemic Change.

School Counsellors around the world are affiliated with national and regional school counselling associations including: Asociacion Argentina de Counsellors (AAC-Argentina), American Counselling Association (ACA-USA), African Counselling Association (AfCA), American School Counsellor Association (ASCA-USA), Associacao Portuguesa de Psicoțerapia centrada na Pessoa e de Counselling (APPCPC-Portugal), Australian Guidance and Counselling Association (AGCA), British Association for Counselling and Psychotherapy (BACP-UK), Canadian Counselling Association (CCA)/Association Canadienne de Counselling (ACC), Centre for Excellence in School Counselling and Leadership (CESCaL) (USA), Centre for School Counselling Outcome Research (CSCOR-USA) Council for the Accreditation of Counselling and

Related Educational Programs (CACREP-USA and international), Counselling Children and Young People (BACP affiliate, UK), Counselling & Psychotherapy in Scotland (COSCA), Cypriot Association of School Guidance Counsellors (OELMEK), European Counselling Association (ECA), France Ministry of Education, Federacion Espanola de Orientacion y Psicopedagogia (FEOP-Spain), Department of Education-Malta, Hellenic Society of Counselling and Guidance (HESCOG-Greece), Hong Kong Association of Guidance Masters and Career Masters (HKAGMCM), Institute of Guidance Counsellors (IGC) (Ireland), International Association for Educational and Vocational Guidance (IAEVG)/Association Internationale d'Orientation Scolaire et Professionnelle (AIOSP)/Internationale Vereinigung für Schulund Berufsberatung (IVSBB)/Asociación Internacional para la Orientación Educativa—Profesional (AIOEP), International Baccalaureate (IB), International Vanguard of Counsellors (IVC), Kenya Association of Professional Counsellors (KAPC), National Board for Certified Counsellors (NBCC, USA), National Centre for Transforming School Counselling (NCTSC) at The Education Trust (USA), National Office for School Counsellor Advocacy (NOSCA) at The College Board (USA), New Zealand Association of Counsellors/Te Roopu Kaiwhiriwhiri o Aotearoa (NZAC), Counselling Association of Nigeria (CASSON), Philippine Guidance and Counselling Association (PGCA), Overseas Association of College Admissions Counsellors (OACAC, an affiliate of National Association of College Admissions Counsellors-USA), Singapore Association for Counselling (SAC), and the Taiwan Guidance and Counselling Association (TGCA).

School Counsellors are also expected to follow a professional code of ethics in many countries. For example, In the USA, they are the American School Counsellor Association (ASCA) Code of Ethics and the American Counselling Association (ACA) Code of Ethics. Additional codes of ethics for other countries may be found in the reference links for the international school counselling professional associations above.

### *Elementary School Counselling*

Elementary professional school counsellors following best practices provide developmental school counselling curriculum lessons on academic, career, college readiness, and personal and social competencies, advising and academic/career/college readiness planning to all students, and individual and group counselling for some students and their families to meet the developmental needs of young children K-6. Increased emphasis is starting to be placed on college readiness counselling at the elementary school level as more school counselling programs move to evidence-based work with data and specific results. Research has shown that school counselling programs help to close achievement and opportunity gaps in terms of which students have access to school counselling programs and early college readiness activities and which students do not. To facilitate the school counselling process, school counsellors use a variety of theories and techniques including developmental, cognitive-behavioural, person-centered (Rogerian) listening and influencing skills, systemic, family, multicultural, narrative, and play therapy released a research study showing the effectiveness of elementary school counselling programs in Washington state.

### *Middle School Counselling*

In middle school counselling, professional school counsellors following best practices provide developmental school counselling curriculum lessons on academic, career, college readiness, and personal and social competencies, advising and academic/career/college readiness planning to all students and individual and group counselling for some students and their families to meet the developmental needs of late childhood and early adolescence according to sources such as the ASCA National Model. Increasing emphasis has been placed on college readiness counselling at the middle school level as more school counselling programs move to evidenced-base work with data and specific results that show how school counselling programs help to close achievement and opportunity gaps in terms of which students have access to school counselling programs and early college readiness activities and which students do not.

Middle School College Readiness curricula have been developed by The College Board that can be used to assist students and their families in this process. To facilitate the school counselling process, school counsellors use a variety of theories and techniques including developmental, cognitive-behavioural, person-centered (Rogerian) listening and influencing skills, systemic, family, multicultural, narrative, and play therapy. Transitional issues to ensure successful transitions to high school are a key area including career exploration and assessment with seventh and eighth grade students. Sink, Akos, Turnbull, & Mvududu released a study in 2008 confirming the effectiveness of middle school comprehensive school counselling programs in Washington state.

### *High School Counselling*

In high school, professional school counsellors following best practices provide developmental school counselling curriculum lessons on academic, career, college readiness, and personal and social competencies, advising and academic/career/college readiness planning to all students and individual and group counselling for some students to meet the developmental needs of adolescents according to sources such as the ASCA National Model. Increasing emphasis is being placed on college readiness counselling at the early high school level as more school counselling programs move to evidence-based work with data and specific results that show how school counselling programs help to close achievement and opportunity gaps ensuring all students have access to school counselling programs and early college readiness activities. High School College Readiness curricula have been developed by The College Board to assist this process. To facilitate school counselling, school counsellors use varied theories and techniques including developmental, cognitive-behavioural, person-centered (Rogerian) listening and influencing skills, systemic, family, multicultural, narrative, and play therapy. Transitional issues to ensure successful transitions to college, other post-secondary educational options, and careers are a key area. The high school counsellor helps students and their families prepare for rigorous post-secondary education and/or training options (e.g. college, trade school) by engaging students and their families in finding accurate and meaningful information on entrance requirements, financial aid, recommendation letters, test-preparation and so forth. Professional School Counsellors at the high school level spend much of their time helping students and their families monitor their progress toward graduation and being adequately prepared for post-secondary options including college.

Some students now turn to private college admissions counsellors specialized in college admissions but the ethics of so doing is open to great debate in terms of who has access to this funding and there is little research-based evidence of effectiveness on the part of these outside parties. The fees for these college admissions counsellors can be as high as $30,000.

A framework for Professional School Counsellor responsibilities and roles is outlined in the ASCA National Model. study showed correlational evidence of the effectiveness of fully implemented school counselling programs on high school students' academic success. Carey et al.'s 2008 study showed specific best practices from school counsellors raising college-going rates within a strong college-going environment in multiple USA-based high schools with large numbers of students of nondominant cultural identities.

### *Education and Professional Credentials Including Certification for School Counsellors*

The education of school counsellors (school counsellors) around the world varies greatly based on the laws and cultures of specific countries and the historical influences of their respective educational and credentialing systems and professional identities related to who delivers academic, career, college readiness, and personal/social information, advising, curriculum, and counselling and related services.

In Canada, school counsellors must be certified teachers with additional school counselling training.

In China, there is no national certification or licensure system for school counsellors.

Korea requires school counsellors in all middle and high schools.

In the Philippines, school counsellors must be licensed with a master's degree in counselling.

Taiwan instituted school counsellor licensure for public schools (2006) through advocacy.

In the United States, a professional School Counsellor is a certified educator with a master's degree in school counselling (usually housed in a Counsellor Education graduate program) with specific school counselling graduate training including unique qualifications and skills to address all students' academic, career, college readiness and personal/social needs through the use of school counselling programs that deliver specific measurable competencies.

About half of all Counsellor Education programs that offer school counselling are accredited by the Council on the Accreditation of Counselling and Related Educational Programs (CACREP) and all are in the USA with one in Canada and one under review in Mexico as of 2008. CACREP maintains a current list of accredited programs and programs in the accreditation process on their website. CACREP desires to accredit more international counselling university programs.

According to CACREP, an accredited school counselling program offers specific coursework in Professional Identity and Ethics, Human Development, Counselling Theories, Group Work, Career Counselling, Multicultural/Diversity Counselling, Assessment, Research and Program Evaluation, and Clinical Coursework in a 100-hour practicum under the supervision of both a school counselling faculty member and a certified school counsellor site supervisor (master's degree in school counselling or higher, and appropriate certification) and a 600-hour internship under the supervision of both a school counselling faculty member and a certified school counsellor site supervisor (master's degree in school counselling or higher, and appropriate certification) (CACREP, 2001).

CACREP released the revision of the Standards for 2009 in 2008, and made a major change moving toward performance-based accreditation including evidence of school counsellor candidate learning. In addition, in the 2009 standards, CACREP greatly tightened and enhanced the school counselling standards with specific evidence needed of how school counselling students receive education in foundations; counselling prevention and intervention; diversity and advocacy; assessment; research and evaluation; academic development; collaboration and consultation; and leadership in K-12 school counselling contexts..

Certification practices for school counsellors vary around the world. School Counsellors in the United States may opt for national certification through two different boards. The National Board for Professional Teaching Standards (NBPTS) requires a two-to-three year process of performance based assessment, and demonstrate (in writing) content knowledge in human growth/development, diverse populations, school counselling programs, theories, data, and change and collaboration. As of February, 2005, 30 states offer financial incentives for this certification.

Also based in the USA, The National Board for Certified Counsellors (NBCC) requires passing the National Certified School Counsellor Examination (NCSC), which includes 40 multiple choice questions and seven simulated cases which assess school counsellors' abilities to make critical decisions on the spot.

Additionally, a master's degree and three years of supervised experience are required. NBPTS also requires three years of experience, however a master's degree is not required, but only state certification (41 of 50 require a master's degree). At least four states offer financial incentives for the NCSC certification (McLeod, 2005). Both certifications have benefits and costs that a school counsellor would want to consider for national certification. NBCC has credentials counsellors in the United States and internationally.

### *Job Growth and Earnings for School Counsellors*

The rate of job growth and earnings for school counsellors depends greatly on the country that one is employed in and whether the school is funded publicly or privately. School Counsellors working in international schools or "American" schools around the world may find similar work environments and expectations to the USA. School counsellor pay varies based on the level of school counsellor or school counsellor roles, identity, expectations, and legal and certification requirements and expectations of each country. According to the Occupational Outlook Handbook (OOH) the median salary for school counsellors in the USA in May 2006 was (USD) $53,750. In Australia, a survey by the Australian Guidance and Counselling Association found that school counsellor salary ranged from (AUD) the high 50,000s to the mid 80,000s. Also, school counsellors can earn additional money working summer months in school or agency counselling positions. Among all counselling specialty areas, public elementary, middle and high school counsellors are currently (2009) paid the highest salary on average of all counsellors. Overall employment for counsellors is average, especially in rural and urban areas. Budget cuts, however, have affected placement of public school counsellors in Canada, Ireland and the United States in recent years. In the United States, rural areas and urban areas traditionally have been under-served by school counsellors in public schools due to both funding shortages and often a lack of best practice models. With the advent of No Child Left Behind legislation in the USA and a mandate for school counsellors to be working with data and showing evidence-based practice, school counsellors able to show and share results in assisting to close gaps are in the best position to argue for increased school counselling resources and positions for their programs.

## School Psychology

School psychology is a field that applies principles of clinical psychology and educational psychology to the diagnosis and treatment of children's and adolescents' behavioural and learning problems. School psychologists are educated in psychology, child and adolescent development, child and adolescent psychopathology, education, family and parenting practices, learning theories, and personality theories. They are knowledgeable about effective instruction and effective schools. They are trained to carry out psychological and psychoeducational assessment, counselling, and consultation, and in the ethical, legal and administrative codes of their profession.

## Historical Foundations of School Psychology

School Psychology dates back to the beginnings of American psychology in the late 19th and early 20th centuries. School psychology is tied to both functional and clinical psychology. School psychology actually came out of functional psychology. School psychologists were not content with what happens to different children and how it happens but focused on answering the question why it happened to children. They wanted to understand the causes of the behaviour and its effects on learning. In addition to its origins in functional psychology, school psychology is also the earliest example of clinical psychology beginning around 1890. While both clinical and school psychologists wanted to help improve the lives of children, they approach it in different ways. School psychologists were concerned with school learning and behaviour problems, which contrasts the mental health focus of clinical psychologists.

### *Social Reform in the Early 1900s*

The late 19th century marked the era of social reforms directed at children. It was due to these social reforms that the need for school psychologists emerged. These social reforms included compulsory schooling, juvenile courts, child labour laws as well as a growth of institutions serving children. Society was starting to "change the 'meaning of children' from an economic source of labour to a psychological source of love and affection,". Historian Thomas Fagan argues that the preeminent force behind the need for school psychology was compulsory schooling laws. Prior to the compulsory schooling law, only 20% of school aged children completed elementary school and only 8% completed high school. Due to the compulsory schooling laws, there was an influx of students with mental and physical defects who were required by law to be in school. There needed to be an alternative method of teaching for these different children. Between 1910 and 1914, schools in both rural and urban areas created small special education classrooms for these children. From the emergence of special education classrooms came the need for "experts" to help assist in the process of child selection for special education. Thus, school psychology is founded.

### *Important Contributors to the Founding*

Lightner Witmer has been acknowledged as the founder of school psychology. Witmer was a student of both Wilhelm Wundt and James Mckeen Cattell. While Wundt believed that psychology should deal with the average or typical performance, Cattell's teachings emphasized individual differences. Witmer followed Catell's teachings and focused on learning about each individual child's needs. Witmer opened the first psychological and child guidance clinic in 1896 at the University of Pennslyvania. Witmer's goal was to prepare psychologists to help educators solve children's learning problems specifically those with individual differences. Witmer became an advocate for these special children. He was not focused on their deficits per se but rather helping them overcome them, by looking at the individual's positive progress rather than all they still could not achieve. Witmer stated that his clinic helped "to discover mental and moral defects and to treat the child in such a way that these defects may be overcome or rendered harmless through the development of other mental and moral traits,". He strongly believed that active clinical interventions could help to improve the lives of the individual child).

Since Witmer saw much success through his clinic, he saw the need for more experts to help these individuals. Witmer argued for special training for the experts working with exceptional children in special educational classrooms. He called for a "new profession which will be exercised more particularly in connection with educational problems, but for which the training of the psychologist will be a prerequisite").

As Witmer believed in the appropriate training of these school psychologists, he also stressed the importance of appropriate and accurate testing of these special children. The IQ testing movement was sweeping through the world of education after its creation in 1905. However, the IQ test negatively influenced special education. The IQ test creators, Lewis Terman and Henry Goddard, held a nativist view of intelligence, believing that intelligence was inherited and difficult if not impossible to modify in any meaningful way through education. These notions were often used as a basis for excluding children with disabilities from the public schools. Witmer argued against the standard pencil and paper IQ and Binet type tests in order to help select children for special education. Witmer's child selection process included observations and having children perform certain mental tasks.

### *G. Stanley Hall*

Another important figure to the origin of school psychology was Granville Stanley Hall. Rather than looking at the individual child as Witmer did, Hall focused more on the administrators, teachers and parents of exceptional children. He felt that psychology could make a contribution to the administrator system level of the application of school psychology. Hall created the child study movement, which helped to invent the concept of the "normal" child. Through Hall's child study, he helped to work out the mappings of child development and focused on the nature and nurture debate of an individual's deficit. Hall's main focus of the movement was still the exceptional child despite the fact that he worked with atypical children.

Bridging the gap between the child study movement, clinical psychology and special education was the first person in the United States to officially hold the title of school psychologist, Arnold Gesell. He successfully combined psychology and education by evaluating children and making recommendations for special teaching. It was Arnold Gesell, who paved the way for future school psychologists.

*Education*

Unlike clinical psychology and counselling psychology, which are doctoral-only fields, school psychology includes individuals with Master's (M.A., M.S., M.Ed.), Educational Specialist (Ed.S.), Certificate of Advanced Graduate Studies (C.A.G.S.) and doctoral (Ph.D., Psy.D. or Ed.D) degrees. Whereas in the past the Master's degree was considered appropriate for practice in schools, the National Association of School Psychologists currently recognizes the 60 credit hour Ed.S. as the most appropriate level of training needed for entry-level school-based practice. According to the NASP Research Committee (NASP Research Committee, 2007), in 2004-05, 33% of school psychologists possessed Master's degrees, 35% the Educational Specialist (Ed.S.) degree, and 32% doctoral (Ph.D., Psy.D., or Ed.D.) degrees. Most school psychology training programs are housed in university schools of education. School psychology programs require courses, practica, and internships that cover the domains of:

1. Data-based decision-making and accountability;
2. Consultation and collaboration;
3. Effective instruction and development of cognitive/ academic skills;
4. Socialization and development of life skills;
5. Student diversity in development and learning;
6. School and systems organization, policy development, and climate;
7. Prevention, crisis intervention, and mental health;
8. Home/school/community collaboration;

9. Research and program evaluation;
10. School psychology practice and development; and
11. Information technology Standards for Training and Field Placement, 2007. Specialist-level training typically requires 3–4 years of graduate training including a 9-month (1200 hour) internship in a school setting. Doctoral-level training programs typically require 5–7 years of graduate training including a 12-month internship (1500+ hours), which may be in a school or other (e.g., medical) setting. Doctoral level training differs from [specialist degree I specialist]-level training in that it requires students to take more coursework in core psychology and professional psychology. In addition, doctoral programs typically require students to learn more advanced statistics, to be involved in research endeavors, and to complete a doctoral dissertation constituting original research APA Committee on Accreditation, 2008;with Doctoral training programs may be approved by NASP and/or accredited by the American Psychological Association. In 2007, approximately 125 programs were approved by NASP, and 58 programs were accredited by APA. Another 11 APA-accredited programs were combined (clinical/counselling/school, clinical/school, or counselling/school) programs (American Psychological Association, 2007).

### *School Psychology Services*

School psychologists are experts in both psychology and education. School psychologists address the educational, emotional, social, and behavioural challenges that many children, youth, and young adults experience. They apply their understanding of human development, psychopathology, the impact of culture, learning theory, the principles of effective instruction and effective schools, and the impact of parent and family functioning on children to serve learners and their families.

As noted by the National Association of School Psychologists (NASP, 2007) and the American Psychological Association (APA, 2007), school psychologists adhere to the scientist-practitioner framework and make decisions based on empirical research.

Although school psychologists understand that schools are important in the lives of young people, not all school psychologists are employed in schools. Many school psychologists, particularly those with doctoral degrees, practice in other settings, including clinics, hospitals, forensic settings, correctional facilities, universities, and independent practice (ABPP, n.d.).

In many states school psychologists with terminal Master's or Education Specialist degrees are limited to employment in school settings. School psychologists employed in schools conduct psychological and educational assessments, provide interventions, and develop and present prevention programs for individuals from birth to age 21. They consult with teachers, other psychological and school personnel, family physicians and psychiatrists, and other professionals about students and are actively involved in district and school crisis intervention teams. They also may provide professional development to teachers and other school personnel on topics such as positive behaviour intervention plans and AD/HD and carry out individual, group, and family counselling.

## Barefoot Social Work

Barefoot social work is an approach to social work that emphasises that workers must be sensitive to the clients' environment, understanding and feeling the client's world and yet remaining detached-as if walking barefoot on rocky ground.

The theory is that this enables workers to be creative and so foster creativity in clients so that they can find their own way out of crisis situations. A variety of tools have been developed for practitioners to use with clients including card games which enable clients to explore their strengths and values and so build the confidence which is necessary to begin the process of change.

### *Creator*

Mark Hamer, a social worker and therapist in the UK, wrote the book *Preventing Breakdown,* based on his work as a solution-focussed social worker with families in crisis. It is a synthesis of Solution-Focussed Brief Therapy, Motivational Interviewing, Cognitive Behavioural Therapy and his own experiences of Taoism which unites all three intervention styles. This idea was developed in a later work, *The Barefoot Helper*.

### *Forensic Social Work*

Forensic Social Work is the application of social work to questions and issues relating to law and legal systems. This specialty of the social work profession goes far beyond clinics and psychiatric hospitals for criminal defendants being evaluated and treated on issues of competency and responsibility.

A broader definition includes social work practice which in any way is related to legal issues and litigation, both criminal and civil. Child custody issues, involving separation, divorce, neglect, termination of parental rights, the implications of child and spouse abuse, juvenile and adult justice services, corrections, and mandated treatment all fall under this definition. Functions of the forensic social work practitioner may include...

Providing consultation, education, or training to:

- Criminal justice, juvenile justice, and correctional systems
- Law makers
- Law enforcement personnel
- Attorneys, law students, and paralegals
- Members of the public.

Diagnosis, treatment, and recommendations:

- Diagnosing, assessing, and treating criminal and juvenile justice populations
- Diagnosing, treating, or making recommendations about mental status, children's interests, incapacities, or inability to testify
- Serving as an expert witness
- Screening, evaluating, or treating law enforcement and other criminal justice personnel.

Other functions:

- Policy and program development
- Mediation, advocacy, and arbitration
- Teaching, training, and supervising
- Behavioural Science Research and Analysis.

Forensic social work practitioners engage only in forensic activities within their areas of competence and expertise.

## Historical Development

### *United Kingdom*

The first appointed psychiatric Social Worker in London was in 1936. The British Association of Psychiatric Social Workers was inaugurated only in 1930. Most of the expertise in England and Wales has been concentrated within the Special Hospitals. Ashworth, Rampton and Broadmoor. at Broadmoor Hospital the first qualified l worker was not employed until 1969.

### *America*

Forensic social work has been done since at least 1899 coming out in part, of the settlement house movement, and the expansion of urban charity work.

### *Role of the Social Worker*

The social worker bridges the gap between the two worlds of hospital and community.

### *America*

In America the Forensic social worker, has a variety of functions, including social assessments for various courts including Family Court, and providing assessments and aftercare for psychiatric hospitals.

### *United Kingdom*

In the U.K. the forensic social worker has several duties, including applications for hospital admission, when necessary, arrange aftercare and social assessments among others. The social worker fulfills the role of the Social Supervisor to specify suitable accommodations for discharged patients, and to assess risk. They provide social care reports to the Mental Health Review Tribunal.

### *Caseworker (Social Work)*

In social work, a caseworker is a type of social worker who is employed by a government agency, nonprofit organization, or other group to take on the cases of individuals and provide them with advocacy, information or other services.

Caseworkers are employed by a large number of organizations in Britain, especially in the voluntary and public sectors. In the United States, most government agencies that provide social services to children in poor or troubled families have a staff of caseworkers, each of whom is assigned a proportion of the cases under review at any given time. In Australia, caseworkers may be assigned to work in child protection, drug and alcohol services or community health organizations.

As of 2004, there were approximately 876,000 child welfare caseworkers in the United States. Seventy-two percent are women, and their mean salary is $30,590. Caseworker turnover is high; every year, an estimated 20 percent of public caseworkers and 40 percent of private caseworkers leave their positions.

### *Case Management (Mental Health)*

Case management is the coordination of community services for mental health patients by allocating a professional to be responsible for the assessment of need and implementation of care plans. It is usually most appropriate for people who, as a result of a serious mental illness, have ongoing support needs in areas such as housing, employment, social relationships, and community participation. In particular, service users with a major psychotic disorder are most often suited to receiving services within this model.

The underlying tasks of case management include.

- assessment of need
- care planning
- implementation
- regular review.

The case management model developed in the USA in response to the closure of large psychiatric hospitals (known as deinstitutionalisation) and initially following a brokeage model, where professionals arranged for the provisions of services, without the need for direct patient care or contact. Clinical or therapeutic case management then developed as the need for the mental professional to establish a therapeutic relationship and be actively involved in clinical care was recognised.

A more intensive form of case management (Assertive community treatment or Intensive Case Management) was also developed for patients with more severe illness who needed a more assertive approach

### *Child Protection*

Child protection is used to describe a set of usually government-run services designed to protect children and young people who are underage and encourage family stability. These typically include investigation of alleged child abuse, foster care, adoption services, and services aimed at supporting at-risk families so they can remain intact.

Most children who come to the attention of the child welfare system do so because of any of the following situations, which are often collectively termed child abuse:

- Neglect including the failure to take adequate measures to safeguard a child from harm and/or gross negligence in providing for a child's basic needs:
- Physical abuse
- Emotional abuse
- Child sexual abuse
- Psychological abuse.

The United States government's Administration for Children and Families reported that in 2004 approximately 3.5 million children were involved in investigations of alleged abuse or neglect in the US, while an estimated 872,000 children were determined to have been abused or neglected and an estimated 1,490 children died that year because of abuse or neglect.

### *History*

The concept of a state sanctioned child welfare system dates back to Plato's Republic. Plato theorised that the interests of the child could be served by snatching children from the care of their parents and placing them into state custody. To prevent an uprising from dispossessed parents: "We shall have to invent some ingenious kind of lots which the less worthy may draw on each occasion of our bringing them together, and then they will accuse their own ill-luck and not the rulers."

Usually the responsibilities are stated within an act of a provincial legislature of provincial parliament. This then empowers the government department or agency to provide services in the area and to intervene into families where child abuse or other problems are suspected. The government agency that manages these services has various other names in different provinces, e.g., child and family services, children's aid. There is some consistency in the nature of laws, though the application of the laws may vary across the country.

### *Worldwide*

***United Kingdom:*** The United Kingdom has a comprehensive child welfare system under which Local Authorities have duties and responsibilities towards children in need in their area. This covers provision of advice and services, accommodation and care of children who become uncared for, and also the capacity to initiate proceedings for the removal of children from their parents care/care proceedings. The criteria for the latter is 'significant harm' which covers physical, sexual and emotional abuse and neglect. In appropriate cases the Care Plan before the Court will be for adoption. The Local Authorities also run adoption services both for children put up for adoption voluntarily and those becoming available for adoption through Court proceedings. The basic legal principle in all public and private proceedings concerning children, under the Children Act 1989, is that the welfare of the child is paramount. In recognition of attachment issues, social work good practice requires a minimal number of moves and the 1989 Children Act enshrines the principle that delay is inimical to a child's welfare. Care proceedings have a time frame of 40 weeks and concurrent planning is required. The final Care Plan put forward by the Local Authority is required to provide a plan for permanence, whether with parents, family members, long-term foster parents or adopters. Nevertheless, 'drift' and multiple placements still occur as many older children are difficult to place or maintain in placements. The role of Independent Visitor, a voluntary post, was created in the United Kingdom under the 1989 Children Act to befriend and assist children and young people in care.

In England, Wales and Scotland, despite the Children Act, there never has been a statutory obligation to report alleged child abuse to the Police. Northern Ireland is the exception to this legislative omission. In 2007 the Department for Children, Schools and Families created the Local Authority Designated Officer,

"LADO" to whom alleged abuse should be reported. The appointee is designated to act as an independent set of eyes and ears to assess situations prior to contacting any other agencies. However, there is no statutory obligation to report alleged abuse to this officer, and no sanction on any setting or organisation for failing to report.

A child in suitable cases can be made a ward of court and no decisions about the child or changes in its life can be made without the leave of the High Court.

### *Effects of Early Maltreatment on Children in Child Welfare*

The National Adoption Centre found that 52% of adoptable children had symptoms of attachment disorder. A study by Dante Cicchetti found that 80% of abused and maltreated infants studied exhibited signs of disorganized attachment. Lessons from research on maltreated infants' attachments to their caregivers. An organizational perspective on attachment beyond infancy.

Children with histories of maltreatment, such as physical and psychological neglect, physical abuse, and sexual abuse, are at risk of developing psychiatric problems. Such children are at risk of developing a disorganized attachment. Disorganized attachment is associated with a number of developmental problems, including dissociative symptoms, as well as depressive, anxiety, and acting-out symptoms.

Children who have experienced such early chronic trauma often require extensive and specific treatment to address multidimensional problems experienced by these children.

### *Criticism*

Despite the benefits of the services of the CPS, in the last two decades, the CPS has come under intense private and public scrutinity as an institution than can and has caused great harm in the name of protection. Although child welfare agencies are generally viewed positively, there has been an increase in the amount of cases where critics believe CPS have reacted out of their bounds.

A notable recent case is the family of Gary and Melissa Gates in Texas. The school called the local CPS and requested the Child Protective Services forcibly remove all thirteen of the Gates children and take them to foster homes under a court order which allowed an Emergency Removal, when there is clear evidence of danger to the physical health & safety of the child. The local CPS gave the explanation that they felt, quote, "Mr. Gates was uncooperative and his uncooperativeness with us put the children at risk." Even though the court ordered the children to be returned, CPS continues to classify the Gates as child abusers. Some have accused the CPS of having too much immediate power leaving the parents feeling lost and aggravated. The CPS has been accused of prejudging parents before proper investigations were done.

Brenda Scott, in her study of CPS concluded, "Child Protective Services is out of control. The system, as it operates today, should be scrapped. If children are to be protected in their homes and in the system, radical new guidelines must be adopted. At the core of the problem is the antifamily mindset of CPS. Removal is the first resort, not the last. With insufficient checks and balances, the system that was designed to protect children has become the greatest perpetrator of harm." Further to that information, several former CPS workers retired from the service, due to increasing circumstances and practices carried out by the organization.

### *Texas 2008 Raid of YFZ Ranch*

In April 2008, the largest child protection action in American history raised questions as the CPS in Texas removed hundreds of minor children, infants, and women incorrectly believed to be children from the YFZ Ranch polygamist community, with the assistance of heavily armed police with an armored personnel carrier. Investigators, including supervisor Angie Voss convinced a judge that all of the children were at risk of child abuse because they were all being groomed for underage marriage. The state supreme court disagreed, releasing most children back to their families. Investigations would result in criminal charges against some men in the community.

Gene Grounds of Victim Relief Ministries commended CPS workers in the Texas operation as exhibiting compassion, professionalism and caring concern. However, CPS performance was questioned by workers from the Hill Country Community Mental Health-Mental Retardation Centre. One wrote "I have never seen women and children treated this poorly, not to mention their civil rights being disregarded in this manner" after assisting at the emergency shelter. Others who were previously forbidden to discuss conditions working with CPS later produced unsigned written reports expressed anger at the CPS traumatizing the children, and disregarding rights of mothers who appeared to be good parents of healthy, well-behaved children. CPS threatened some MHMR workers with arrest, and the entire mental health support was dismissed the second week due to being "too compassionate." Workers believed poor sanitary conditions at the shelter allowed respiratory infections and chicken pox to spread.

### *CPS Problem Reports*

The Texas Department of Family and Protective Services, as with other states, had itself been an object of reports of unusual numbers of poisonings, death, rapes and pregnancies of children under its care since 2004. The Texas Family and Protective Services Crisis Management Team was created by executive order after the critical report Forgotten Children of 2004. Texas Comptroller Carole Keeton Strayhorn made a statement in 2006 about the Texas foster care system. In Fiscal 2003, 2004 and 2005, respectively 30, 38 and 48 foster children died in the state's care. The number of foster children in the state's care increased 24 percent to 32,474 in Fiscal 2005, while the number of deaths increased 60 percent. Compared to the general population, a child is four times more likely to die in the Texas foster care system. In 2004, about 100 children were treated for poisoning from medications; 63 were treated for rape that occurred while under state care including four-year old twin boys, and 142 children gave birth, though others believe Ms. Strayhorn's report was not scientifically researched, and that major reforms need to be put in place to assure that children in the conservatorship of the state get as much attention as those at risk in their homes.

# Bibliography

A K Malkani : *Social Work for the Poor*, Mohit Pub, Delhi, 2008.

A K Rizwi : *Social Policy and Social Work*, Mohit Pub, Delhi, 2008.

A S Kohli : *Human Rights and Social Work, Issues, Challenges and Response*, Kanishka, Delhi, 2004.

Abha, Vijai and Prakash: *Voluntary Organisations and Social Welfare*, ABD, Delhi, 2000.

Agarwal, L.B.: *The Harijans in Rebellion*, Taraporewala, Bombay, 1934.

Ahir, D.C.: *Dr B.R. Ambedkar: Buddhist Revolution and Counter-Revolution in Ancient India*, B.R. Publishing, Delhi, 1996.

Ahmed, Akbar : *Pakistan : The Social Sciences' Perspective*, Oxford University Press, Karachi, 1990.

Akash Gulalia : *Social Work Practice : With Mobile Population Vulnerable to HIV/AIDS*, Mohit, Delhi 2008.

Anand, J. H. : *Dalit Literature is the Literature of Protest*, Delhi, ISPCK, 1995.

Ankit Prasad: *Social Welfare and Social Action : YMCA at Work*, Mittal, Delhi, 2005.

Atal, Yogesh: *The Changing Frontiers of Caste*, Delhi, National Publishing House, 1968.

B.T. Lawani and I.S. Subhedar : *Social Work Perspectives*, Om Pub, Delhi, 2006.

Bailey, F. G. : *Caste and the Economic Frontier: A Village in Highland Orissa*, Manchester, University of Manchester, 1957.

Bakshi, S. R.: *Gandhi and Hindu-Muslim Unity*, Deep & Deep Publications, New Delhi, 1987.

Baldwin, Peter: *The Politics of Social Solidarity: Class Bases of the European Welfare State, 1875–1975*, Cambridge, Cambridge University Press, 1990.

Barnes, Bob.: *Social Survey Division in the 1990s*, Population Trends, 1991.

Benjamin, Joseph: *Scheduled Castes in Indian Politics and Society*, New Delhi, Ess Ess Publications, 1989.

Berger, P. L. : *The Sacred Canopy, Elements of a Sociological Theory of Religion*, Garden City, Doubleday & Company, 1967.

Beteille, Andre.: *The Backward Classes and the New Social Order*, Oxford University Press, Delhi, 1981.

Bhagwat, Vidyut: *Dalit Women in India: Issues and Perspectives - Some Critical Reflections*, New Delhi, Gyan Publishing House, 1995.

Bhai, P. N.: *Harijan Women in Independent India*, B. R. Publishing, New Delhi, 1986.

Bhatt, Anil: *Caste, Class and Politics: An Emperical Profile of Social Stratification in Modern India*, Delhi, Manhohar Book Service, 1975.

Bose, N. K.: *The Scheduled Castes and Tribes and Their Present Conditions*, Calcutta, University of Calcutta, 1969.

Bose, Pradip Kumar: *Social Mobility and Caste Violence: A Study of the Gujarat Riots*, Delhi, Adjanta Publications, 1985.

Brijesh Mishra: *Glimpses of Social Welfare in India : Problems and Perspectives*, ABD Pub, Delhi, 2006.

Campolo, T. & Fraser, D. A. : *Sociology through the Eyes of Faith*, San Francisco, Harper & Row, Delhi, 1992.

Carsten, F. L. : *The Rise of Fascism*, London, Methuen and Co., 1967.

Chaklader, Snehamoy : *Sociolinguistics: A Guide to Language Problems in India*, New Delhi, Mittal, 1990.

Charles D Garvin; Lorraine M Gutierrez and Maeda J Galinsky: *Handbook of Social Work With Groups*, Rawat, Delhi, 2007.

Chhaya Patel: *Social Work Practice : Religio Philosophical Foundations : Essays in Honour of Professor Indira Patel*, Rawat, Delhi, 1999.

Cravens, Hamilton: *Before Head Start: The Iowa Station and America's Children*, Chapel Hill, University of North Carolina Press, 1993.

D K Lal Das and Vanila Bhaskaran : *Research Methods for Social Work* : Rawat, Delhi 2008.

D.K. Lal Das : *Practice of Social Research : Social Work* Perspective, Rawat, 2000.

David Lewis and N Ravichandran: *NGOs and Social Welfare : New Research Approaches*, Rawat, Delhi, 2008.

Debotosh Sinha : *Aspects of Industry and Occupational Social Work*, Abhijeet Pub, Delhi, 2007.

Dennis Shirley: *Community Organizing for Urban School Reform*, Austin, University of Texas Press, 1997.

Dietrich, Gabriele: *Dalit Movements and Women's Movement*, Horizons India Books, New Delhi, 1992.

Donaldson, Gordon A. : *Cultivating Leadership in Schools*, New York, College Press, 2001.

Dumont, Louis: *The Caste System and Its Implications*, London, Granada Pub. Ltd., 1970.

Edward Chambers: *Roots for Radicals*, New York, Continuum, 2003.

Elisabeth Relchert: *Social Work and Human Rights : A Foundation for Policy and Practice*, Rawat, Delhi, 2003.

Ellul, J. : *The Technological Society*, Grand Rapids, Eerdmans, 1990.

Fisher, Michael : *A Clash of Cultures: Awadh the British, and the Mughals*, New Delhi, Manohar, 1987.

Frederic G. Reamer : *Social Work Values and Ethics*, Rawat, Delhi, 2005.

Freeman, James M.: *Untcuchable : An Indian Life History*, CA, Stanford University Press, 1979.

G.R. Madan : *An Eminent Scholar, Saint and Social Worker*, Radha Pub, Delhi, 2008.

Ghurye, G. S. : *Caste and Class in India*, Bombay, Popular Books, 1950.

Gibson, R. : *Critical Theory and Education*, London, Hodder & Stoughton, 1986.

Glass, Joseph W.: *The Pennsylvania Culture Region: A View From the Barn*, Ann Arbor, UMI Research Press, 1986.

Gorhe, Neelam: *Social Development and Dalit Women*, Gyan Pub. House, New Delhi, 1995.

Gorringe, H.: *Untouchable Citizens : Dalit Movements and Democratization in Tamil Nadu*, Delhi, Sage Publications, 2005.

Grunlan, Stephen A. and Milton Reimer : *Christian Perspectives on Sociology*, Grand Rapids, Mich., Zondervan, 1982.

Gurukal, Rajan: *The Formation of Caste Society in Kerala*, Rawat Publications, New Delhi, 1994.

Hajira Kumar : *Social Work, Social Development and Sustainable Development*, Regency, Delhi, 1997.

Hana Nagpaul : *Social Work in Urban India*, Rawat, Delhi, 1996.

Harry C. Boyte : *Commonwealth, A Return to Citizen Politics*, New York, The Free Press, 1989.

Heinsath, Charles : *Indian Nationalism and Hindu Social Reform*, Princeton, Princeton University Press, 1964.

Hopkins, Thomas J. : *The Hindu Religious Tradition*, Encino, California, Dickenson, 1971.

I. Sundar: *Social Work Practices in Health and Medical Profession*, Sarup Book Pub, Delhi, 2009.

I.S. Subheda : *Fieldwork Training in Social Work*, Rawat, Delhi, 2001.

Jaffrelot, Christopher: *Dr. Ambedkar and Untouchability: Fighting the Indian Caste System*, New York, Columbia University Press, 2005.

Jainendra Kumar Jha : *Social Welfare and Social Work*, Anmol, Delhi, 2002

Jogdand, P. G.: *Dalit Women in India: Issues and Perspectives*, New Delhi, Gyan Publishing House, 1995.

K. Chakraworthy: *Untouchable Social Work in India*, Sumit, Delhi, 2006.

K.D. Gangrade : *Gandhian Perspective on Global Interdepen-dence, Peace and Role of Professional Social Work*, Authorspress, Delhi, 2008.

K.K. Jacob: *Social Work Education in India*, Himanshu, Delhi, 1994.

Kamble, N. D.: *Deprived Castes and their Struggle for Equality*, Ashish Publishing House, New Delhi, 1983.

Lakshmanna, C.: *Caste Dynamics in Village India*, Nachiketa Publications, Bombay, 1973.

Lal, Shyam: *Caste and Political Mobilisation: The Bhangis*, Jaipur, Panchsheel Prakashan, 1981.

Lindburg, Donald: *Social Organization of the Kutenai.* Chicago: University of Chicago Press, 1962.

M A Khan : *Social Work and Social Policy, Concepts and Methods,* Book Enclave, Delhi, 2007.

M R Kamble : *Social Work With Children,* Aavishkar, Delhi, 2007.

M.N. Parmar and Jagdish Solanki : *Social Work Perspective on Depressed Class Population,* Anmol, Delhi, 2006.

M.S. Bedi : *Social Development and Social Work* , Himanshu, Delhi, 1994.

Mallik, Suneila: *Social Integration of the Scheduled Castes,* New Delhi, Abhinav, 1979.

Manju Gupta : *Child Abuse, A Social Work Perspective* , Mangal Deep Publications, Delhi, 2001.

Margaret Alston and Wendy Bowles : *Research for Social Workers : An Introduction to Methods,* Rawat, Delhi, 2003.

Marshall, P. & VanderVennen, R. : *Social Science in Christian Perspective,* Lanham, MD: University Press of America, 1988.

McGivney, V. : *Informal Learning in the Community, A Trigger for Change and Development,* Leicester, NIACE, 1999.

Moberg, D. : *Wholistic Christianity, An Appeal for a Dynamic Balanced Faith,* Brethren Press, 1985.

Moddie, A.D.: *The Brahmanical Culture and Modernity,* London, Asia, 1968.

Mohammad Naqi : *Social Work for Weaker Sections,* Anmol, Delhi, 2005.

Murli Desai : *Methodology of Progressive Social Work Education,* Rawat, Delhi, 2004.

Murli Desai and Siva Raju: *Gerontological Social Work in India : Some Issues and Perspectives,* B.R., Delhi, 2000.

N.C. Dobriyal : *Social Work for Older and Sick People,* Sumit Enterprises, Delhi, 2008.

Narain, A.K. & Ahir, D.C.: *Dr. Ambedkar, Buddhism and Social Change,* BR Publishing, Delhi, 1993.

Omvedt, Gail : *Reinventing Revolution: New Social Movements and the Socialist Tradition in India,* New York, Sharpe, 1993.

P Murugesan: *Social Welfare Programmes and Fertility Decline,* Abhijeet Publication, Delhi, 2009.

P.K. Bajpai : *Social Work Perspectives on Health,* Rawat, Delhi, 1998.

P.M. Parmar : *Social Work and Social Welfare in India,* Sublime, Delhi, 2002.

Pamela Trevithick: *Social Work Skills : A Practice Handbook,* Rawat, Delhi, 2009.

Patnaik, Nitayananda: *Caste and Social Change: An Anthropological Study of Three Orissa Villages,* National Institute of Community Development, Hyderabad, 1969.

Pekka Himanen: *The Information Society and the Welfare State: The Finnish Model,* Oxford UP, Oxford, 2002.

Perkins, S. & Rice, C. : *More than Equals: Racial Healing for the Sake of the Gospel,* Downers Grove, InterVarsity, 1993.

Prakash M Katare : *Social Work and Folk Culture,* Arise Pub, Delhi, 2006.

Prasanta K. Pattanaik: *Essays on Individual Decision-making and Social Welfare,* Oxford University Press, London, 2009.

Pratima Chaturvedi : *Social Work : Theories and Practices,* Book Enclave, Delhi, 2005.

Premanand Choudhary : *Child Survival, Health and Social Work Intervention,* ABD Pub, Delhi, 2008.

Profulla C Sarker : *Issues and Perspectives on Social Work and Social Development,* Serials Pub, Delhi, 2008.

R.B.S. Verma, H.S. Verma and Raj Kumar Singh: *Empowerment of the Weaker Sections in India : Interface of the Civil Society Organizations and Professional Social Work Institutions,* Serials, Delhi, 2006.

R.P. Arya : *Training for Social Work and Rural Development,* Manglam, Delhi, 2007.

Raj Bala Mathur : *Modernisation of Social Work, Planning and Administration,* Book Enclave, Delhi, 2007.

Raj Bhanti : *Field Work in Social Work Perspective,* Himanshu, Delhi, 1996.

Ramesh Chandra, *Government and Politics of India,* New York, St. Martin's Press, 1995.

Rameshwari Devi and Ravi Prakash: *Social Work : Methods, Practices and Perspectives,* Mangal Deep, Delhi, 2004.

Ranjna K. Devi : *Social Work, Philosophy, Concepts and Dimensions*, Omega, Delhi, 2009.

Rao, M. S. A.: *Social Movement and Social Transformation: A Study of Backward Class Movement*, New Delhi, Macmillian Press, 1978.

Ritter, Gerhard A.: *Social Welfare in Germany and Britain: Origins and Development*, Kim Traynor, New York, 1986.

Robert Fisher and Peter Romanofsky: *Community Organizing for Urban Social Change, A Historical Perspective*, Greenwood Press, Delhi, 1981.

Robert Fisher: *Let the People Decide, Neighborhood Organizing in America* 1984, Twayne Publishers, Delhi, 1997.

Roy Burman, B.K.: *Beyond Mandal and After Backward Classes in Perspective*, New Delhi, Mittal, 1992.

S K Sen : *Social Work Practices*, Book Enclave, Delhi, 2007.

S.K. Bhalla : *Social Work With Lawbreakers of Society*, MD Pub, Mumbai, 2008.

S.P. Ramachandran : *Social Work for Minorities*, Sumit Enterprises, Delhi, 2008.

Sandhya Joshi: *Child Survival Health and Social Work Intervention*, Concept, 1996.

Sangwan, Satpal : *Science, Technology, and Colonisation: An Indian Experience, 1757-1857*. New Delhi, Anmika Prakashan, 1991.

Sanjay Bhattacharya: *Social Work : An Integrated Approach*, Deep and Deep, Delhi, 2003.

Sarat C. Joshi : *Gandhian Social Work*, Akansha, Delhi, 2009.

Seerveld, C. : *On being human: Imaging God in the modern world*, Lanham, MD: University Press of America, 1989.

Shaikh Azhar Iqbal : *Principles and Practices of Social Work*, Sublime, Delhi, 2005.

Shaikh Azhar Iqbal: *Problems of Social Welfare and Social Work*, Sublime, Delhi, 2005.

Sherry Joseph : *Social Work Practice and Men Who Have Sex With Men*, Sage, Delhi, 2005

Shilaja Nagendra : *Social Work and Social Welfare in India*, ABD Pub, Delhi, 2005.

Silverberg, James: *Social Mobility in the Caste System in India,* Mouton Publishers, The Hague, 1968.

Simon, Robert Leopold: *Spiritual Aspects of Indian Music,* Delhi, Sundeep, 1984.

Singh, S. N.: *Reservation: Problems and Prospects,* New Delhi, Uppal Publishing House, 1987.

Skillen, James W. : *A Covenant to Keep : Meditations on the Biblical Theme of Justice,* Grand Rapids, MI: CRC Publications, Center for Public Justice, 2000.

Stephens, S. : *Children and the Politics of Culture,* Princeton, Princeton University Press, 1995.

Tejomayananda, Swami : *Hindu Culture: An Introduction,* Chinmaya Publications, Piercy, CA, 1993.

Tripathy, R. B.: *Dalits: A Sub-Human Society,* New Delhi, Ashish Publishing House, 1994.

V.V. Devasia and Ajit Kumar : *Social Work Concerns and Challenges in the 21 Century,* APH, Delhi, 2009.

Vijendra Kumar : *Problems and Perspectives on Social Work and Social Welfare,* ABD Pub, Delhi, 2002.

Whitley, O. R. : *Religious behavior: Where sociology and Religion Meet,* Engelwood Cliffs, Prentice-Hall, Inc, 1964.

Wolterstorff, N. : *Until Justice and Peace Embrace,* Grand Rapids: Eerdmans, 1983.

Wuthnow, R. : *God and Mammon in America,* New York: Free Press, 1994.

Yolton, J. W.: *John Locke: Problems and Perspectives,* Cambridge Uni. Press, 1969.

Zelliot, Eleanor: *From Untouchable to Dalit: Essays on the Ambedkar Movement,* New Delhi, Manohar, 1992.

Zimmer, Heinrich : *The Art of Indian Asia,* New York, Pantheon, 1955.

# Index

## L



## M



## N



## O



## P



## Q



## R

## S



## T



## U



## V



## W



## Y



□□□